THE CRAFT OF
Decoupage

Patricia Nimocks

CHARLES SCRIBNER'S SONS

NEW YORK

Abridgement Copyright © 1972 Patricia E. Nimocks

Unabridged version entitled Decoupage
Copyright © 1968 Patricia E. Nimocks

*This book published simultaneously in the
United States of America and in Canada—
Copyright under the Berne Convention*

*All rights reserved. No part of this book
may be reproduced in any form without the
permission of Charles Scribner's Sons.*

A-1.72[M]

*Printed in the United States of America
Library of Congress Catalog Card Number 75–179551
SBN 684–12741–5 (trade paper, SL)*

Contents

INTRODUCTION

The History and Origins of Découpage

Découpage is the art of decorating surfaces with applied paper cutouts, according to Webster's International Dictionary. It comes from the French découpage, from *découper*—to cut up, cut out. Webster uses an excerpt by Leo Lerman, "(She) would coil up on the frayed needlepoint of a rosewood sofa and spend her time making découpage." Even in such a brief excerpt one can sense the antique and elegant environs of découpage.

Découpage is the name of a style of work and is preceded usually by a preposition—in découpage or with découpage—being synonymous with cutouts. One who does découpage is a découpeur—not a découpager. One who is cutting is découping—not découpaging. Work finished is done with découpage—not découpaged. Découpage is always spelled as one word.

This is a skillful art in which one achieves a dimensional quality by cutting an irregular edge. This serrated edge blends optically and is more easily applied to a surface. Découpage is an art of elegance. Work produced in this manner should reflect an exquisite quality. It is easy to identify immediately as découpage and doesn't look like any other art. There is a crisp refinement about découpage that distinguishes this work the moment you see it. The stylish appearance is uncommon, mellow and usually antique in character. Découpage is always an individual creation. It can be identified as an extension of one's own personality. The pieces one creates will reflect one's own love of beauty, choice of subject, and care of finishing that is typical of one's own character.

There are three main types of découpage:

The 18th Century découpage—true découpage—classic in feeling, is made of originals or reproductions of hand-colored 18th century prints.

5

19th century scrapbook pages, using German embossed and die-cut designs. Although intended for the scrapbook, they became ornaments for boxes, screens, panels, valentines, and furniture.

This is done in the character of the antique work. Trompe l'oeil (fool the eye) was done in this manner; however, it can be done also in Victorian or Modern découpage.

The Victorian découpage is done with precolored and cutout embossed scrapbook pictures and gold paper braid. During this period, the gay home-loving Victorians made use of these cutouts on practically everything. This is the introduction to découpage for many who are shy about coloring or cutting.

The Modern or Contemporary découpage makes use of currently printed papers—such as calendars, gift cards, magazines, and wrapping papers. This is another form of découpage for the beginner who has a favorite illustration or some greeting cards that would do very well for a first project.

18TH CENTURY DÉCOUPAGE

The découpage work in which we are most interested today relates closely to the "arte povero" of 18th century Italy. It was given the name because "arte povero", *the poor man's art*, was an imitation of the fine lacquer work brought in from China and Japan. The English succeeded in making the closest replicas of the lacquer furniture. The Italian work, however, became such an imaginative and colorful form of decorating that this technique was copied and local designs, as well as styles, came into being all over Europe and the British Commonwealth.

The French découpage was done in the most intricate and lacy cutting. The subjects used were dainty flowers, butterflies, birds, cherubs, musical

A page from a late 18th century scrapbook from England. The center engraving is hand colored. The surrounding cut-out designs are freehand drawings, which are water colored.

instruments, garlands and traditional little trophies. Their découpage was in the stylish character of the 18th century furniture—quite fanciful and ornate.

The German découpage, as well as some Austrian, was a little heavier following the character of Biedermeier furniture. The scrapbook pictures of embossed flowers, birds and all types of tiny miniature embossed tradespeople, children, cherubs, ribbons and so on decorate work by the Germans. They preferred solidly pasted together geometric forms—medallions, octagonals, diamonds, circles and squares. Their colorful work with the embossed scrapbook material has never been surpassed. The embossed printed and precut motifs were invented by the Germans, so their supply was accessible. Caroline Duer—a distinguished editor of Paris *Vogue* magazine—was a noted designer of découpage, using the embossed paper scrapbook flowers, hanging baskets, and gold paper braid on her furniture and little boxes. Cooper Union Museum in New York acquired one of her original chest-cabinet creations.

The English découpage is feathery, beautifully and intricately cut. Much of their work was done on various colored fine papers. Their large screens, which were used in so many places, were lavish and decorative. They were particularly active découpeurs during the early 19th century with this delicate work. At the middle and toward the end of the 19th century, the English turned to the use of embossed paper scrapbook pictures. Queen Victoria was one of the most famed of the collectors of découpage. Her extensive collection included miniature architectural works of castles, palaces, cathedrals and historical buildings. These were reminiscent of the intricate fold-out valentines—and may have been the forerunners. This type of cutting and mounting to give the illusion of depth is called vue d'optique, whether it is framed or in a deep box.

About 160 years ago an invalid by the name of Amelia Blackburn created garlands of flowers and birds so exquisite, original and so unique, that the paper cuttings she did were called "Amelias." For many years after her death they were still called by this name. The craftmanship she displayed was quite phenomenal. The feathers of the birds were each cut with such deftness that close inspection reveals no less realistic a feather. The ordinary white paper that she used for the cuttings was drawn very carefully, cut accurately and colored to closely resemble nature. The feathers and tufts on the birds were no thicker than a hair. Pin pricks were used on the bodies where scissors could not get the desired effects. Her remarkable delicacy of cutting and accuracy of detail must have taken indomitable patience. When one considers her personal handicap, it seems these cuttings were a triumph of the talented and persistent Amelia Blackburn.

Few examples of "Amelias" are in the British Museum, but there are two large black cases of paper mosaicks by Mrs. Delany. This very fashionable lady was born in 1700. In one of her letters dated Dublin 1758, she described her wanderings among the herbs and flowers of Dublin Mountains, and how delighted she was to see a white robin. Fifty-eight was a very advanced age for women in the 18th century, but she still delighted in making her paper mosaicks. King George III was utterly fascinated by her work. Around her tea table, many of the luminaries of her day gathered to see the beautiful flowers. Erasmus Darwin, engaged in his great work *The Loves of the Plants,* inserted a very flowery compliment to her in his poem, and doubtless made the old lady very happy.

Mrs. Delany's flowers were cut from many colors of papers, pasted layer on layer to achieve the final effect of a flower. Upon close examination one can see some natural plant material in the form of leaves which were used with her cutouts. They would not be noticeable except they have faded more than the paper.

Her work is remarkable for its close imitation of nature and the flowers have a graceful quality. I believe that bits of leaf were placed among the paper cutouts as timeless evidence of her subtle wit.

As you can see with Amelias and paper mosaics, the many names for découpage are varied in each language. The arte del povero and arte povera as well as scrivan, scriban, and incised ornament are all découpage but one must possess the persistence and dedication of a sleuth to track down the various names in many countries. I suspect there are many yet to discover.

The Italian découpage follows the style of furniture and the city in which it was done. The Venetian pieces were ornate, opulent, lavishly bedecked with delicate flowers, scrolls, birds and other ornamental creatures. From Genoa comes découpage furniture, a little more sturdy and much less flamboyant. The colors are richer and the style is firmly established here. A great deal of découpage furniture is now made in Italy for export. The principal towns manufacturing are Genoa, Florence and Rome.

In Sicily, découpage is used in gayest profusion with bright paper cutouts on the festival carts, depicting historical and religious highlights. Sometimes other materials are used with cutout paper such as metallic paper in bright glossy accents.

Swedish découpage is done in earthy monotones. Black and white engravings are gently enriched with burnt apricot, forest green, dark salmon, and peach umber. The black and white prints are used on dark painted backgrounds or natural deep wood tones. It is astonishing how effective these muted colors can be.

Norwegian découpage is confined almost without exception to mythological subjects since this country is steeped in the tradition of the Vikings.

A museum in Nordscia has examples of découpage which appear to have been colored or tinted with watercolor, producing a dim glow. The work was serene in its rich coloring.

Portuguese découpage is as brilliant and dazzling as a tinsel-strewn Christmas tree. Brightly colored paper is used for their cutout work. They have traditional designs interpreted in skillfully cutout foil and tinsel paper. Provincial patterns used are similar to Pennsylvania Dutch; however, much more delicately done. The effect of the rich colors and tinsel foil is reminiscent of the late afternoon sunlight shining through a stained glass window.

Polish découpage craftsmen have been doing cutouts for generations. Their work is usually done in colored papers superimposed to make exacting designs, immediately recognized as cut paper motifs. Most of this work is provincial and it is done in bisymmetric patterns.

Mexican découpage is bright, colorful and used as ornamental motifs at the many holiday festivals. Mexican artists have been very adept in the use of papier mâché in recent years and more and more découpage can be expected from this artistic country.

Belgian découpage was usually cut with a knife and done in the manner of silhouette cutting except for pierced work and reverse cutting. Little information is available on their découpage which was done at the turn of the 18th century. The tiny cutouts look like faded threads and are unbelievably delicate.

Découpage has always been a craft to share. If you could imagine the great undertaking of a journey in 18th century France or England, you know why the families who got together prolonged their visits. Weeks of being together before they returned home created an opportunity to share many hours. The hostess would plan to use their time imaginatively. Often the guests would bring along new ideas. Fine scissors were a basic tool in every lady's work table so it was only natural to begin cutting pictures for a scrapbook. This time-consuming art was very popular throughout Europe and England. The local printers around London made every attempt to produce prints that would catch these ladies' favor. The small prints were very delicate and they covered every subject.

Robert Sayer collected the works of many artists, Martin Englebrecht, Jean Pillement, and others not signed. He bound his volume of about two-hundred pages and called it *The Ladies' Amusement Book.* I am sure these little inspirations were used as basic design material for more than scrapbook pictures. They lend themselves well to needlework pictures and could be very suitable in repeat patterns for textile design or enlarged for repeats in wallpaper design.

Découpage was beginning in Italy also in the 18th century, but in an entirely different way. The first pieces of paper which were pasted onto a surface in the very earliest works of découpage were done by artists who may have been unable to do a handsome line drawing but could do a very good job of cutting and, therefore, they pasted prints onto their furniture. The backgrounds of these pieces were often done in egg tempera, using cloud effects in many muted tones. In some backgrounds trees and shrubs were painted. The foreground was filled with the cutout figures of people in a typical setting. Of all the Italian work done in cutout ornament, many of the classic examples are desks or secretaries.

The woods which were used in Italian furniture generally were soft because in Italy there are very few hardwood trees. It is also possible that the pieces of lumber imported from nearby countries did not always match and, therefore, the surfaces of these odd pieces of wood were covered with gesso. Gesso is a combination of Spanish whiting similar to chalk and it is bound with rabbit skin glue or perhaps hide glue available in Italy at the time. The entire secretary was covered with this gesso and a smooth ground was laid for the application of prints. These prints were previously hand-colored in a technique resembling our watercolor.

The secretaries were known as arte povero (the poor man's art). The name became a classic designation for the cutout prints. In the books that are available describing the 18th century secretaries, the work is referred to as incised or appliqué. The witty and graceful art of découpage furniture (arte povero) was born in or near Venice. The largest number of beautiful secretaries done in découpage are credited to the Venetian craftsmen. This beautiful city was, of course, the center of a great deal of commercial activity and it was by far the most opulent of the cities in Europe.

The Italians were as active commercially as the Spanish and British in trade with the Far East. The treasures brought from the Orient had a very strong influence on European designers. The original works were rare and extremely expensive; therefore, imitations, adaptations and variations of the Chinese and Japanese pieces were produced according to the limitations of materials or imagination of the artist. The delicate gold line work, latticed design motifs, and other exquisite tracery of the oriental motifs were adapted to furniture used in fashionable homes.

The early Italian secretaries were more than ornamental. They were of great utility value and importance to the master of the house. Such a piece provided storage for fine letterpaper, documents of importance, reference and correspondence. It was always placed prominently as it represented the finest personal furniture possession of the master of the household. A very small percentage of the people were literate and those few who had a good education were highly regarded. Since the secretary identified the educated, it was selected by the bride to take to her new home. The Italians strengthened their political position by intermarriage of the leading families in the neighboring city-states. They also made matrimonial alliances with foreign rulers, and frequently would include the scriban or secretary in the collection of furniture the bride took to the new court. This practice of taking a dowry collection into another country spread the cultural commodities of the Italian courts. They were very enthusiastically received in France by such ladies as Marie Antoinette, Madame DuBarry, Madame Pompadour. Each of them commissioned work done in the exclusive manner of the Italian scriban.

The engravings of Pillement, Watteau, Boucher, Englebrecht

It is quite certain that some prints were cut out before the 18th century. Few have been authenticated for use on furniture or accessory objects before the year 1700. Ever since paper and prints have been available to man, these creative materials have been used as ornaments. How far back the art goes or where it was done and who did it are not nearly as important as what material relates directly to découpage as we know it today.

Until the use of engraving and etching, the only line work for reproduction was block printing done with wood blocks. These were used primarily as illustrations for religious works or for educating in the religious context. Most of this work was done by monks or sponsored by the church. Therefore, we could conclude that the earliest forms of printing were predominantly religious and educational. The earliest ornaments and vignettes were religious symbols since so much relating to the church was transferred from pagan or old worship practice and embraced in the Christian tradition.

The engravings, etchings, stone lithographs, aquatints, mezzotints, and other reproduction methods used in the 18th century provided a wealth of material on many subjects. These prints, highly ornamental and of decorative quality, would provide a great temptation to the découpeur. Engravings were not highly regarded by the collector or the patron. They were widely done as reproductions of masterpieces and paintings of great value. The engravers were a group of highly skilled people whose work was unique. Often a single plate could take up three years of a dedicated engraver's life. The beauty and precision of their work has paid off in the long run, as these works which were earlier scorned are now prized by museums, which have special curators of prints.

The 18th century artists, whose works were copied, scorned the engravers and sought to have them barred from the artists' guild. There were a few artists who did direct etching and engraving of their own and who were far more broad-minded about the profession or art of engraving.

The most notable French engravings were created from the year 1710 to the end of the century. Aging Louis XIV saw a new era of rejuvenation. Watteau was to be a dominant figure throughout the century. In many books on 18th century French engraving there is no mention of Pillement at all. He rarely did his own engraving and much of the work that he designed was engraved by someone else. This designer, who in his own time was not especially noted, has since been recognized as the inspired genius whose work is preferred by the découpeur. Also, there were many crayon and pen sketches from both Jean Pillement and François Boucher. Reproductions of these sketches are highly regarded by those currently engaged in the art of découpage.

In France the flowering of découpage was linked with the prints of the engravers and artists of this 18th century period, who were creating elegant designs suitable for ornamentation of all types in the spirit of the new decor. Jean Pillement was most prolific; he created exotic flowers, birds, cartouches, borders, and small scenic vignettes. Pillement's wonderful world of fantasy was largely designed for repeat uses—such as fabrics, textile design and wall ornamentation, wallpaper, wall panels, bas relief plaster. For this reason, we see his characters climb ladders into the scene above where there are other characters in a balancing act or perhaps fending off a dragon. His ornamental people were for the most part in the Chinese style, called by the French name—chinoiserie. He designed many fantastic insects, butterflies, birds and floral garlands. These flights of the imagination prove his mastery of drawing and his real creative genius. It seems certain that Pillement did not design with the idea of his prints being cut. They were to be inspirations for plaster work for the textile designers and other decorators of the day.

Pillement's chinoiserie is not always popular with those new to découpage. On the contrary, it is rather ignored as the novice "oh's and ah's" at the marvelous drawing Boucher exhibits in his cherubs and well-rounded drawings of Venus. Boucher was an engraver and artist as well. As you become more familiar with découpage you will have a deep and growing appreciation of Pillement's chinoiserie.

Martin Englebrecht's sturdy characters, made to represent the trades, show a humorous collection of people who are constructed from their own wares. A clockmaker and his wife made from clocks and clock parts, a pastry vendor made up of tiers of goodies, and others immediately recognized by symbols of their occupation, were original and popular engravings sought by the collector and now are of permanent importance in découpage.

VICTORIAN DÉCOUPAGE

During the latter part of the 19th century, die-cutting and embossing made colored scrapbook pictures easy to use and very popular. About this time gold foil was embossed and die-cut in the same manner. These companion materials were produced in Germany and used extensively there; however, they were produced with the idea of being used in scrapbooks and for other ornamental uses. They were used in Germany on furniture—generally these embossed cutouts were pasted together in geometric shapes—following the contours of the furniture. Biedermeier furniture was the style most frequently used. The English used scrapbook pictures on screens, frequently in a dense concentration of material.

This tabletop screen is 9 inches high and shows panels of the Twelve Days of Christmas. The gold-embossed borders provide attractive ornament. The script is mounted on the back.

A cameo medallion, used uncolored, is pasted on a turquoise ground and decorated with silver-embossed paper braid. Many coats of varnish create a beautiful finish for this piece of Victorian découpage.

A collection of Victorian découpage using gold paper braid for decoration on the tree, tea caddy, wastebasket, stamp holder, flower vase and cruet.

CONTEMPORARY VICTORIAN
DÉCOUPAGE

Victorian découpage is identified by the embossed die-cut material that is used. If hand-colored cutouts accompany the scrapbook embossed material, it is still called Victorian because of the predominant use of border designs and fill-in ornaments. If small borders are used in gold paper braid and the majority of the cutout material is from current full color prints, it is called modern découpage because of the large proportion of modern material that is used. When gold paper braid border material is used on a piece which is predominantly a reproduction of

18th and 19th century prints, the work is referred to as 18th century découpage. There are many combinations in which all three kinds of material are used and you would call this simply découpage, and avoid trying to estimate how much of one or another is used and what to call it. Think of the situation in terms of fabric—silk, cotton, and nylon. If you have a predominantly silk costume you will call it silk even though cotton trim is used. If you have a cotton dress with nylon lace it is called a cotton dress. If you have a combination of all three you refer to it by the type of design, such as a daytime costume or an after-five dress. So, in the instance of the use of all three types of découpage refer to it as "a three-panel découpage screen with Chinese motifs," or "a trinket box done in découpage with an apricot background."

In using Victorian scrapbook pictures, they too can be cut apart for better placement—or to make the design less static. They can be cut apart to make an open composition, or to make two pieces about the same size. The gold paper braid is cut apart for greater versatility. A horizontal scroll border can be cut apart and made into a vertical design.

The most important facet of découpage is the idea—which basically begins with the designs you use, how you use color, and the relationship of sides and top in a three-dimensional piece. In the instance of a screen or two-dimensional piece the total design impact is the thing to observe.

Generally, you will use Victorian embossed material for its color and ornamental quality. Many designers of small pieces such as boxes and trays use the gold paper braid to add an embossed texture to the piece on which they are working. A neat beaded or scrolled border, after being glued in place, is painted with two base coats along with the remainder of the box. The whole embossed area is glazed with an antiquing mixture and wiped to give an ornamental effect without the color of the metallic border.

Use borders imaginatively—they will greatly enhance your work. They can be used to alter the appearance of a geometric shape. A rectangular box is not as intriguing until a spandrel shape is placed around the central figure. Spandrels can be used as a completely solid frame or only the oval frame without the triangular corner ornaments. In picture frames for photographs, the oval mat is called a spandrel mat. In framing 18th and 19th century portraits, the wooden oval cut-out was called the spandrel.

On a very long box—3″ x 12″—break the surface into three rectangular areas with borders. The larger center rectangle should be horizontal and the two ends vertical. This is almost the effect of a double window with a pair of shutters. When using octagonal boxes it is best to use an oval or octagonal design on the top. A rectangle or a square on an octagonal box is an awkward use of space.

The beautiful designs and lovely cutting on this box are repeated in an interior design plan. A very narrow gold border is used to define the contours of this well-made box. The oriental flowers are quite suited to the box which shows oriental influence. Pale pink ground is used for the natural colored flowers and figure.

Many of the borders will contour in long arcs but it is difficult to make one turn a short curve. If you want to use a narrow border up to a half-inch wide to turn a curve, cut through the border seven-eighths of the way across, just leaving a thin strip to hold the border together. Continue this clipping every quarter of an inch closer or farther apart according to the contour. Now bend gently to the curve. Practice this on a strip of paper.

It is a good idea to use sealer on the back of all embossed work to help keep the contoured motifs crisp. Apply white glue to both surfaces, the box and the border, let set about a minute to become more tacky, then press together. This makes a firmer contact and it dries faster.

QUESTIONS AND ANSWERS

Victorian Découpage: Gold Paper Braid

1. Q. How can I make the gold paper border flat so it does not take so much varnish to cover it?
   A. Use a roller or burnishing tool to press the embossing and flatten it after you paste it into place.

2. Q. What do you use to make the gold turn silver color?
   A. Lacquer thinner or denatured alcohol (Solox) will remove the stain, leaving silver foil exposed.

3. Q. What is the best way to put the narrow gold borders on?
   A. Apply white glue to the surface you are decorating and to the gold braid; allow to dry a little, then press together.

4. Q. How do you soak gold paper braid off when you use white glue?
   A. You can't. White glue is waterproof.

5. Q. What do you use to antique the braid? Can the same be used for brass feet?
   A. You can use artist's oil paints in black and Van Dyke brown, thinned with turpentine. Apply and wipe off. Antiquing glazes are also fine. You can use acrylic or even watercolor for the antiquing stain on any gilded surface and brass accessories. Burnt umber and burnt sienna are also good antiquing colors. Raw umber is favored by many. When using watercolor, protect with acrylic spray.

6. Q. Do the gold paper braids tarnish?
   A. No, they are aluminum foil stained with yellow, which gives the appearance of gold or brass.

7. Q. I have a lot of paper braid in different colors of gold. Will this show under the varnish?
   A. Yes, all the color variations will appear as different after many coats of varnish.

8. Q. How do I make all the gold braid the same color?
   A. Remove all the stain to silver and stain them again with a yellow stain in a lacquer base, or use many coats of orange shellac to obtain the same tone on all the braid.

9. Q. Is the gold paper braid back in style now? How about embossed scrap book pictures like flowers and cherubs?
   A. For a long time Victorian fancy work was scorned. It was not collectible. Antique dealers assured customers they didn't even have a piece of Victorian around. Today, the craft work and the

ornaments of this opulent and ornate decorating period is again in style. Regardless of how good or bad a period of design is, history shows that styles do return a generation or two later.

10. Q. Was there much découpage work done in gold braid and embossed paper cutouts?

A. The Austrians and Germans made lovely ornate decorations in tight geometric styles on furniture in the 19th century. Much Biedermeier furniture was done this way. Caroline Duer, once fashion editor of Paris *Vogue,* was the best known modern designer of découpage using this material. Her work was lovely and fashionable—purchased by museums and private collectors alike.

11. Q. How do you prepare the gold braid for Victorian découpage or to use as borders for other things?

A. It is a good idea to spray acrylic over the gold braid when you first get it. Spray it over the foil side first in an even spray—passing over back and forth at a steady moderate pace. The plastic spray will hold the yellow dye in place, which is rather easily removed when you seal over the braid with sealer or shellac. Also, spray the back side of the whole piece. If you always prepare the gold paper braid this way, it will be ready to use with no loss of time preparing it just before you use it.

12. Q. Is gold paper braid called by any other name?

A. Yes. It is given many different names by the many people who sell it, either prepacked or in open stock. It is called Dec-it by Harrower House, Decorets by Taylor House, Fools Gold by East House, and other trade names. It all comes from Germany and Austria.

13. Q. Can the antique material be obtained anywhere?

A. Brandon Memorabilia in New York City has a good selection of antique gold braid and scrapbook pictures.

Marbleized Papers, Tortoise Shell and Gold Tea Chest Paper

1. Q. Where do you use marbleized paper in découpage?

A. Usually, these papers are not used except for lining. They can be used as a background if the pattern is very subtle. Marbleizing is a lot of design competition for cutout pieces.

2. Q. Do you seal this paper before you use it?

A. Use sealer on the front before pasting. Some of the marble colors may be water soluble or may bleed with the use of sealer. Seal the piece before using because it will not stretch when wet with paste. Lacquer or acrylic sprays as well as shellac can be used as a sealer for marbleized paper.

3. Q. How do I prepare gold tea chest paper to use for a découpage background?

    A. Use varnish or acrylic spray on the gold side. Use sealer or shellac on the back. This paper can be very fragile when moist with paste. Also, remember you will have to level the paste underneath—which means you will press the excess paste to get it out.

MODERN DÉCOUPAGE

Modern découpage is distinguished by the use of currently printed flowers, birds, little figures and a whole world of subjects which are printed in full color. The beginners in découpage find this material gets them started without spending the time required to color a print. It opens the door for many who would never do any découpage if they had to color a print. Most of these people do learn to color later and find it wasn't so difficult after all. A most pertinent fact about modern découpage (other than opening the door for the beginner) is that it is very inexpensive. It is possible to find greeting cards to cut out, even gift wrapping papers or pictures from discarded magazines. These materials can be very beautiful and easy to work with; however, there are a few hazards. One important caution is to obtain colored prints which do not bleed under the sealer. The way to test for bleeding is simple and a standard step in preparing your material. Apply sealer. If it doesn't bleed or make a halo of color from the printed area, it is satisfactory. If one sealer doesn't work, try an alternative. First, try the alcohol soluble découpage sealers, or even shellac.

If the print bleeds, there is yet another possibility. Try an acrylic spray. In some instances acrylic sprays make inks bleed but the découpage sealer works well. Try it both ways. If neither prevents the problem, dispose of the print. It just can't be used.

Another caution is to work with papers of the same weight. Heavier and lighter papers rarely work well together and very likely the character of the material is different on the various weights of paper.

A very important caution is that you should not use aluminum spray paint on the back of a print. It may correct the problem of ink showing through but you encounter a greater problem. Rarely does a print hold well if it has aluminum paint on the back. The most frequent problem découpeurs have asked me about is that of the print lifting or having a blister under it. In nearly all these cases they had used aluminum paint. Under the many coats of varnish, much stress is created as the varnish

This handsome and easy-to-do box has a red-brown painted background, items cut out of a yachtsman's mail order catalog and a durable varnish finish.

dries and shrinks. This blister may occur as early as three months after being finished or as late as two years.

I am sure many people work out methods of using magazine prints. What works one time may not work the next time. The many types and grades of paper used in modern printing are as different as the varieties of printing inks. Most of the inks are not alcohol soluble or soluble in mineral spirits, which is the vehicle in many acrylic sprays. We're just worrying about the few inks that do bleed and how to control them.

Since the most important material for modern découpage is the print and how to prepare it, I've tried to acquaint you with some problems. Generally, you should not have any problems if you seal the print on the front, let it dry, and cut it out. Apply paste to the surface and press the print in place. After many coats of varnish, you'll have a very lovely piece.

Combine gold paper borders and corner ornaments with motifs cut out of greeting cards which are embossed. This Victorian material helps extend the few designs one can obtain from a greeting card. Very charming little trinket boxes can be made from cutout greeting cards, especially if a message or little poem is placed inside the lid.

Many of the beautiful and very exclusive découpage basket purses are done with modern découpage materials. The loveliest prints from Switzerland, Germany, Austria and England are available in series of Gould's Birds, Redouté's Fruits and Flowers, and Audubon Bird Prints. These are found in inexpensive books or portfolios and are a very good buy. There are also books of Austrian folk costumes and people from many other countries done in a decorative style very suitable for découpage.

Around Christmas time many inexpensive children's books are available in gay colors and charming subjects. The animals are beguiling and are large enough to be very easy cutting. This is wonderful material for some small piece of furniture. Once at an auction we found a sturdy little toy box, which could double as a child's seat. It was in good sound condition so we painted it a teal blue flat enamel, which was a perfect background color for bright animals, birds, and Santa Claus with his ornate sleigh. A fireplace with stockings, bright bricks, and glossy new toys made

The little trunk-shaped box is painted shell pink and has prints from a child's song book.

A thriving community of sea ceatures is set against a celadon green background. The color prints are cut out from a children's nature book.

An old footbath is painted yellow ochre and decorated inside with cut-out prints of Audubon's chipmunk, squirrel, and outside with game birds.

Color prints of wildflowers provide related design material to accompany Audubon prints of birds. The black background is a lovely contrast color for this wastebasket.

a good print for the back, which is where we began the design. Santa and his reindeer were on the left side, all the little animals and birds were placed on the front and the right side, so Christmas was not evident from the front. The same toy box could be used through the holiday season as a log box in years to come. It was necessary to buy two books (under a dollar each) to have sufficient material.

The three types of découpage materials are as different as if they were entirely unrelated. In the world of the 18th century prints, the delicate material and fabulous engravings are a real inspiration to work with. Relaxing with a Victorian découpage project is yet another world. It is entirely different from 18th century work to use ornate gold paper motifs cut apart and reassembled to suit your needs. The modern materials are as new as today and offer a truly inspiring selection of prints.

When you use a large print or magazine picture with very little cut out of the center, try to make some small cutouts so the varnish can tack the print down to the surface. This should be helpful in preventing any later release of the print from the surface.

Sometimes you can combine a very attractive print from a magazine with black and white prints in the right scale, which you color to match. If the additional prints are used on the sides and not right next to the colored book prints, the illusion will be that they are all alike.

QUESTIONS AND ANSWERS

Modern Découpage

1. Q. Why don't you recommend wallpaper for découpage?
   A. It is pulpy and coarse. The patterns are never fine. Often the layers of heavier paper will stratify and come loose. It is impossible to cut intricate patterns and it is difficult to cover with varnish. Avoid heavy prints and wallpaper. They weren't made to be covered with layers of varnish.

2. Q. What about using fabrics, real butterflies and flowers? Some people do découpage with these materials.
   A. This is not découpage. Avoid this kind of thing.

3. Q. What do you do with a magazine picture that you want to use, but there is black type on the back?
   A. Erase as much as possible--gently. Place on a medium to dark shade of background. This camouflages the type. If you still see the type, do not use the picture as the varnish will exaggerate the type. After all, you can't use everything you can cut out.

Understanding the Materials You Work With

The materials you work with are really not difficult to understand. There are a few rules to go by but your best teacher may be yourself. You learn the most from your own mistakes. There aren't many that will baffle you. A problem faced by many new to découpage reminds me of a patient who sees many different doctors and only finds out he is more confused than before. Please use one book for reference and bear with the author until you understand the material. Do not quote from many different sources and follow the advice of each person you consult. Everyone is working for the same result but the methods may be a little different. After you understand one approach, then branch into another author's work. Each one will cover something you haven't learned before. But do not mix them all together! Your own keen observation is the answer to your search for knowledge.

Read the labels on everything you buy. Notice the percentages of solids in varnish, get what you pay for. Ask questions of the people who sell you material. Write letters to people who write articles. They expect to answer questions—they can answer yours, too. All paints, varnishes and sealers should have clear labels explaining drying time, solvents, what to clean your brush with, and the number of fluid ounces must be accurate. Read all of this information. Buy only products of reputable manufacturers. Nationally advertised brands are the best buy.

UNDERSTANDING PASTE, GLUE, MUCILAGE, ADHESIVE

The more delicate and intricate cutting is done on lighter weight paper. This fragile cutting should be pasted down with a light découpage paste. It holds very well and is easy to move out from under prints as it sets more slowly than white glue.

Heavier paper, such as is found in hand-made paper of antique prints and other papers used for prints in color, requires heavier paste or glue, such as the white glue—Elmer's, Duratite, and so on. Paste is also used for these heavier prints, but the white glue *is not* used in fine cutting. It is sometimes difficult to remove excess white glue after it is hard and set because it is waterproof. Adhesive is a name generally given to the whole group of paste, glue, cement and other compounds used to adhere materials to each other. It comes from the Latin meaning "to stick." Read all labels. This should tell you what you need to know.

You do not use cements or heavy duty wood and laminating adhesives except for wood repair or some special glass-to-wood use. Do not use paste for heavy repairs—only on papers.

"Adhesium" available at paint and wallpaper stores is widely used on glass before application of a pasted print. A thin coating of this clear material is wiped on clean glass and allowed to dry. After the print is pasted on the surface and is dry, a damp sponge or cloth is used to remove the "Adhesium" and excess paste from the glass surface. If you use tea chest paper over all the background you leave all the "Adhesium" to help the paper adhere to the glass. It is not a paste or glue itself but is used to help prints adhere to glass. This sticky material would be good used on any gloss surface such as a lacquer tray or a prefinished metal.

SEALERS

There are many kinds of sealers. The oldest and most traditional is shellac. Orange shellac is bleached for "white" shellac, which is pale in color. Rectified shellac is an artist grade which is refined to remove certain impurities. Any of these three types has a limited shelf-life, which means the time between manufacture, sitting in a warehouse, on a dealer's shelf, and finally in the customer's possession. The shelf-life of shellac is only about six months under most favorable conditions. If it is not fresh when applied to a surface it becomes gummy and is very slow to dry or even may not dry for weeks. This is very bad because in using solvent alcohol to remove the old shellac you may damage the prints, and surely you will remove stain from the gold paper braid which will turn it silver.

Modern sealers developed for découpage are the result of modern chemistry. They have indefinite shelf-life and always dry as they should. They will require only one caution, do not use them in a moisture-laden atmosphere. Alcohol, which is the solvent for all sealers, attracts moisture, thereby accumulating water in the sealer film and appearing to be a frosty coating.

Découpage sealers are important in preventing dark paint colors from bleeding. It is a good idea to apply sealer to the entire surface of the work you are doing before varnishing. If you know the paint color you have used does not bleed under varnish, it is not necessary to seal before varnishing. You can make a test panel to determine which paints bleed.

Sealers have another advantage. They act as a paint bonding adhesive on glass or other very slick surfaces. Découpage sealers remain slightly plastic and prevent paint chipping from a glossy metal or glass surface.

The découpage sealers are important in penetrating the surface of the paper to change the porous surface into a non-porous surface. A sealed print will not be discolored by varnish. Paper which is sealed is stiffer and easier to cut. Most important, the sealer-saturated paper will not disintegrate when it is wet with paste and moved with the fingers for removal of paste or to flatten the print. Finally, when you clean off excess paste, the print, though delicately cut, will remain intact.

WHAT PAINT TO USE

The flat enamels are by far the most suitable paints to use for découpage. You can easily see any extra paste that is yet to be removed, as it is glossy on a flat paint surface. But the greatest advantage of the dull surface is that varnish adheres to it much better. Semi-gloss paints are used as a second choice. It is wise to avoid rubber base or water base paints. It is possible to obtain flat enamel or flat oil paints everywhere paint is sold. It is not always easy to find the right color, but these can be mixed by the merchant who sells you the paint. If you'd like to experiment in mixtures, it is possible to do this quickly and with no waste of paint. Dip a few drops of paint from one can, a touch from another, and blend on a piece of wax paper or newspaper. This way you can see if the colors you are blending will become the color you hope to obtain.

Paint basically is varnish with colored pigments added. Since you will be working with turpentine or mineral spirits as thinners, do not hesitate to add one or the other if your paint seems too thick. It is very important to have paint level out flat. If it doesn't, you are using too much or it is too thick. The best application procedure in paint and varnish is to apply thin coats, be frugal. You cannot have drips or runs if there is no excess paint build-up.

KNOWING YOUR MATERIALS CHART

Product	Thinner	Drying Time Between Coats	Remove With	Type of Drying	Flammable
Shellac	Alcohol	45 minutes	Alcohol	Evaporates	Yes
Varnish	Turpentine	24 hours	Paint remover	Oxidize	Yes
Acrylic Spray	Mineral Spirits	1 hour	Turpentine	Evaporates	Yes
Lacquer	Lacquer Thinner	4 hours	Lacquer Thinner	Evaporates	Yes
Epoxy Varnish	See Label	8 hours	Not soluble	Polymerize	Yes
Oil Paint Flat	Turpentine or Mineral Spirits	24 hours	Paint remover	Oxidize and Polymerize	Yes
Enamel	Turpentine or Mineral Spirits	24 hours	Paint remover	Oxidize and Polymerize	Yes
Metal Primer	Turpentine or Mineral Spirits	24 hours	Paint remover	Oxidize and Polymerize	Yes

THINGS TO AVOID

Types of material that are difficult to work with:
1. Wallpaper, post cards, photographs
2. Fabrics, printed embossed wrapping paper
3. Wood fiber, crepe paper, tinted tissue paper
4. Natural plant material—leaves, petals, butterflies

Types of material that bleed:
1. Some magazine, calendar and greeting card prints
2. The watercolors which are aniline dyes. These are liquid—ready mixed in small bottles.
3. Some of the *leaves* of color which are soluble in water.
4. Alcohol soluble inks

How to test:

If the alcohol soluble sealer causes these materials to bleed, try an acrylic spray. If no color comes through to the back of the colored print now and no halo of color from the ink, then it can be used. If you still have doubt, brush the varnish on a small test area before you cut. If a print bleeds do not use it.

SILICONE AS A HAZARD

Be sure to notice what is in any spray you use to keep the fabric soil-resistant. If you use a silicone spray you can contaminate a good varnish finish. Silicones in hand creams or anywhere else act as a separator and may prevent adhesion of future coats of varnish. This is a caution measure. If you are going to refinish a piece of furniture which you know has had a furniture polish spray used often, this piece should be checked. If the spray can label reads, "contains silicone," it may not hold a varnish or paint at all once the finish is worked on. There is very little that can be done. See your paint dealer. There is always hope that some product will be available to neutralize this penetrating separator.

WHAT SCISSORS TO USE AND WHY —KNIVES AND BLADES

Découpage scissors: the most popular and best scissors are the fine steel cutlery known also as cuticle scissors. They stay sharp the longest and this is important. These are held with thumb and third finger with the blades resting against the index finger. Usually the blade is held pointing out.

Silhouette scissors are very convenient for cutting fine work or straight lines. Many people prefer these easy-to-use scissors. Generally, the finger hole is larger and suits men better than the découpage scissors.

Embroidery scissors can also be used if they are small, sharp and well adjusted; that is, not too loose. The turn screw can be tightened or loosened to make cutting easier. A tiny amount of oil or vaseline in the hinge and rubbed over the blade is helpful. Never use rusted scissors —or permit them to rust.

Shears and larger scissors are used only for cutting large prints in two or occasionally for long strips of border material. They are heavy and not suited to fine cutting.

Oiling and Adjusting the Scissors: New scissors are rather like new shoes—they look well but they need to be broken in. A good machine oil will keep the blades and hinge in perfect order. If the scissors need to be loosened, the set screw can be released slightly. If, after cutting awhile, the scissors seem to drag or resist cutting, gently touch each of the blades with a tiny amount of oil. Even the tiny amount of natural skin oil on the face is enough to lubricate the blade. After your scissors are broken in, the cutting seems much easier. Natural wear is the best way to break them in. Do a lot of practice cutting.

Knives and razor blades are invaluable for certain types of cutting. If you cut well with a knife or have always used a razor blade, it may be difficult to sell you on the idea of scissors. Take my word for it—much of the cutting done in découpage is easier, more attractive and much less strained with the right scissors.

BURNISHING TOOLS

Special tools to bevel the edges of the print, or press it into the background wood, may save half the effort of burying the print in varnish. The burnishing tool is pressed along the edges of the cutout print after it is pasted in place and dried. In softer wood or on a gesso finish it may be possible to embed the print level with the surface before applying the sealer. Then proceed with the varnish finish.

The steel burnishing tool has a choice of two ends: the spoon-shaped end is for working on a flat surface. The other end is for narrow crevices and right angles such as along the molding at the bottom edge of a box.

The agate burnisher, used for polishing gold leaf, is superb for burnishing the print edge in découpage work. Agate, being a semiprecious stone,

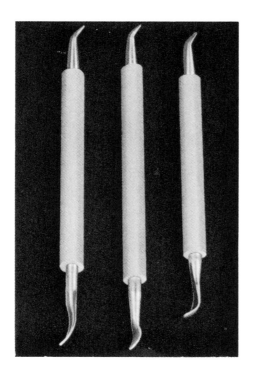

Three burnishing tools are shown. The spoon end is used to press the print edge into the background. The point end is used on embossed border edges.

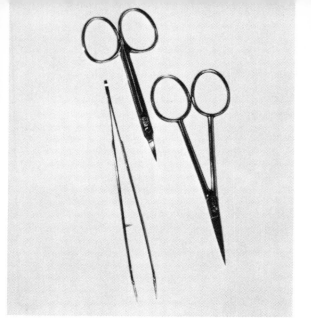

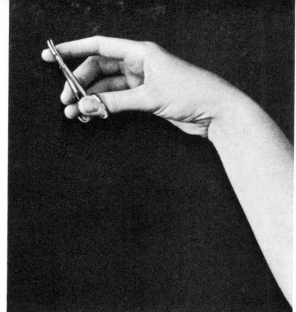

Either the curved découpage scissors, or slender silhouette scissors are essential; tweezers are necessary to handle delicate cuttings.

The scissors are held with thumb and third finger in a very relaxed manner.

when shaped, hand-polished and mounted in a metal ferrule is a very expensive tool. It is possible to use small smooth agates not mounted to accomplish burnishing, but it is tiresome and not as effective.

QUESTIONS AND ANSWERS

Burnishing

1. Q. How can I flatten a print and embed the edges into the wood before varnishing?

   A. Use a steel or agate burnisher. Press the edges gently, then more firmly with increasing pressure until you barely feel the edge.

2. Q. Can this be done right after pasting?

   A. Wait an hour at least. You can burnish *before applying sealer or after.*

3. Q. Will this help flatten wallpaper cutouts?

   A. Yes, but it is a job. Avoid wallpaper.

4. Q. Can I use any other object for burnishing, such as a silver spoon?

   A. Stainless steel is hard and won't wear off. Silver may be soft enough to wear and leave dark marks. Stainless is better. Test the object

31

you have in mind. A nut pick, used on the back side, may work for you if you don't have a burnisher.

5. Q. Where can I obtain a burnishing tool and what do I ask for?
   A. Art and craft stores have these supplies. Any découpage supply store should have them.

6. Q. Will a burnisher work on metal and glass?
   A. Yes, it will bevel the edges but obviously it can't embed the print. Masonite and other hard dense surfaces come in this category, too.

7. Q. Will a burnisher help embed fabrics cut out for découpage?
   A. Do not use fabric cutouts. This is not découpage.

8. Q. For what is the narrow end of the burnisher used?
   A. Crevices and inside corners, such as along a box with a base molding or narrow contours.

TWEEZERS

This handy tool will prevent damage to your prints. If you have small pieces to place into paste, the tweezers are an invaluable tool. They assist you in lifting a print from the pasted surface, if it is necessary. Curved-nose tweezers are by far the best to buy; however, if you have a pair of the spade-nose tweezers, the kind stamp collectors use, these are useful in handling the prints. Cosmetic tweezers are also useful, but they are much stiffer. A pair of tweezers I enjoy very much are longer and finer than the short curve-nose tweezers. These were purchased at a dental supply house, which I'm sure will sell you if you don't mind spending a little more money for this very fine tool.

BRUSHES

There are many kinds of hair and bristle that are used to make brushes. The small brushes used for little boxes are probably squirrel, ox, pony, camel, sable, or some other soft hair. They should be cleaned in a proper solvent, shampooed, shaped and set aside to dry. The larger brushes, one inch to two inches wide, are ox hair or other combinations, and are more difficult to clean after use. Dip them in their solvent and clean until no more color comes out. Then, wash with detergent and water—a couple of good sudsy shampoos—wrap in a *paper* to make the chisel shape end. Dry the brush, bristle end down, so water will not dry in the ferrule causing rust.

Brushes used in sealer are cleaned thoroughly in alcohol and shaped to dry. If your brush dries a little stiff, it wasn't stored clean. Alcohol will always soften this brush. More sealer used on the brush will dissolve the previous sealer. The same is true of lacquer brushes, cleaned in lacquer thinner.

Varnish brushes are the most tedious to clean because they are used daily during the build-up of a découpage finish. It is very satisfactory to leave the brush in turpentine from day to day until you are finished. This will prevent varnish from drying along the shafts of hair, which is one thing that causes a poor varnish finish. The dried varnish always seems to work out, coat after coat. Don't let it happen to begin with. Use the varnish brush only for varnish. Label the sealer brush and the brush used for paint and don't use them alternately.

PUMICE AND ROTTENSTONE

These are two different materials coming from two very different places. The largest deposits of pumice are in Sicily. Pumice is a volcanic ash, a silicate, and a sharp abrasive used also as scouring powder. It is used with oil as an abrasive to smooth down a varnish finish. Pieces cut from an old felt hat are excellent to be used for a rubbing pad—and re-used for a long time. A pound of pumice costs about thirty cents.

Rottenstone is a clay deposit which is dried, ground into a powder, and also used as a rubbing abrasive. Its cutting action is not as severe as pumice.

The advantage of using pumice or rottenstone is that they are much less expensive than wet or dry sandpaper and will contour more easily when used with a felt pad for rubbing. They are a little less convenient to store and messy to clean up. After all, an abrasive is an abrasive. Use the one which seems to work best for you—or whatever you feel does the job. I am inclined to use the #400 wet or dry sandpaper because there is a wider choice of abrasives in the grades of sandpaper and steel wool.

THE MAGNIFYING GLASS

Sometimes it is difficult to see the work you are doing and you wish to use a magnifying glass in preference to reading glasses. The precision ground glass that hangs from a cord around the neck is very practical and light weight. You may prefer the sand unit—to be placed on a table. Be sure to have a suitable light wherever you do your work.

Preparing Furniture for Découpage, Painting, etc.

The beginner must learn to discriminate between the bad dents and charming irregularities which contribute natural distress and the look of antiquity to a piece. By all means remove ring marks and geometric shapes of accident. Sandpaper must be changed when it fills. The disposable sandpaper is of less value than human energy.

The final coats of paint will show up irregular sanding. Sand in the direction of the grain. When sanding on the edges of painted surfaces, you must be very careful not to rub through the paint. Develop a sense of touch. Use the tips of the fingers to feel the surface lightly, without pressure. If the pressure is heavy you will feel only your own pressure, not the surface texture. It is possible to feel roughness that cannot be seen. Care must be taken to sand absolutely even and level. This makes the ideal surface for découpage.

FILLERS USED FOR FURNITURE WORK

Any repairs that are badly done are obvious. This is as unacceptable as the original damage. Minor repairs are filled with spackling compound —ready mixed or the kind to which you add water; use for cracks, holes, or any gouges. This material can be molded for replacement of broken mouldings. Larger cavities should be laid with glue first so the spackling will remain in the hole. When this material shrinks—and it will with a large hole—it must be brought back up to the surface and allowed to dry again, sanded, and sealed. Plastic wood can also be used for repair of holes. Allow to dry and sand level.

Vinyl filler (by various trade names) is made to fill open grain wood. This is wiped across the grain. It will fill small holes and cracks as it surfaces the wood. Sand when dry, and seal with shellac.

GLUE JOINTS OR SWELL WOOD

A good glue should be used to tighten joints or make other repairs before work proceeds. At the time a joint is glued you must apply pressure. It is a good idea to wrap old innertube rubber strips around the piece of furniture. It does not scratch and will contour to the piece on which you are working. A furniture vise should be used on large pieces.

If you have loose joints which can't be glued easily, swell the wood. This is done by a single application of one-half alcohol and one-half glycerin. Mix these and place eye droppers full in the dowel holes. It may take a few days for this to be tight, but it will hold.

SHELLAC—THE ORIGIN OF LAC

In Siam and India the lac trees are host to many small insects which cause the tree to "bleed" or secrete a sticky substance. This substance is the lac flake that is gathered or harvested only at night. After being melted, purified, and finally graded, it is exported. When it arrives in the United States, various manufacturers buy it and "cut it" with alcohol. A four pound cut should be diluted fifty percent with alcohol when you use it. This means you're using a two pound cut. Four pounds of lac, or solids, are added to a gallon of alcohol to make the four pound cut; only two pounds of lac are added to a gallon for the two pound cut.

Shellac deteriorates and is apt to become gummy after six months. It is absolutely necessary to use only fresh shellac. Write the date purchased on the label. Metal containers darken shellac—store it in glass containers. Shellac should be stirred, never shake it—this creates bubbles. In damp weather the alcohol will cause shellac to bloom. Milky shellac is anhydrous and attracts water like salt. If shellac gets cloudy, an application of alcohol should remove the bloom—then let dry. Do not work in a moisture-laden atmosphere when using shellac or varnish. After an hour of drying time, shellac may be coated with paint.

Good studio practice demands a brush used only for the sealer. For boxes and small projects you will need a small brush about one-half to one inch. If you are doing furniture or other large pieces, you will need a one-and-one-half inch to two inch thin bristle brush. A thick brush discharges too much shellac or other sealer. You will be able to do a better job using natural bristle brushes. My feeling is that my own limitations in talent are sufficient. I can't be hampered further by less than the best tools.

How to Apply Shellac to New Wood

Load the brush. Press out the excess on the inside of the container. (Drawing it across the edge of the can creates air bubbles.) Use quick even strokes, being careful not to overlap. The strokes should begin with a full brush in the center of the area to be covered; continue with light strokes across to the outer edge. Follow quickly by stroking from the center to the opposite edge. The brush will generally hold enough shellac to repeat this procedure on the following stroke. When the brush is less full, pressure is needed on the heel of the brush to discharge the remaining shellac. Reload the brush to complete the coverage and repeat the procedure. For carved pieces, use a minimum brush load. Tap the end bristles into the deep places to assure complete coverage. Pick up any runs or excess in the gentle tapping. A fine shellac coat requires precision, quickness, and a deft touch. If the shellac brush should become hardened—and alcohol doesn't do the job—it may be cleaned in a solution of half and half ammonia and water. NEVER SOAP. Shellac is the most used sealer; however, if you use lacquer sealer, sanding sealer, or pigmented sealer, they are to be applied in the same way as shellac.

HOW TO PREPARE THE SURFACE FOR PAINT

Raw Wood

Unpainted furniture fresh from the store or cabinet maker still requires sanding. There are often whiskers of wood or tool dents which should be sanded with 2/o garnet sandpaper. Sink any nail heads with a nail set and fill with a good wood filler or vinyl filler. Also, fill any joining cracks. These cracks should be sanded. Check for any leftover glue—chip off with razor blade and sand smooth. Dust the piece or clean up with a vacuum cleaner brush, use a tack rag, and then seal. The sealer closes the surface of thirsty raw wood and prevents uneven absorption of the paint. Only raw wood is sealed before painting.

Varnished Wood

Many new products are available for surface preparation of old varnish. These are mostly solvents. These will have names like Prepare-it, Sur-

Three tiny trinket boxes are done on pastel grounds of ivory, powder blue and shell pink. The 18th century palette of colors is used for the prints. Very narrow gold borders are used at the top, bottom, and at the edge where they meet.

facene, or Liquid Sandpaper. They do not do the job of sandpaper but they soften the old surface, which makes it more receptive to paint.

If you have a piece which has raised or blistered veneer, cut a narrow slash with a razor blade, fill with glue and weight the area, using wax paper to prevent sticking to the weight. Edges should be clamped with a C-clamp, using wood blocks. Fill any chips with wood filler, seal the chipped area with shellac and sand. Refer again to the use of fillers, if needed. Your piece is now ready to paint.

Painted Wood

A previously well-painted piece needs little work. It is wise to wash it with turpentine or mineral spirits to remove any grease or old wax. A light sanding assures best adhesion. The surface preparations such as Liquid Sandpaper, Surfacene, or Prepare-it are good insurance that your paint will hold well.

Drips and rollovers (the ridge of paint sometimes seen on the edges) should be chipped and sanded off. Chips in the paint should be carefully feathered out with 2/o and 6/o garnet paper. After sanding, wash off remaining residue with alcohol or mineral spirits. If filler is needed for holes, fill and sand. Shellac this area to seal it.

Glass or Glossy Metal Surface

Though you don't often paint over mirrors, glass or glossy metal, such as chrome, it is a good idea to include this information here. A penetrating sealer* should be used on these surfaces first, as the sealer will stick tightly to the slick surface and act as an adhesive for the paint. Any sealer labeled as "penetrating" will do this job.

* See supply source

Metal

It is a good idea to use a metal primer as an undercoat on all metal. This specially designed paint will protect the surface and prevent rust. It provides a good surface for the paint. Metal primer must dry overnight. Hardware should be primed before painting. Old painted hardware should be left in a can of lacquer thinner till clean, or use paint remover. You may need a wire brush—a suede cleaning brush is handy. Emery cloth is good for removing rust; also, wet or dry sandpaper can be used. Wash the surface with alcohol, apply a metal primer and dry overnight. Your metal is now ready for painting.

Metal preparation is really easier than wood but it does require some different materials.

OLD METAL—PAINT CHIPPED, DAMAGED, DENTED METAL

Use paint remover to clean metal. Hammer the dents out as smooth as possible. Wash with alcohol. Apply metal primer. Dry overnight and you are ready to paint.

OLD METAL—PAINTED

If the paint is in good over-all condition, you need not remove the paint. Simply wash with alcohol to remove the wax or oils. Sand lightly with very fine sandpaper if the surface is glossy. You are ready to paint.

OLD METAL—NOT PAINTED

Use sandpaper and steel wool if there is rust on the tin. Wash with alcohol and apply one coat of metal primer. Dry overnight and sand lightly. You are now ready to paint.

NEW METAL—GALVANIZED

Wash with a diluted acetic acid or vinegar. Diluted acetic acid is found at drug stores and sometimes paint stores. This etches the surface to cause good adhesion. No primer is necessary. Apply two or three thin coats of paint. A smooth surface is vital. Thin paint flows out easily and makes a level surface. Sand very lightly (just like whisking off fingerprints) between coats. Caution: diluted acetic acid may be dangerous to use. (see label.)

NEW METAL—NOT GALVANIZED

Wash with alcohol and apply metal primer. Sand and apply paint.

NEW METAL—PAINTED

On a tray with screened or lithographed scenes or flowers—use fine sandpaper over all to remove gloss and create a surface for good paint adhesion. Apply three thin coats of paint.

GOLD LEAF—JAPANESE PAPIER MÂCHÉ

Do not sand, but apply four coats of two pound cut of shellac—one hour apart. Alternate coats of shellac—one vertical, one horizontal, or use two coats penetrating sealer, such as Treasure Sealer.

Antique Gesso

The white thick layer on old frames and furniture that looks like plaster is likely gesso. This material was used in Europe to cover the surface of patching and joining odd pieces of wood. The scarcity of cabinet wood and the fact that hardwood was not easily available, brought about the need for an attractive finish. This gesso is made of whiting—a chalk-like powder and glue. It does not shrink, but the wood is likely to. The old pieces in Europe are not prone to cracking and shrinking as they are kept in places cooler and more humid. When these antiques are brought into our heated homes, they dry out and shrink.

The antique tray is ornamented with the prints of Jean Pillement. The 18th century palette is quite authentic for color. The epaulette cask at the right has a ground of palladium leaf and the prints are colored in the grisaille palette.

39

Delicate cut-outs are carefully placed on this footed box. The brass ring on the front is especially effective because of the ornaments surrounding it. Subtly antiquing the brass fittings makes the whole effect more authentic.

RESTORING ANTIQUE GESSO

Chip off all loose pieces with a knife. Sand and feather out these places down to the wood. There will be some places, such as carvings, where this is not possible and the piece must be filled with a vinyl filler —such as the ready-to-use spackling. It is helpful to use a small artist paint spatula for little filling jobs. The small tool is good for smooth repairs. After filling the holes, sand, and seal with shellac. On such a piece, you will have to decide if an over-all shellacking would be wise. In most instances, the piece should be shellacked all over. It is then ready to receive paint.

Plaster—Marble—Stone and Leather

In order to prepare these materials for paint the surface must be cleaned thoroughly with alcohol.* This will remove old wax and oils. Fill any holes or cracks with a vinyl filler, allow to dry, and sand smooth. You are ready for the shellac. Use a two-pound cut. Apply four thin coats forty-five minutes apart. This will thoroughly seal the surface preparing a perfect base for the paint.

TO REPAIR A TEAR OR HOLE IN LEATHER

When a hole must be repaired in a leather panel of a screen, glue a round patch of fabric on the *back* side of the leather. A synthetic resin

* Alcohol-solvent alcohol, wood alcohol, denatured alcohol, the same as you use in a chafing dish burner.

or vinyl glue is used to hold the fabric. Fill the front area of the hole with a vinyl filler for a patch. Stain it with oil color thinned with turpentine—the color you will be using on the front. Seal with shellac when dry. Basically, this procedure would be followed in repairing a hole in a leather covered table top. If the hole was made by a cigarette, the charred portion should be scraped out and underlaid with a thin coating of glue to hold firmly the vinyl filler patch.

Replacing Molded Pieces—Casting in Plaster

A good impression can be obtained usually by pressing modelling clay or kindergarten oil clay against the piece to make a mold. Water will act as a separator. When you have the mold ready, mix a little plaster to fill the cavity and the replacement is made.

TO MIX PLASTER

Use a small plastic bowl or half a rubber ball to mix the plaster. Fill with the amount of water that the finished project will take. You can pour water into the cavity to measure this. Usually, a two part plaster to one part water is a good ratio. Pour plaster into the water until it appears to be saturated; do not stir until all the plaster is in the water. After stirring, the mixture begins to form and thicken in approximately five to ten minutes. As soon as the forming begins, pour the plaster into the mold. After twenty to thirty minutes you can remove the model from the mold. It may take forty-eight hours to dry the plaster—then, seal with shellac.

REMOVE DUST, SANDING RESIDUE
OR RUST

This is very important. Your paint job depends on being done over a clean—not dusty—surface. It is also possible to contaminate the rest of the paint in the can if you transfer dust into fresh paint. Use a magnet to pick up steel wool particles. A vacuum cleaner attachment is very good to use on a sanded piece. A tack rag is a valuable "tool" for the painter. They are inexpensive and ready to use, and are available at hardware or paint stores. You may prefer to make a tack rag, using cheese cloth and a little slow drying varnish. Keep this in a glass jar between uses to prevent drying. The ready-made tack rags stay tacky.

Metal

Wastebasket—previously painted:	Sand lightly to create a surface for adhesion of paint. Wash with alcohol, then paint it. Use a contrasting color inside. Make a cardboard bottom board—seal and paint.
Wastebasket—raw metal:	Wash with vinegar. Dry and paint an undercoat of metal primer. Make a cardboard bottom board—seal with shellac and paint. Attach pull ribbon to edge to remove bottom for good cleaning.
Teapot—needs plating:	Wipe off with alcohol and apply paint directly to metal.
Aluminum Pitcher:	Apply penetrating sealer directly to aluminum to create a bonding base for the paint. One even coat is adequate.
Watering Can—raw metal:	Wipe with vinegar. Apply metal primer—one coat, then ready for paint.
Tray—unpainted:	Wipe with alcohol. Apply metal primer. Sand when dry and apply paint.

Ceramic Unglazed—Bisque Ware

Box and Lid:	Apply two generous coats of sealer to close porous surface. Then you are ready to paint. Ceramic stains may be used as a paint.
Picture Frames:	Apply two generous coats of sealer to close porous surface. Apply base color.
Rose Bowl—other bowl shapes:	Apply two generous coats inside and out of sealer to close porous surface. Apply base color.
Vase or Cylinder Urn:	Pour sealer on the inside—roll around to cover all inside surface. Apply two coats to the outside and dry. You are ready now for base color.
Switchplate—Socket Plate:	Apply two coats of sealer and dry. You are ready for base color.

Découpage Procedures

ASSEMBLING THE COMPOSITION

As you lay out your design, there may be too much foliage or other material in one area and a need for some extra material at another place. Cut it from one place and use where it is needed. This redesigning of the print material is unique in découpage and a tremendous design advantage.

For your first design projects, I would suggest cutting a piece of paper the size of your box lid or tray and complete the temporary composition tacked onto this paper. Then, you can pick up the pieces one at a time to paste them into place rapidly before your pasted surface is dry.

It is best to remove all hardware from the box and put the hinges in to fit the finished dimensions of the box. If the hinges fit before the box is decorated and varnished, it is unlikely they will fit perfectly when you reassemble the box. It might be necessary to raise the hinge with a piece of cardboard slipped between the box and the hinge—not noticed when the screws are replaced.

Planning a Focal Point

A good composition emphasizes good design. We have an inborn sense about design and we let this guide us when we place design materials in a harmonious relation to each other. When creating a design, let intuition guide you in the decisions about the placement and arrangement of the cutouts. One has an intuitive feeling that things balance; that colors are harmonious and that the scale is well coordinated. Good design is harmoniously arranged around a point of interest. The balance and rhythm which you create depend on carrying out a well laid plan. Sometimes your plan will be quite simple; although you do not use a great many motifs, the placement of your cutouts emphasizes the focal point and attracts the eye.

Some pieces which you plan will not have a point of interest or focal point. This type will have repeat motifs in a balanced relation to one another but they emphasize the importance of the structure of the furniture itself.

In the case of a very plain piece you can build an important scene as a focal point. On an ornate bombé or galbé piece it may be impossible to establish a focal point without detracting from the furniture structure, so the designs will decorate the surface and point up the basic form.

COLORING WITH OIL PENCILS

When you begin to use oil pencils you are forced to observe closely how color blends occur. You will note that even though you always knew leaves of trees and other foliage are green—try coloring a flat green leaf —something is missing. It just doesn't have any character or direction. Now let me help you observe something about the leaf and how to color it. Use a terra cotta #64 pencil softly as an undercoloring. Make the upper farther edge stronger, tapering to a light tone at the lower nearest edge. Now color with #46 grass green. Next, use terra cotta over the deep coloring again—gently but enough to note a deeper tone. Use zinc yellow #1 at the near edge of the leaf. If you hold this drawing out at arm's length, you will see your leaf has direction; it tends to be horizontal instead of vertical. You have control over depth and direction—you must guide color to make it work for you.

Let's try another example of form. Color a peach a nice flat peach color, an even coloring over all. Again, you'll observe a completely flat peach—it has no shape—even though it is the right color. If you add warm colors to ripen it, the peach will still remain flat. Get a peach, an orange, or other round fruit—notice why it has a round appearance. It has a source of light which highlights the surface nearest the source of light. If there is a light directly overhead, the highlights will be nearest to the light—move the light bulb. The source of light and the highlights follow the bulb. Just as the sun hits one side of the earth to make it bright, the opposite side is its darkest in the absence of light. Sometimes a reflection can give underlighting to make a second source of light and enhance the shape—just as sunlight reflecting from the moon lights the dark side of the earth.

Let us color the peach again with an understanding of color—an observation of form. Use terra cotta #64 to make a color foundation darker in the shadow—very pale to no coloring on the highlight. Use #17 pink to establish the apricot color, blending gently from dark to light. Use straw

The pencil is held at an angle and is used following the lines in the engraving. Gentle blending is done so that no pencil mark can be seen.

#58 to blend over the middle tones between light and dark. Use red #17 and burnt carmine #65 to augment the shadow. Zinc yellow #1 is used for the highlight, and last blend a little white #72 over the top half of the peach. This frosting with white can give the illusion of softness like the downy covering many peaches have.

Before you indulge in the delightful experience of coloring trees and buildings, observe them. You will be surprised how flat the forms are on an overcast day and how sculptural the form when the sun is near the horizon. Early in the morning the sun gently molds and shapes form, lighting the landscape from relatively flat forms to rich voluptuous forms. There is no greater thrill than the observation of beauty. It is abundant and around you all the time.

Color has perspective, too. The things nearest you are strongest in color; those at a distance are pastel; at the greatest distance they are muted by the mist in the atmosphere. An important observation in a sunlit scene is that the lightest light, such as the corner of a building, is next to the darkest dark. Using this knowledge, you will gain perspective dimension when you color buildings.

In many of the 18th century prints, the ground around the figures and animals could be very uninteresting if you use only green. The roadways or paths would not be grassy; traffic would have worn the grass down to the earth. Use terra cotta and straw color, as well as pearl gray and burnt carmine, along with three colors of green.

Coloring a Print

Découpage is an art involving a great deal of learning. First, it is necessary for you to master coloring the prints. This phase of découpage is of utmost importance because it is the foundation for so much of the work you will do. Understanding color and using color is more than an exciting experience; the whole world of sight is involved in our response to color.

The 18th century or Classic découpage is done with hand-colored reproductions or with original prints. The antique examples were all hand colored. You will enjoy coloring once you gain courage through a little practice. The beginner is apt to want to use all the colors available on the first print. This is frustrating and not practical. When you color flowers use a book with good color plates for a guide. Encyclopedias have butterflies, shells, flowers, and costumes which you can use. Borrow books from the library to help you when you start coloring. In no time you will be very pleased with your coloring ability, and delighted with the prints you've completed. You will find that you continue to gain confidence and improve your color knowledge with each bit of coloring.

After you have colored quite a few prints you will discover you are just beginning to learn. The art of coloring is not accomplished quickly. If you abandon coloring for a while, it takes a little practice to get back to your previous standard. Do not expect to do one print and be an expert any more than to bake a cake from a mix and feel you are now a pastry cook.

What Color Schemes to Use

These six palettes are suggestions which will help you, but are by no means the limitations of coloring. The beginner or advanced student appreciates color suggestions and these selections should prove to be invaluable. You need not use *all* the colors in the palette. Eventually, you will be able to develop your own color techniques and in some instances abandon the palettes suggested, replacing colors to your taste. My personal philosophy in teaching découpage is to boost your courage, talents and curiosity to the point where you are able to carry on in your own individual way, no longer needing instruction but instead creating freely and with great personal flair.

The 18th Century Palette: Begin coloring your figures, trees and all subject matter with a terra cotta pencil, coloring lightly and *only* in the shadows. With this color as underlay in the shadow area of the print, there is a lovely unity of tone. Use your pencils in the direction of the lines in the engraving. Notice that the shadows actually carry the color and give dimension to your work. Now, very gently add light green to the tops of trees and grasses, blending to darker green. Add touches of blues, pink, red, yellow and straw. Last, accent shadows and make crisp details with the burnt carmine. Have an extra piece of paper beside your print to try out blends with your pencils. When you discover certain tones that especially please you, write down the name or number of your combination so you can do it again. I like to do flesh in a fragile pink and accent the shadows lightly with a yellow green. This results in a blend very near skin tone. Try this on a piece of paper first to see how it works. Sometimes, I like to add, also, a bit of pale blue for cold highlights *over* the yellow green. Look at the back of your hand. Try to identify the many colors that make up real flesh. Use blue over green for some leaves; blend pink over them to subdue the color. Use pink and brown for tree trunks; go over these with yellow ochre. It is possible to erase if it is ever necessary. Use a gentle pencil eraser. The Pink Pearl eraser is recommended. If you have a black and white print with very dark shadows, *erase the dark inky shadows* before you begin, to make it easier to color.

The Toile de Jouy Palette: In France, the Southern region became quite noted for its interpretations of fabrics printed with pictorial line drawings. These repeat motifs were inspired by the engraver's work and were very desirable for casual fabrics. The toiles are done in a single family of colors. In the reds we could use light, medium, and deep colors to capture the essence of the print. A group of three blues or three greens can be used in the same way. Or perhaps the grays would suit you best in three different colors for the *Grisaille Palette.* The Grisaille is usually used to imitate the tones of marble sculpture and its shadows. Therefore, it may be a bit more formal in comparison to the casual monotone of blues, reds, or greens. The colors in the toile de jouy palette are very effective on a background of off-white or a tint of the colors used. The Grisaille Palette is most stunning on black, but it will do equally well on any vivid color background.

The Empire Palette: In the year 1800 Josephine Bonaparte had just acquired the mansion, Malmaison. She was bent on making the gardens there the finest in Europe. Ultimately, this splendid extravagance covered 4,500 acres and was the great triumph the Empress Josephine had hoped for. Her official artist for recording the beauty and variety of every known rose of the time was Pierre Joseph Redouté. This very talented artist had previously enjoyed the patronage of Marie Antoinette. His undying fame was earned by publication of *Les Roses* following a series of eight folios of *Les Liliacées.* The Empire Palette is taken from this period with the Empress Josephine at the center of the fashion scene. Gold and ivory, with apple green, royal blue, and exotic woodtones were predominant on furnishings of the period as accent colors.

The Boucher Palette: If coloring the cherubic designs and prints is your choice, you should learn to handle this palette. It is excellent for the delicate cherubs and flesh tones in François Boucher's drawings and similar subject matter. #16 flesh pink is used in the light areas, terra cotta in heavy shadows. Use pale green for foliage and pale blue for ribbons and other ornaments. This color effect originally was produced by using the sanguine pencil or oil chalk as in a line pastel. A watercolor wash in blue or green was used to accent ornamental features. This delicate coloring accentuates the beauty of the drawing and was a technique employed by many 18th century artists. If your preference is those prints showing cherubs and others which are drawings in an informal mood, this is a palette you will use a great deal and enjoy more as you use it. See Coloring a Boucher Print, next page.

The Pompadour Palette, blue and apricot—This group of colors is inspired by Madame de Pompadour's love for the cool blues, using warm colors as complimentary accents. Though two centuries old, this is still a favorite choice of many of us today. Some of the most stylish furnishings can be accomplished in the Pompadour Palette. A cabinet with two doors above and drawers below could be done with a central panel painted in apricot for background and the cartouche made of cut-out prints using this palette. The background border around the cartouche could be painted a soft pale blue. The varnish finish will mute and relate these colors with a subtle overtone. During Madame de Pompadour's residence at Versailles, her personal suite was decorated in this color scheme.

The Provincial Garden Palette, lavenders and fragile blues, pink, and green—Many of the smaller flowers of the French countryside are in lilac

1. Zinc Yellow
2. Lemon Cadmium
3. Gold
4. Primrose Yellow
5. Straw Yellow
6. Deep Cadmium
7. Naples Yellow
8. Middle Chrome
9. Deep Chrome
10. Orange Chrome
11. Spectrum Orange
12. Scarlet Lake
13. Pale Vermilion
14. Deep Vermilion
15. Geranium Lake
16. Flesh Pink
17. Pink Madder Lake
18. Rose Pink

19. Madder Carmine
20. Crimson Lake
21. Rose Madder Lake
22. Magenta
23. Imperial Purple
24. Red Violet Lake
25. Dark Violet
26. Light Violet
27. Blue Violet Lake
28. Delft Blue
29. Ultramarine
30. Smalt Blue
31. Cobalt Blue
32. Spectrum Blue
33. Light Blue
34. Sky Blue
35. Prussian Blue
36. Indigo

37. Oriental Blue
38. Kingfisher Blue
39. Turquoise Blue
40. Turquoise Green
41. Jade Green
42. Juniper Green
43. Bottle Green
44. Water Green
45. Mineral Green
46. Emerald Green
47. Grass Green
48. May Green
49. Sap Green
50. Cedar Green
51. Olive Green
52. Bronze
53. Sepia
54. Burnt Umber

55. Vandyke Brown
56. Raw Umber
57. Brown Ochre
58. Raw Sienna
59. Golden Brown
60. Burnt Yellow Ochre
61. Copper Beech
62. Burnt Sienna
63. Venetian Red
64. Terra Cotta
65. Burnt Carmine
66. Chocolate
67. Ivory Black
68. Blue Grey
69. Gunmetal
70. French Grey
71. Silver Grey
72. Chinese White

This series of colors is used in making up the palettes.

colors, fragile blue, and mingled with the daisy-like marguerites. These colors are in such happy company together, you will see them used often in the daytime fashions of the period. Color the ladies' garden costume frocks in flower tones. The Provincial Garden Palette is a favorite color group when you use a soft pastel background color on furniture or boxes.

Coloring a Boucher Print

The Boucher Palette for coloring cherubs and other prints with flesh tones.

1. Following the lines of your engraving, color with #64 terra cotta all deep shadows on the clouds, people, ribbons, etc. Lightly warm all mid-tones with this pencil—you will have a lovely sanguine coloring when you have completed this step. If there is an area too dark, use an eraser to tone down the shadow.

2. Do not rush, color carefully. Using #16 flesh pink, color all pale skin tones, even up into the hair; however, not all of the hair area. This pale tone will cover a great deal of the ink in case you need to tone down some of the engraving.

3. Subtly blend pink madder lake #17 over the pale flesh at the knees, toes, above the eyes and in the shadows. If you get too much color on these fragile angels, use a Pink Pearl eraser to diminish color.

4. Now, using #58 raw sienna color the hair and wings, also any basket, arrow quiver, or other natural color material. Do not cover up the highlights. Later you can accent these with white. Go over areas of skin to enhance the natural skin tones.

5. Use #47 grass green to go very lightly over the pinks—not the light skin tones—the contrast color will bring a vibrance to the skin. Look at the back of your hand—see the many colors that can be distinguished, particularly the illusion of blue for veins.

6. Terra cotta #64 will add a sculptural quality to the figure when you again go over each shadow area—this time covering any possible ink from the background.

7. Zinc yellow #1 should bring dancing lights to the gold of the hair, if you have not covered the highlights. Blend into the surrounding hair. Do the wings now with the same color. Don't forget the basket and quiver of arrows. The arrow feathers can be #39 turquoise blue.

8. Water green #44 is used heavily on the shadows of all the ribbon and fabric flowing about the cherubs.

9. Pink madder lake #17 is used over the flowers in the basket. Select a few, go over flowers and leaves, also use #39 turquoise blue. Do not blend over the pink but use the blue as little tufts of blue flowers. It must keep its identity. Go over the blue garlands to color the darkest

shadows with #46 emerald green. CAUTION: DO NOT color without regard as to what is happening to your forms. The build-up of color is meant to enhance form as well as local color. Hold the print back a little—turn it upside down to evaluate your work. Hold it to a mirror—this is the test!

10. Emerald green #46 is good for leaves. Color in circles, letting up pressure so the green becomes just a mist of color around the edges. Go over the edges to be sure you do not have a white line on the edge when you cut. Do this with your skin tones, as well. These color run-overs tend to make the shapes softer. Outline makes a hard crisp edge and shape. (Sometimes you need this to distinguish texture. Use it only when you wish to denote crisp shape—out of place in the Boucher cupid setting.) A contrast of light and dark also adds crispness to form. This should be noted in the blue ribbon garlands. It is soft but rather shiny like satin. Use #72 white over white highlights. This shows up later *under the varnish*—not now as you color.

11. Use #34 sky blue to color all cloud forms. Use circular strokes, round and round in small circles, leaving the white *all* white. Do you notice the substance given by the terra cotta which you laid on when you started? This blends and gives depth and richness to the cloud forms. The white in this pale blue mutes the ink and makes the clouds even more misty—or even a little smoky. Keep turning your pencil so it doesn't flatten out too much on one side.

12. Raw sienna #58 should be used in long lines to follow the engraving for sky and background—do a light color application. Go over the pale blue with #58 raw sienna. This will pick up the sky color and make the clouds more interesting.

13. Go back with #17 pink madder lake to pink any toes, fingers, or shadows that need a little more color and warm up the clouds and sky a little.

14. Kingfisher blue #38 should be used on grape and other leaves, over the green you already have on them.

15. A final detail—deepen the quiver and thongs with terra cotta #64 —also, any stems and twigs, even go over skin shadows if there is any ink showing.

16. Burnt carmine #65 can be used very lightly to distinguish certain details on ribbon garland and shadows, but be careful with this strong color.

17. Use #72 white to blend any skin tones which are too warm.

18. My coloring is a little intense in the shadow. I'll erase a little to tone it down. Are you pleased with your coloring? A little practice and you'll be surprised with your ability to make color behave and form come alive.

ABOVE: *Abbé de St. Non basket—see page 52.*
BELOW: *Boucher cherubs—see page 49.*

Coloring a Basket of Flowers

(A Print by Abbé de St. Non)

1. Color *all shadows* lightly with #64 terra cotta.

2. Do all leaves lightly in #46 emerald green. Fill in tiny areas with green, so you do not have to cut them out. Connect leaves with ladders.

3. Color the ribbons #33 light blue, draw in additional ribbon with a pencil and color blue.

4. Color bell flowers #33 light blue, also accent blue ribbon.

5. Large roses—color #58 raw sienna lightly over terra cotta #64; use #17 pink madder lake heavily in the shadows to bring up the color and tone down the engraving. BE SURE TO LEAVE HIGHLIGHTS.

6. Color a balanced group of smaller accent flowers in #15 geranium lake.

7. Go back with #17 pink madder lake, do apples and other fruit which should be a rosy color. Then accent with #15 geranium lake.

8. Color the basket with #58 raw sienna, also, spade and wood the same color.

9. When coloring grapes with #48 May green, make little ovals with the highlight left in.

10. Use #40 turquoise green for small flowers.

11. On the large single flowers partly colored with #5 straw yellow, accent centers and shadows with #64 terra cotta. Go back with #5 straw yellow to do any tiny accents or flowers which should be in this color. Also, go over the previously colored green leaves around the outside to give a sunlight glow.

12. Do fruit in the bottom of the basket with #15 geranium lake. Do flowers with #33 light blue. Go back over all outside leaves with #4 primrose yellow, then strengthen the colors of other leaves with #46 emerald green. This is an opportunity to fill in areas which will be very intricate to cut. Be sure no leaves have white edges. After you finish cutting you may have to go back and color if this step is not done now.

13. Accent highlight on wooden walking stick with #17 pink madder lake; color the remainder of the stick with #64 terra cotta.

14. Last of all, use #65 burnt carmine for your shadow accents, particularly behind leaves and in darkest areas of the garlands and basket.

By now you have fully developed your coloring and the last deep accents bring greater depth and contrast to the coloring. Your print should be a lovely medley of color without anything outstanding—an over-all pleasing effect.

Coloring French Chinoiserie
(A Print by Jean Pillement)

The 18th Century Palette plus #22, #41, #58

1. Use #64 terra cotta as a light coloring: the trees, children, rocks; stronger in the deep places as the shadows carry the color. If you find an area too dark to accept color, use an eraser to diminish the ink. Always color in the direction of the lines of the engraving. Leave the lightest areas for highlights—we'll color these white later. When this step is done you should have a sanguine coloring which would be complete as is.

2. Use #46 emerald green to color all leaves and other greenery. Since there is a lot of green to color keep turning your pencil to maintain the point. Make the shadows deeper. Do the distant foliage in circular motions, developing soft green puffs of delicate leaf structures. Fill in areas between branches that would be hard to cut. Go beyond the edges so the color spills into the background. This makes it possible always to have a colored edge when you are cutting. You can color after the sealer has been applied, even after your cutting is done.

3. Use #5 straw yellow to light the background trees with a sunny hue. Color the ground lightly and any flower centers. Some of the Pillement trees are really just outsize flowers in magnificent exaggeration.

4. #58 Raw sienna looks like the color of bamboo poles. Color delicate little fences, ground, and some rock ends with this color.

5. The Children Playing Badminton, print A, and the large flower petals to the left are done with #5 straw yellow. This color easily covers the ink. In print B, Children With a Top, the large flower trees to the left are centered with #5 straw yellow. The flowers themselves should be overlaid with #18 rose pink, especially the shadows. *DO NOT color the highlights yet.* Go over #18 rose pink with the stronger #17 pink madder lake. Use #15 geranium lake to make a fringed outline, nearly around the flower. Back to #17 pink madder lake and color the twigs and highlights on back of trees with this pink.

6. In the Children Playing Badminton, print A, use #17 pink madder lake over the large yellow trees to accent the outline edge in a deep sawtooth. Also, tip the cascades of foliage on the trees to the right with #17. Doing the tops of the crescents will make the tree appear to be in bloom.

7. Coloring the costumes: Make a strong base color of #5 straw yellow on the tunic of the child. Accent neck and armbands with #15 geranium lake.

8. On another child's tunic, color #33 light blue strongly in the

French chinoiserie prints by Jean Pillemont—see page 53.

shadows. Use #40 turquoise green for the rest of the mid-tones, still leaving all highlights. Color the hat to match.

9. Now color the oriental skin; first, with #58 raw sienna, using a little strength on the hands and face. Go over this with #18 rose pink, lightly. Accent the blue costume with #65 burnt carmine; also, identify the eyes and shadows on the figure, making leggings this same color.

10. Use #33 light blue to cool the leaf shadows under the lower frame structure at the bottom of the cartouche. Also, go over cascading leaves of the tree from the underside. The cool shadows make the children seem more animated in their bright warm colors. Work this color in many shadow areas with the dimensional qualities of a shadow on an overcast day. Do not make it too definite.

11. Color rackets #15 geranium lake, badminton bird #33 light blue and #65 burnt carmine. Use #15 geranium lake for sticks for the top spinners.

12. The one remaining child should have his tunic done in #58 raw sienna with a color developed by overlaying #15 geranium lake. Use #64 terra cotta for shoes, as well as #15 geranium lake for the other pair.

13. With #5 straw yellow again, warm the background clusters of trees, also, do tops of the chunky cartouche* structures and some of the tree trunks where a sunlight glow can be seen.

14. With #48 May green subdue the pinks on lower cartouche area; also, the pink on the fences and tree branches.

15. With #64 terra cotta tone the blue shadows on the tree bark, *blending to keep colors from being streaks.* Color in soft little circles or in the direction of the engraving to avoid pronounced coloring.

16. Greatly strengthen the red tunic by blending #17 pink madder lake over all. Then define deeper red with #15 geranium lake.

17. Use #22 magenta for shadows on the blue tunic. Be cautious with this color, use just a little. Gently blend over the red tunics and trousers to relate all these costumes. #41 jade green is used to tone the tree leaves.

18. Last, we'll use #65 burnt carmine to define forms. Use it on the branches next to flower or leaf forms to make the distinction between tree and leaf. This color helps with perspective. It is necessary to prevent these forms from all being in the same plane. Some are near, others fade back. The nearest shapes are more clearly defined. Look out the window to see distant forms hazy, close ones crisp. Pick up the edge accents of the tree flowers, also their stems. Color any sticks, twigs, strings, toys, not already in color. This is the time to draw in any final ladder or attachment to make the composition hold together while cutting.

* Cartouche—The stylized frame or border motif enclosing the subject matter.

19. You will note we did not use white at all in this design so far. It can now be used on the skin tones and over the light areas of the tree flower as well as the ground. Having blended these areas, your picture is complete.

The chinoiserie prints are the most difficult to color. If you can handle this coloring, you can master any print. Guidance cannot be underestimated; however, you are the one who renders the coloring and since you can interpret directions into a beautiful picture, one day you will do without this aid and be on your own!

The Limited Palette (Grisaille)

If you would like to enhance and add a sculptured look to the black and white print, it will take just two colored pencils and white. Use terra cotta #64 first in the shadow areas only, color many of the outlines as well. With this completed you have a print which appears to be a sanguine drawing—it has rather an antiqued quality. Use a pale blue #34 pencil on the areas tangent to the terra cotia shadows. The lightly tapered terra cotta coloring blends with the pale blue on some contours. The pale blue gently rounds the scrolls and figures by it self in others On the contours, where you have not used any color, press the white to add highlights. The white is distinct under the varnish but does not seem to be there at all before it is sealed and varnished.

Prints for which we suggest using the limited palette are crests, scrolls, cherubs, architectural, processional groups, sculpture and frieze motifs —often seen in borders. This subtle sculptured color is called grisaille—meaning gray in French. Under the varnish the colors have life and are more beautiful than just black and white.

Other Color Groups

All of the limited palettes will be used in the same way as grisaille. First, color the shadow areas with the darkest pencil, always following the lines in the engraving. Then, gently blend next to it the middle tone, and last, use the lightest tone as a blend toward the highlight or palest area of the contoured form. It is a good idea to use white as color on the highlight. (No color should be under white.) You will not see this colored area show up until after the varnish. In all the things we do at the time of coloring, we must consider the color under varnish, if varnish is to be used. Sealer will also bring the white into focus. The only times you do not use varnish over the print will be when pasting the print under glass or in ribbon découpage when the print is not pasted to anything.

PALETTES

18th Century Palette

#19-5	Straw Yellow		#19-40	Turquoise Green
#19-15	Geranium Lake		#19-46	Emerald Green
#19-17	Pink Madder Lake		#19-48	May Green
#19-18	Rose Pink		#19-64	Terra Cotta
#19-33	Light Blue		#19-65	Burnt Carmine

Suggested background colors: pale blue, apricot, pale green, royal blue, apple green, old gold, Venetian red, pink lake, Venetian yellow, shell pink.

Limited Palettes

PINKS

#19-15 Geranium Lake
#19-17 Pink Madder Lake
#19-18 Rose Pink

GRISAILLE

#19-39 Turquoise Blue
#19-64 Terra Cotta
#19-72 Chinese White

BLUES

#19-36 Indigo
#19-38 Kingfisher Blue
#19-39 Turquoise Blue

YELLOWS

#19-4 Primrose Yellow
#19-3 Gold
#19-7 Naples Yellow

GREENS

#19-41 Jade Green
#19-44 Water Green
#19-47 Grass Green

ORANGES

#19-5 Straw Yellow
#19-10 Orange Chrome
#19-13 Pale Vermilion

Background colors: off white, pale blue or green. For the grays: onyx black, cherry red, apple green, royal blue, old gold or Venetian yellow.

The Provincial Garden Palette

#19-1	Zinc Yellow		#19-39	Turquoise Blue
#19-15	Geranium Lake		#19-40	Turquoise Green
#19-17	Pink Madder Lake		#19-41	Jade Green
#19-22	Magenta		#19-46	Emerald Green
#19-25	Dark Violet		#19-47	Grass Green
#19-26	Light Violet		#19-65	Burnt Carmine

Suggested background colors: Periwinkle blue, pale blue, frost green, antique white, shell pink.

Pompadour Palette

#19-11	Spectrum Orange	#19-34	Sky Blue
#19-13	Pale Vermilion	#19-35	Prussian Blue
#19-16	Flesh Pink	#19-38	Kingfisher Blue
#19-17	Pink Madder Lake	#19-40	Turquoise Green
#19-33	Light Blue	#19-58	Raw Sienna

Suggested background colors: Pale blue, royal blue, apricot, old gold or Venetian yellow.

Boucher Palette

#19-1	Zinc Yellow	#19-46	Emerald Green
#19-16	Flesh Pink	#19-47	Grass Green
#19-17	Pink Madder Lake	#19-48	May Green
#19-18	Rose Pink	#19-58	Raw Sienna
#19-34	Sky Blue	#19-63	Venetian Red
#19-38	Kingfisher Blue	#19-64	Terra Cotta
#19-39	Turquoise Blue	#19-65	Burnt Carmine
#19-44	Water Green	#19-72	Chinese White

Background colors: Apricot, old gold, ivory and an antique white.

Empire Palette

#19-16	Flesh Pink	#19-57	Brown Ochre
#19-29	Ultramarine	#19-60	Burnt Yellow Ochre
#19-30	Smalt Blue	#19-66	Chocolate
#19-46	Emerald Green	#19-70	French Gray
#19-47	Grass Green	#19-72	Chinese White

Suggested background colors: Ivory, antique white or onyx black.

There are numerous suitable ground colors that will occur to you. It would be a long list indeed if all the possible colors were listed. Use your own good judgment and plan within the framework of your chosen color scheme.

QUESTIONS AND ANSWERS

Understanding Color and Coloring

1. Q. What is the difference between oil pencils and water color pencils?
   A. Derwent, Prismacolor, Paradise and Venus are brands of pencils which are not soluble in water. You can't blend or dissolve the

color by wiping a wet sponge across the page. Mongol and other water color or water soluble pencils will bleed if you wipe a damp sponge across a page colored with this type pencil. Be sure to seal all coloring with a good sealer. This will prevent their bleeding when in contact with paste and water later.

2. Q. Can water color be used to color prints?

    A. Yes, it is faster—perhaps easier for many people and quite controllable. The colors can be more brilliant, but it is not easy to seal them so the color doesn't come off when you paste. This is the only place that you'll have trouble. Seal water color at least two coats, top and one on the back. Test a print in water after you seal, if you're not sure the print is adequately protected. Two coats of découpage sealer or acrylic spray should be used for water colored prints.

3. Q. Can water color and pencils be used on the same print?

    A. Yes, but seal with two coats on the top and one coat on the bottom if much water color is used.

4. Q. Will all water colors work equally well?

    A. You must test each brand. Water color was not made to have a sealer or varnish brushed over it but you must always seal. Make a test of all your colors on typing or bond paper, and seal. This should be a good test.

5. Q. Are poster colors or tempera good water colors to use?

    A. No, they are opaque and will obliterate the engraving lines.

SEALING THE PRINT

Before cutting, you must seal the color into the paper. This is done with an application of sealer over all the colored areas. Gently flow the sealer onto the print and blot off the excess with a crumpled paper towel. This step is important for three reasons: 1. Sealing the color into the print prevents the varnish from discoloring the print. 2. The sealer also prevents the cutout paper from shredding apart when it is wet with paste and pushed around with the fingers. 3. The sealer makes the paper stiffer and delicate cutting is much easier. The colors appear to blend very subtly as soon as the sealing process is begun. Uncolored prints must be sealed to protect the ink, prevent varnish discoloration, and stiffen the paper for cutting.

CUTTING

Pick up the découpage scissors with the blade curve pointing away from you and in a very relaxed way slip your third finger and thumb into the scissors. Rest the scissor blades on your index finger. Open and close the scissors many times to get used to it. This is the way you will hold your scissors for almost all cutting. Take a practice piece of paper and feed it into the scissors, move the paper round and back with your other hand. The hand holding the scissors doesn't move back and forth, it only opens and closes the scissors in a very relaxed but exacting way. After some practice you are anxious and likely ready to cut out your print.

The first cutting will remove all excess paper from the outside of the print. Your straight scissors will do this more rapidly. You will cut next the inside details. After you have the inside areas cut out, begin to do the outside contours. Hold your scissors so the curve is pointed out—most people cut better this way. If this just doesn't suit you, try it with the curve pointing in.

Generally, you should cut the inside areas first. There are some prints in which the outside areas would be cut out first—doing some *incised* cutting when you are done. In this creative craft, you will learn by practice what is best for you to do in a given circumstance.

Avoid very long straight line cutting; instead, cut a *serrated* edge by wiggling the paper back and forth as you cut so as to produce a softer, blending edge. You will readily see the advantage of this preferable cutting technique when you compare the hard line with the *serrated* line. These details make for distinguished cutting.

Do not cut corner details so you destroy the crispness. For example, if you have stair steps to cut, each step should be squared and crisp on the leading edge, as well as a right angle where the riser joins the tread. This will appear to be a zigzag instead of rounded scallops.

All of your cutting should be done so that you further identify the material you are cutting. Clusters of leaves and satin fabrics should be rounded and soft. The character of trees and other hard materials should be cut to identify their texture.

Occasionally, it is necessary to turn the scissors—with scissors' curve cutting in the opposite direction. Whenever it is better to change scissors, by all means do. Some instructors feel it is best to hold the scissors at an angle so as to cut a bevel edge. This is not likely to produce a very different edge from straight cutting, as the scissors cut it the same from any angle. If you believe you cut better at an angle or a bevel, do it that way. I believe it is most important to be as relaxed and comfortable as possible to make cutting a pleasure. You will have a greater appreciation of your découpage when you appraise your cutting from the reverse side.

Découpage is the art of distinguished cutting. Accomplishing this superb cutting is possible for anyone who has good enough vision to thread a needle. Practice is of ultimate importance. Fine cutting doesn't happen when you try your first practice print. It is mastery of the scissors that makes the most beautiful découpage. The accomplishment of découpage can hold you a captive forever.

Hold the print with the left hand, cut from underneath so you can see your work. Uncut strips of paper "ladders" are left intact until ready to paste. Ladders are seen on scrolls at right.

The four English découpage pictures are cut from colored paper. The feather cutting is so delicate it appears almost lifelike. The light-colored birds are yellow; the dark ones are blue and wine, gray and lavender. Bright red flower blossoms and green foliage make a lively and colorful "painting." Circa 1800.

Styles of Cutting

Creative cutting is not done following the lines of the engraving. It is rarely shown in the print at all. For the most part you must decide where to use these cutting styles and how much detail to add. These styles of creative cutting make your work much more interesting to look at, and the art of cutting prints, distinguished as fine découpage.

1—Straight cutting—ladders
2—Reverse cutting—positive
3—Reverse cutting—negative
4—Reverse cutting—shadow
5—Feathering or feather cutting
6—Drybrush cutting.

7—Serrated cutting 10—Outline detail cutting
8—Incised cutting 11—Bannister cutting
9—Foreground detail cutting 12—Stencil cutting

1. *Straight cutting* is usually confined to border designs. This is accomplished by feeding the paper straight into the scissors with no movement of the hand holding the paper. Straight cutting is done on ladders as it is quicker.

2. *Serrated cutting:* This is the type cutting done on most figures, animals, flowers, trees and other designs which give a soft edge. It makes a much firmer bond when pasted down. The paper is moved back and forth as it is fed into the scissors to produce this type cutting.

3. *Feathering or feather cutting:* This is the same thing and the cutting is done in a manner to imitate feathers. Usually you determine where to place the feathering, which occurs most often at the lower right and left of a print motif.

4. *Drybrush cutting:* This type of cutting is an alternate to feather cutting. It is used at the lower right and left for the purpose of producing an imaginative lower edge detail. It is done to resemble a drybrush technique often used in watercolor and other artistic brush work. This cutting is done to appear to be an arc with a downward sweep.

5. *Foreground detail cutting:* This style of cutting is done to produce an attractive front edge. The grass tufts and other motifs you invent will make the print more exciting and produce an edge which will hold much better when pasted. Although this is usually done at the front edge of prints, it is also a suggested technique to finish a print motif which is cut off at one side or the other, such as buildings and trees. By doing this, it is possible to blend prints from one to another to make a continuous horizontal design, hiding the fact that many prints have been used in a line. This is convenient when designing a lamp shade or paper basket.

6. *Reverse cutting—negative:* This type of cutting creates an opening which appears to be a small plant or tuft of grass. This innovation in cutting is useful for many reasons. It offers an opportunity to accent a bland area of print. Gold tea chest paper can be used behind the opening,

creating a tuft of grass, or to enliven the same area with the background color paint. It is an opening which enables the varnish to hold to the paint—assuring you of continuous adhesion of the varnish film.

7. *Reverse cutting—positive:* Used for the same cutting advantage, and the same varnish adhesion advantage as reverse cutting negative. You see the positive motif or design cut in the paper with the paper tuft shown against the opening. It is possible to accent either type of reverse cutting by pasting metallic paper behind the reverse cutting. Both positive and negative can be used together. They add variety and interest.

8. *Reverse cutting—shadow:* This technique offers further variety to the découpeur. A motif or tuft of grass is cut out of the print as if it were a shadow in which the cutout opening repeats the design in the print.

9. *Incised cutting* is usually done after a print is entirely cut out. The purpose of this cutting is to open up areas in a print which are entirely solid. The openings may be any size or shape—and are camouflaged in the print so as not to be noticed. The reason you should open up areas in a print is that this provides a hole to remove excess paste, and most important provides a spot where the varnish can touch paint and firmly tack the varnish film to the paint surface. This one trick can prevent many "blister under print" heartaches.

10. *Stencil cutting* is done with a knife or razor blade. It is difficult to handle this type of cutting with scissors. The openings produced are long crescents or S curves. When using a razor blade or a knife, cut against a hard surface for the best cutting (masonite or glass). Stencil cutting is done along lines in a scroll or parallel to accent lines.

11. *Bannister cutting:* This type is done with a knife or scissors. There are few opportunities to use this style but you should be aware of it when you need it. Many short vertical lines are cut between two lines. The bottom horizontal is cut from end to end, releasing all bannisters. They are then broken loose on alternate shafts to produce a series of bars—unattached at the bottom until they are glued.

66

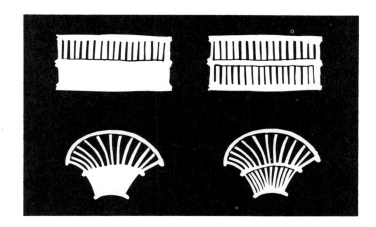

12. *Outline detail cutting:* Narrow crescents cut to accent the outline of flowers, fruit, figures, cloud formation, and other curves. A straight outline is accented with straight cutting. Either a knife or scissors is used for outline cutting.

Cutting Two Prints at Once

Sometimes there is a need for many of the same print. This is especially true of borders, ornaments and scrolls. It is not good for the beginner, who needs practice, to cut two prints at a time. As the experienced découpeur works on larger pieces, some monotonous cutting can be eliminated. Superimpose the printed images and pin right through the print with a very fine silk pin. The tiny hole is not noticeable when pasted down, and it is a good escape hole for air or trapped paste. Be sure to mark the ladders on the top print.

Drawing Ladders

As you look at your lovely colored print, you may feel you do not know where to start cutting. Do not cut until you determine where to draw the ladders. Take a colored pencil and draw in the *ladders* that you will need to keep the print intact while you are cutting, and to make it possible to handle them prior to pasting the prints into position.

Ladders are your third hand, which hold delicate tendrils of paper together until you are ready to paste. They are placed by the découpeur in strategic places to hold long stems or appendages intact while cutting. You draw in the connection with a pencil; then you cut around the ladder which you drew. The ladder remains in place until just before you paste. Then you snip them off as they have served their purpose. Sometimes ladders are left in place if they become part of the design. In this case, the ladder should be the color of the connecting motifs.

Study the print and join portions which will be weak or isolated on a long stem. In the cutting photograph, you can see a ladder between the scrolled curves at the right of the illustration. Make all these connecting ladders with a colored pencil before you begin cutting. Store the prints with the ladders intact as this facilitates handling.

PASTING THE PRINTS
IN PLACE

Before you open your paste—get a small bowl of water, sponge, and a small damp cloth. You will need them as you work. Dip your finger or two fingers into the paste and go over the entire area to be covered with cutout designs. Smooth this paste as evenly as you can, adding drops of water when necessary to have a good surface to receive the cuttings. Pick up your pieces from the temporary composition and place them on the pasted surface, working as rapidly as you can. Use a barely damp piece of cloth over the freshly pasted work. Roll over the entire surface with a small roller. Rinse the paste out of the cloth and repeat, removing all traces of paste. If the cloth is too wet it will dissolve the paste under the prints, making it necessary to add paste later. The slight dampness of the cloth draws the paste up rapidly and leaves the surface clean.

Paste one side of a box at a time; however, relate each area to the next side or top. Sometimes a flower stem trails off the top to the sides —you may have a design start on the lid and follow down the sides to surround the subjects on each side. Occasionally, you may use the side as one design unit and a separate but related composition on the top.

Don't paste one layer upon another. This heavy build-up will make it necessary to add many extra coats of varnish. *Carefully* cut and fit edges next to each other. Remember the smoother your box, paint, and print, the easier it will be to apply the varnish evenly. One hazard in sanding is that thin spots in the varnish will be sanded through quickly with possible damage to the print. This will happen only if the print humps up here and there or overlapping prints make a high place. Another place to watch is the edges.

The paste referred to is the water-soluble découpage paste. It is removable, if the need arises. *Glue* is not water soluble and not removable. Paste is used exclusively on prints. Glue is used on fabric lining, gold tea chest paper and gold braid.

QUESTIONS AND ANSWERS

Paste

1. Q. I have heard of wonderful mixtures of something like Elmer's glue and some other paste where you have the advantage of both— what is this called?

A. Trouble. You may end up with the advantages of neither. Use the right adhesive and don't alter it. Don't mix your own and expect good results. It may work sometimes. The right paste, glue or adhesive is one made for découpage. Buy from a specialist. Use materials that are made to go together. A complete collection of materials for découpage that work together and fit the job right is like buying the right size clothes to fit an individual.

2. Q. I like to buy one brand of paste, another brand of sealer, and I just buy whatever varnish I can find. I have never had any problems. What about that?

A. Some people have all the luck!

3. Q. I had a magazine cover print lift after it was glued down flat. I used a heavy duty glue and I had sprayed the back of the magazine cover with aluminum paint to keep the printed type from showing through. What caused the trouble?

A. Aluminum paint or gold paint should not be used under prints. The glue holds to the metallic powder and the inadequate binder for the paint is absorbed in the paper. You may have trouble with metallic sprays of this type. It is best to put magazine prints on a darker background or not use them at all if you have type showing through. If you spray or paint a box with gold or other metallics, use Treasure Sealer* as a paint bonding adhesive.

4. Q. Why should I avoid vinegar water as a cleaner when I glue the prints on?

A. Vinegar is acid and can react on many things. It can give you problems with metal leaf or tea paper that cannot be corrected. If your glue or paste is not easily cleaned with plain water, change adhesives. You should *not* use a waterproof glue—it can't be cleaned off when dry.

5. Q. Why did my gold tea chest paper come loose after I was done with the box? I used glycerin to slow the drying so I could glue evenly.

A. Glycerin may slow the drying but it does damage the adhesion of the glue. The glycerin can prevent varnish from adhering, too. It acts as a separator. Do not alter your paste or glue with anything—unless directions on the label say so. Change paste, work faster, or work on smaller areas if the paste you use dries too fast.

* See page 128.

THE VARNISH FINISH

Almost everyone is astonished when you say, "It has thirty coats of varnish." This alone would set you apart from the crowd, but it is neither complicated nor difficult to apply a number of coats of varnish in order to achieve an incomparable finish. After your pasted découpage is thoroughly dry, assemble brush, varnish, soft cloth and paint thinner or turpentine for brush cleaning. Apply the varnish to your work in long flowing strokes. Do not brush too rapidly or in short choppy strokes. Be generous but not to the point that the varnish will sag or run. Pick the brush stroke up at the edges of a box or tray in order to avoid rollover (an accumulation of varnish on the edge of the box). Inspect your box each time you apply a coat of varnish, so you do not allow a sag or a drip to dry. Remove drips with the brush or a turpentine-dampened cloth.

Apply one coat of varnish every twenty-four hours or follow the instructions on the varnish can label. When you have applied ten coats, begin sanding with wet-or-dry sandpaper #400, available at most paint stores. You will be pleased with this sandpaper that you can use so effectively. Dip it in water; always keep the surface and the sandpaper wet. No dust is created to make you sneeze. After a thorough leveling with the sandpaper, begin the last series of six to ten varnish coats. If you are satisfied with a few more coats, this is your decision to make. If it takes sixteen or more coats to achieve the rich depth of varnish comparable to a fine deep porcelain glaze, continue until you are satisfied. You can apply too few coats, but it is unlikely you will apply too many. The last two coats of varnish should be a low lustre.

By adding a little detergent when you are wet sanding it is possible to obtain a smoother finish, as it tends to help eliminate small scratches.

Cleaning the brush: After each use of the brush, you should clean it with a solvent and shampoo the bristles thoroughly. Then squeeze the water out gently, setting the bristles in place to dry. Or, you can keep your varnish brush suspended in a glass baby bottle filled one-third deep with turpentine. Cut the rubber tip from the nipple so the brush will fit snugly and stay in place. A plastic bottle will not hold the solvent—use only glass.

Découpage, being the art of cutting out paper, has nothing actually to do with a specific finish. Varnish wasn't used on the original works. The 20th century examples are largely exhibited with many coats of varnish or other clear finishes which protect and enhance the lovely cuttings. Of the many examples which are currently done, the most effective are not antiqued or fly-specked. Those two finishes are connected with painted furniture and somehow have been added as an unnecessary conceit in découpage. It is best not to antique or color glaze in dark tones when finishing works of découpage. It is also best not to spatter with black paint to create artificial fly specks.

A subtle antique coloring is achieved with amber varnish. After a few years most varnishes will deepen in color and artificial antiquing also becomes much darker. For this reason, one should create a finish in as natural a coloring as is possible. If you use antiquing at all, it should be so subtle that an expert would find it difficult to detect. Any obvious anachronism is as bad as an artificial finish effect. The beautiful deep lustre of varnish is the most desirable and durable finish for découpage.

How to do the Varnish Finish

Assemble supplies for varnishing: Brush—varnish—small pan
                                   Tack rag—paint cloth—turpentine
                                   Brush saver bottle

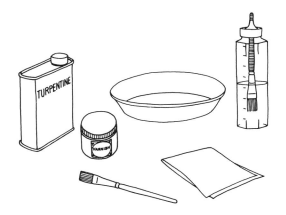

Assemble supplies for sanding: #400 wet or dry sandpaper—sponge—
                                  bowl of water
                                  Steel wool—découpage wax

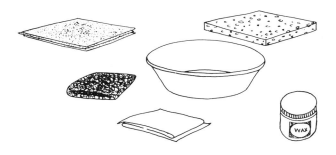

1. Pour a small amount of varnish into a pan. It is easier to hold and no evaporation or contaminating dust will damage the varnish remaining in the can. Pour in more as needed. Also, you can thin with turpentine as needed.

2. Dip your brush halfway up the bristle in the varnish. Lay the brushful of varnish on your work, draw it toward the edge, and lift it up from the edge. Do not draw down or apply pressure as you will deposit excess varnish. Work rapidly—do not rebrush when the varnish is beginning to set. Always remove bristles as they fall from a brush.

3. When the varnishing is done, set it aside to dry where no lint or dust will fall into the film as it dries.

4. Use your tack rag to pick up dust particles, as a regular ritual—before each coat of varnish is applied. Wait twenty-four hours between coats (unless otherwise specified on the label). Apply about ten coats before you begin to do any sanding.

5. *First Sanding:* Dip sandpaper in water and begin to level the varnish. Sand with the grain. As a paste is worked up from the water and sanding, remove with wet sponge. Be careful not to sand through a print edge or the paint at the outer corners of boxes. These are danger points for beginners. When the surface is reasonably level—use your tack rag to pick up any stray dust particles and apply six to ten more coats according to how thick or thin your layers of varnish are applied.

6. *Second Sanding:* This is done much the same as the first sanding except it must be very level this time. Use steel wool #0000 to get low places.

7. *Final Varnishing:* Apply two coats of low gloss varnish twenty-four hours apart, and use steel wool for a smooth surface.

8. *Waxing:* The final coating is a découpage wax or fine furniture wax. Apply very sparingly with a damp cloth. After ten minutes polish to an incomparable sheen.

QUESTIONS AND ANSWERS

Understanding Paint, Varnish and Lacquer

1. Q. Why does the enamel paint I'm using leave ridges? It seems too thick.

   A. It needs to be thinned. Use turpentine or mineral spirits.

2. Q. Are turpentine and mineral spirits the same? Where do they come from?

   A. Turpentine is made from the southern pine tree. Pure gum turpentine is made from the sap. Steam distilled is made by heating the stump of the tree to get the turpentine. Mineral spirits is also a solvent for paint but it is a petroleum product, distilled from crude oil. It is much weaker in its solvent strength than turpentine but is a comparable material for thinning. The products distilled from petroleum include mineral spirits, kerosene, naphtha, gasoline, acetone, xylene, and toluene. The last ones listed are the strongest solvents—used as lacquer thinner (in given proportions). Mineral spirits is much less expensive and lower in odor. It is also available as odorless mineral spirits—used in odorless paints.

3. Q. My paint seems to build up ridges when I apply the second coat. I have already thinned it. Does it need to be thinner?

A. Not likely. This happens when the undercoat is not fully dry. If you didn't wait twenty-four hours this will happen. You may also find you didn't mix the paint well and you are into a denser material near the bottom. If so, then it may need more thinner.

4. Q. How do I get a mellow old look? What varnish do I use?

A. The amber-colored varnish will build up to a mellow old look. You may also add a small amount—¼"—out of the small tube of oil colors, Van Dyke brown or burnt sienna. Mix this oil color with a teaspoonful of turpentine and add it to one-half cup varnish for one coat. If you want it deeper, do another coat. The darker the varnish and the more coats the deeper the antique coloring.

5. Q. How can I tell if I'm buying varnish that will go over flat enamel paints?

A. It will be labeled varnish—low luster, or gloss. If you learn to read labels carefully it will help you learn a lot about the materials you use. The harder the varnish, such as spar or deck varnish, the tougher it is to sand. This type must be sanded every coat or two. If you use a varnish made for découpage it will be much easier to sand. It has aluminum stearates and silicas which do not make a tough surface—these are built-in for easy sanding. So, many coats can be applied for a more rapid build-up, and you don't have to sand until ten to fourteen coats have been applied. Then, you can apply a spar or semi-gloss varnish for the last few coats. The varnish suitable to apply over flat enamel will usually have a typical varnish odor. If it smells like lacquer or nail polish—check the label—you will find a special solvent or lacquer thinner is used to clean the brush. This type of material will shrivel the enamel or oil paints.

74

6. Q. When do you use a sealer over the paint and why?

A. If you buy a paint you've never tried before—and it is not made for découpage—or if you use paints left over from other things—seal it. Sealer will prevent the varnish from causing the paint to bleed. Many paints will not bleed and you do not need to worry about this problem. You can always test this if you have a panel of the paint in question, by brushing on a varnish and stroking back and forth many times. Then apply the varnish left in the brush on white paper. If there is a pink coloring evident, the paint bleeds. This is assuming there is red pigment in the paint.

7. Q. How do I get a muted soft-colored varnish finish that is not amber or antique coloring?

A. There are many brands of varnish now available for découpage which are cloudy in appearance; some are a creamy gray color. These are usually alkyd resin varnishes that are pigmented slightly. They are easy to sand, give a rapid build-up and a lovely muted mellow color. For a final tough finish, it is best to use two coats of a low gloss varnish.

8. Q. Will lacquer give me an absolutely clear finish?

A. Yes. However, it *cannot* be used over flat enamel or oil paints. It can be used over poster paint, tempera, rubber base, and other water base paints. Ask for brushing lacquer.

9. Q. I have a piece two years old that has begun to get wide cracks in it. Why? I used lacquer.

A. Many coats of lacquer are apt to crack in this manner. It happened to me and I found out why. Most lacquer when sprayed on, such as a factory finish, is very thin and eight coats sprayed is the equivalent of three coats brushed on. From 18% to 34% solids are in brushing lacquer. Only 8% to 12% solids are in sprays because they must be thinned so much to prevent clogging the nozzle. Therefore, many coats of lacquer hand-applied cause a stress which eventually shows up as cracks in the finish. I am told this is true of clear lacquer in general. The pigmented lacquers used in import ware are very different from U.S. clear lacquer. I would not use lacquer for more than six coats to avoid cracks.

10. Q. Why sand between coats of paint?

A. A smoother finish is the result of careful sanding, especially between coats of paint. Be sure to use a tack rag to pick up dust from sanding.

11. Q. What is a tack rag? Why is it used?

A. It is a cloth (commercially ready to use) which is slightly sticky or tacky and it will pick up the dust from sanding paint or varnish. It is essential to a good finish. If you have dust on a varnished piece and do not remove it, your next coat of varnish merely embeds the dust and causes unnecessary little irregularities. Do not varnish while wearing a wool sweater, because it sheds lint and statically attracts dust.

12. Q. How can you tell what color a paint will be when it dries? Mine seems a shade darker.

A. Most paint dries a shade darker when it is dry and cured. You can tell after twenty-four hours. Make a test and dry it.

13. Q. How does the amber varnish affect colors of paint?

A. If you could look at colors through amber-colored glasses you would be able to gauge how your paint will be affected by varnish. The reds are intense and attractive as are orange, mustard and yellow orange. The pale pink becomes salmon. The pale yellow becomes deeper and white or off white seems yellowed. The blues all become slightly green and the greens seem richer and mellow. Brown is not affected. Lavender seems to become a neutral gray. Violet is also neutralized and seems brownish. The amber tone of varnish will change every color.

14. Q. In my varnish finish there are darker and lighter streaks. Why?

A. Uneven coats is the answer. If the base color of paint wasn't smooth, varnish will flow into the crevices and appear darker. If you apply heavy overlaps of varnish, the overlaps may be darker. If you use a brush which does not discharge the varnish well, you may have irregularities. Use a good brush—apply even coats. It is all a matter of experience and learning. Streaks and color variation can always be traced to inexperience or being in a hurry. An exception could be: using inferior materials.

15. Q. What causes sags in the varnish? How can I correct it?

A. If you understand the cause you should never have this happen. Too heavy an application of varnish will sag. If the varnish dries quickly on the surface, the under layer may slip to a sag. This can not happen if thin layers are applied—or if you let the varnish set to dry in a horizontal position. An ounce of prevention is worth a pound of cure.

16. Q. What causes edge build up, especially on boxes?

A. The brush continuously is discharging varnish at the edge because of the way you use your brush. Think of touching the brush down near the middle of a box lid and making an arc as you lift the brush near the edge. Finish each edge by attempting to pick up excess varnish at the edge.

17. Q. What is rollover and how is it caused?

A. Rollover of paint or varnish is caused by a brush stroke which discharges the varnish at the edge. It builds up on this outside edge or runs down and drips. You are brushing in the wrong direction or you have not checked the edge for possible drips or rollover. Be aware of this fault—it is easy to prevent—terrible to sand off!

18. Q. There are drips around the edge of a lid on which I am working. They are not dry enough to sand, too dry to remove with turpentine, how do I get them off? How do I prevent them?

A. Prevent this happening to start with by using a cloth dampened with turpentine all around this underside—before you leave it to dry. You remove these semi-dried drips with a knife or even your fingernail. Then wipe with a turpentine-dampened cloth. When dry, sand.

19. Q. Do you need as many coats of varnish on furniture as you use on boxes?

A. I would try to make a table top or desk top as smooth as you can, using more varnish on the horizontal surface as this will get the most wear. Boxes are easy to handle, easy to do and should be well finished. A large secretary may be difficult to have all designs buried in varnish. The originals and the reproductions available from Italy today have very little varnish.

20. Q. How do present-day varnishes differ from those used during the 18th century?

A. The earlier varnishes in the 18th century were often more like shellac or lacquer, called seed lac. These products dry by evaporation, which means a dried-out brush could be softened in its own thinner, a shellac brush in alcohol, a lacquer brush in lacquer thinner. The resins used in the 18th and 19th centuries dried by evaporation, such as the picture varnishes, damar varnish and spirit varnishes. Spirit varnish is one thinned with alcohol. Modern varnishes, if they dry in a brush, are not soluble in turpentine as they have polymerized—or changed their molecular structure—

77

and a stronger solvent must be used. Some paints and varnishes oxidize when they dry. Basically, paint is varnish with a pigment added. Latex paints are rather like the natural rubber latex for which they are named. They cure into a different material than they were in the liquid state. Varnish as we know it today is a 20th century product.

21. Q. Were the varnishes of the 18th century made to last?

A. Shellac was generally used as a finish, and we know now as they did then, that this resin will become very dark brown with time and dust embedded. Many of these pieces were cleaned off regularly and new shellac applied. Not everyone who inherited this furniture knew how to take care of this finish a generation or two later, so the finish became dark and often the piece was set aside as unattractive and not used. This happened also to paintings which were varnished with a turpentine soluble light varnish. Many people knew enough to have the varnish removed every thirty or forty years and fresh varnish applied to preserve the painting. Only recently some museums are restoring the varnish on paintings and other works of art which should have been treated years ago. So you see the varnishes used then were not identical to those we use now.

22. Q. I prefer to use a water base paint. Can I still use the antique varnish if I want the old amber color?

A. Yes. Varnish can be used over water base paint. The strongest objection to water base is the time necessary for it to cure out before the varnish or lacquer is used. The problems involved do not show up immediately. They start happening two to six years after you put in all that work, so I just feel it is best to use the oil base paint known to hold up under many coats of varnish.

23. Q. What is the main difference between spray can products and those you brush on?

A. The paint or varnish, lacquer, sealer, or acrylic, which is packaged in spray cans is very convenient and more people turn to these products daily. You can't beat them for many things you need to paint. They are much more expensive for the amount of paint, et al, you will use. You must use many more coats for the same coverage. Let's look at the label on the spray can. You will see 8% solids—92% vehicle and propellent, or some such ratio. Look at a paint can label—34% solids, resin, pigment, modifiers, etc. and 66% vehicle—thinner, driers, etc. This is one reason the aerosol paints dry so fast, a thin coat and fast drying vehicle. It may take four coats spray to equal one brush-applied. I believe you should enter into the spirit of découpage, an antique craft, with the idea that there is no big rush. Here is one refuge where there is no hustle-bustle. You do your best work and relax while doing it.

24. Q. What is varnish?

A. The natural and synthetic resins form the solids of a varnish. These are diluted with a solvent, turpentine or mineral spirits, and modified as to gloss, drying time, plasticity and resistance to abrasion and other external forces. The resin is generally amber in color. Many layers of varnish of this type add a soft antique glow to the work underneath.

The synthetic varnishes are less amber. Some are nearly water clear. When the resin is modified, a milky or translucent liquid results. Either of these two basic types of varnish depends upon a solvent being evaporated and the layer of modified resins building a coating on the surface. The solids content is usually 34% to 45%. Turpentine or mineral spirits can be added to aid in leveling of the varnish. This information about varnish is much too simplified, but it does perhaps bring a little better understanding of this material. Basically, it is a natural product being used as a protective on wood. It bonds perfectly to the paint, being of similar material, and protects as well as enhances the surface.

25. Q. What is lacquer?

A. The lacquers, having nitro-cellulose solids, may be easier to understand. They dry by evaporation. They can be dissolved again in *their own* thinner. Varnish cannot; however, varnish can be dissolved by a stronger solvent system, such as the lacquer thinner.

Alcohol does not dissolve lacquer nor, in many cases, varnish. It will dissolve shellac, which is its solvent. Mineral spirits is the weakest solvent and will not dissolve varnish, shellac, or lacquer. Turpentine is about twice as strong a solvent as mineral spirits and is by no means the same. Fumes from lacquer thinner should be avoided. They may seem mild but some people are easily overcome. Sprays in general are very handy and easy to use for many jobs.

26. Q. What is mineral spirits?

A. It is a petroleum distillate, like naphtha, gasoline, kerosene, xylol and toluol. It is used as a paint thinner and has a very weak solvent power. It is much weaker than turpentine as a solvent, but an equally good thinner. It dries from a surface without leaving a residue. It is often given other label names such as paint thinner, enamel reducer, varnish reducer. It costs half the price of turpentine.

27. Q. What is odorless mineral spirits?

A. It has much the same properties of mineral spirits but it is a different petroleum distillate. It has no odor and is very pleasant to use; however, it does give off the same vapors that mineral spirits does and must be used in a ventilated area.

28. Q. What is acrylic?

A. Acrylic is a water clear plastic—used as a synthetic resin. It can be used as a clear spray for many different surfaces. It is usually in a petroleum solvent vehicle.° Sometimes it is in a water base emulsion. The water base emulsion looks milky. When dry, it is perfectly clear. Sometimes this is used as a sealer—such as the bright drying floor "wax", self-polishing. Water base sealers must not be used on raw wood. They are suitable for plastic or use over painted surfaces. Avoid water base products for découpage—except, of course, the paste and glue.

29. Q. How do you make paint crackle?

A. Add a slow drying oil such as raw linseed to the base coat and a drier or fast drying solvent to the top coat. The top dries rapidly and cracks away from the base coat. All crackling of paint is a flaw and is rarely controllable—so even if you have a successful crackle once, it may not be consistent.

30. Q. How do you make very fine gold lines with paint?

A. Liquid Leaf paint can be used in a ruling pen and the fine lines ruled onto a box or other surface. It is then protected with Treasure Sealer and the varnish coats applied.

31. Q. I have a wooden box that warped. Why? How do I unwarp it?

A. Uneven drying or lack of equal varnish on the outside and inside can cause a box to warp. The concave surface is the one which dried into the warp. On this surface, place two coats of one-half alcohol and one-half glycerine, mixed together. Forty-eight hours later, repeat. This action is slow but it works. Do not rush it.

° Krylon acrylic, Blair acrylic, Devoe acrylic, Sherwin Williams, Glidden, and many other clear plastic spray manufacturers.

32. Q. I have a dust free area to varnish, new varnish and I clean my brush carefully. I still have a lot of trouble.

A. You probably have varnish dried up in the ferrules of the brush, even if you have cleaned it as well as you can. Suspend it in clean turpentine between varnish coats. Experience will overcome all these problems.

33. Q. Explain what makes the best finish.

A. Use materials made for découpage. Use as thin a paper as is practical, a layer of paste worked into the surface before pasting the print, removal of excess paste from under the print and the edges, and thin layers of varnish, dried properly between coats. The final rubbed finish can be as smooth with 3M paper and steel wool as with rubbing compounds. It's your own experience that makes the difference. By all means, use découpage wax to protect your finish.

34. Q. What causes the print to have a blister under it after applying twenty-five to thirty coats of varnish on the box?

A. If you have a blister the paste or glue did not adhere. As the varnish dries and cures, it shrinks. This happens *after* six weeks, usually. The more coats of varnish, the greater the stress. This is like a slow drying skin on a drum head—it can pull up a print.

35. Q. What can I do to prevent blisters?

A. Use the right paste or glue for the right job, and press out all excess. Découpage paste is used for light-weight paper. A heavier glue is used for heavier paper. It is advisable not to overdo the varnish build-up. That is—most varnish available at the paint store is made to be built up to no more than four coats. The large number of coats, twenty-five or thirty, cause immense stress. The varnish may pull apart and crackle or lift the prints. Be sure to use thin coats. This makes it possible to dry thoroughly between coats—this causes less stress. Varnish made for découpage has been modified so it builds up rapidly but doesn't shrink after many coats. Spar or gloss varnish does give a good finish but was not made for the build up.

Varnish made for découpage is not as tough as other varnish, i.e., spar varnish, bowling alley varnish. The tough film you expect to last on a gym floor or traffic area should repel or resist abrasion. It is extremely difficult *to sand* these varnishes. They were not meant to be sanded. They would be usable for one top coat, but not for coat-on-coat application.

36. Q. What is the best way to keep varnish?

A. When you buy it in a large can, put it into several two ounce jars, which are absolutely clean and dust free, or buy the smaller sizes already packaged. This way a skin doesn't form over the whole can of varnish and waste so much and you can't contaminate the unused varnish with dust particles.

37. Q. Will antiquing or glazing with a darker tone make a découpage piece more authentic?

A. No. It is not a good idea to do any antiquing. This dark muddy effect will not improve the appearance in any way and it will continue in nearly all instances to get darker with age. Most varnish will deepen as it matures.

38. Q. Can you antique a finish a little?

A. Yes, if you need a tone to bring out contours in a particular piece of furniture or a box. Antiquing colors should be used in a very subtle manner—so you do not see streaks but a gentle accent on the old distresses. I would advise against it in general as the work will gain a used look naturally, if it is used.

39. Q. How do you do the spatter or fly specks?

A. Fly specks and faux texture of this type are a hangover from antiquing and they do not generally add to the finished work. In fact, most times when you see speckling or spattering it detracts from the design. I have seen some diluted color used so subtly that the antiquing spatter was attractive. Immediately after the spatter is applied, it was blotted so it was hardly evident. Then a spatter of plain naphtha or even lighter fluid was done, leaving tiny clean spatters. Do this only on old furniture and boxes.

40. Q. How do you make a piece look like a real antique?

A. If you are accustomed to seeing the real antiques (made before 1830) and the very fine objets décoratifs—you will not see any spatters or speckles. Indeed, the finest were well cared for and look old and authentic because of the exquisite workmanship and superb materials. If you want the appearance of a fine antique piece, do a real craftsman's job with designs of the period and do not antique or glaze at all! Rub wax into the finish.

41. Q. Why do you use steel wool in some instances and wet or dry sandpaper in others?

A. Wet or dry sandpaper is flat and will level out a varnish finish. If the varnish used was gloss, you will have some glossy depressions. Use steel wool to get into these areas. You must have an even surface to make an even gloss when you apply the wax. If you want a contoured surface, use the steel wool because it follows the embossing into high and low places.

42. Q. Do you like to see a smooth surface or one with the contour of the découpage?

A. In 18th century work one should try to have a smooth finish. On large pieces, it is possible to have a print contour showing on the sides, but the flat planes should be as level as you can make them. On Victorian découpage the embossed surfaces of the work are attractive if the finish is deep. Do not use sandpaper if you want a contour; use only steel wool, as it will not flatten any of the embossing. You can also do a final rubbing with pumice and oil.

THE WAXING

With a single coat of wax a magnificent transformation will take place. The slightly etched and dusty finish will assume the smooth texture of elegant porcelain and polishing will reveal depth and a richness only acquired in the classical method of a deep varnish finish. This hand-made, hand-finished piece may well be your proudest possession—a special piece you have made.

There is a wax made for découpage, different from all other waxes, and yet it can be used on any fine furniture. This is Royal Parquet découpage wax. Use a damp piece of knitted cloth or cheesecloth, wring all water from it, pick up a little wax and apply to the varnished surface. In about ten minutes polish with a dry cloth to a lustrous sheen.

BRIEF SUMMARY OF
THE VARNISH FINISH

1. Apply ten coats of gloss varnish before first sanding. All varnish coats must dry twenty-four hours between each.

2. The first sanding is done with #400 wet or dry sandpaper dipped in water for the sanding operation. Ever-soft sponge removes the sanding residue. The tack rag is used just before applying a coat of varnish.

3. Apply four to ten more coats according to the richness of finish and coloring you want. Sand smooth with #400 wet or dry sandpaper. This final sanding should leave a perfectly level finish.

4. Use a tack rag before final two coats of low luster varnish. Gently steel wool the surface with #0000 to remove the minute scratches as a result of sanding.

5. Application of wax: Use a découpage wax which is a varnish wax or a fine furniture wax. A SLIGHTLY DAMP CLOTH is used to pick up a small amount of wax. Rub firmly into the finish and polish shortly after application with a damp soft cloth first, a dry cloth last. Do a small area at first to get the feel of this procedure. It is a very important step.

QUESTIONS AND ANSWERS
Waxing

1. Q. Can any wax be used on the varnish finish?
   A. If your work is sanded or rubbed down it needs wax and any paste wax is better than none. The best wax to use is pure white and has a gentle fragrance of French spices. It will not distort the finish as yellow or brown wax does and the illusive fragrance remains.

2. Q. Why is it necessary to wax?
   A. After using sandpaper or abrasive rubbing powder and oil, the finish is minutely scratched all over. It has an etched surface. Scratches can more easily mar this finish and it can collect small amounts of dirt to make the appearance less attractive. After all your work so far, it is a shame to leave the surface open instead of finished with wax. A smooth finish is smoother after waxing. This is a time-honored procedure with all fine furniture or varnish technicians—the final waxing. It feels better and it looks richer. The real distinction between an ordinary finish and an extraordinary finish is how it looks and especially how it feels to the touch.

UNUSUAL TECHNIQUES

There are many exciting effects that are closely related to découpage. They cannot be placed in any of the three main areas of 18th century, Victorian, or Modern découpage as they are not any of these. We categorize this collection of methods as "unusual techniques." They are meant to expand your curiosity, to present a broad scope of imaginative ideas with which you can combine découpage cutouts, gold paper braid, marbleized paper, gold tea chest paper, and other materials. This is not a traditional collection of authentic types. Some of them can become traditional. After all, every tradition started somewhere. The traditions we have in découpage now will be the basis for ideas in new traditions of the future.

Finishes—Unusual Techniques on Glass

THE MOONSTONE FINISH—USING CLEAR DRYING WHITE GLUE

A mirror is used for the background. Paste prints on mirror with a coat of white glue. Brush a coat of white glue over the print and set aside to dry completely clear. Apply a total of six coats with no attempt to be perfectly smooth. Do not thin the glue at any time. The uneven surface is ripply over the mirror and it is softly diffused—giving the appearance of a mysterious inner light. Give three coats of gloss varnish; steel wool, and wax for finish.

SEEDED GLASS

Apply white glue on glass—not mirror. Set print or gold paper braid into glue and coat also with white glue. After being allowed to dry clear, apply six more coats capturing or creating bubbles by brushing fresh glue into a partly dried surface.

SMOKED GLASS MIRROR FOR DÉCOUPAGE

Hold a mirror above a candle allowing carbon to collect in a random pattern. Move the mirror slowly—raise and lower it to produce the effect you want. Frame this mirror as it is under a piece of thin picture glass. The picture glass should be ornamented with découpage before you frame.

The double switchplate shows the moonstone finish bordered in gold and using Victorian découpage material. A mirrored switchplate is covered with six coats of white glue and dries to a nearly clear finish, which resembles moonstone. The pushplate is hand colored and backed with gold leaf.

85

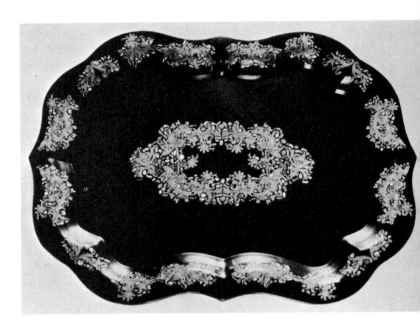

A large tray, using the Chippendale scrolls for the border and cente designs, features lustrous accents of carefully cut-out mother-o pearl. The use of mother-of-pearl adds great dimension to the elega tray.

OPALINE

This iridescent coloring is relatively easy to do and is accomplished by the use of pearl paint or pearl spray. On a lamp base the sea shells and stylized scrolls make fine companion designs. After being colored in nacreous pastels and pasted to the inside of the glass, two coats of the pearl lacquer, or four coats of the spray are applied. Allow ample drying time between coats. The last step is to apply one coat of flat white or a pastel color to back up the pearl. An especially interesting illusion is created by using a metallic foil, silver leaf or Treasure Silver as a final step instead of the flat paint.

SMOKED GLASS DÉCOUPAGE

On a well-cleaned glass, spray an even coating of acrylic all over the backside. Dry thoroughly. Hold this glass over a lighted candle and move gently to accumulate the candle smoke where you want it to be. A beeswax candle will not smoke very much so use an ordinary one. When the coloring meets your approval, spray a fine mist of acrylic over the smoked surface to embed the carbon. Paste brightly colored découpage on a mirror and install behind the smoked glass, in a frame.

Bright reflections from mother-of-pearl add considerable interest to a switchplate. The very thin veneer sheets are easily cut after being soaked in hot water.

Mother-of-Pearl

The illusion created by using mother-of-pearl is incomparable. Glints of opalescent fire accent the print in strategic contours and add a dimension that cannot be achieved any other way. The best mother-of-pearl comes from the South Pacific. It is layered in a very thin veneer measuring about two inches by five inches.

To Prepare: Use a pencil to trace the pattern onto the translucent shell. While it is dry, the shell is brittle. Pour hot water over the shell, soak ten minutes, remove from water and begin cutting with the découpage scissors. Leave the shell in water during a long working period to avoid soaking from day to day. The left-over pieces can be used in many designs. Use the natural irregular bits on any contour without cutting a pattern.

To Apply: A thin coat of white glue is applied to the surface of the print and the mother-of-pearl. Dry to create a tacky instead of wet surface. A firm bond is made on contact. For small bits of mother-of-pearl, apply glue only to the print and press the shell into place. The white glue will dry transparent so there is no need to remove the excess. Apply a coat of clear sealer before you varnish.

Gold Leaf—Metal Leaf

First, we should distinguish between gold leaf and metal leaf, which is widely but erroneously called gold leaf. Real gold leaf is always packaged in squares 3″ x 3″. It comes in very few shades. The main two types of real gold leaf are standard and patent (or gild-in-the-wind) leaf. The latter is very lightly adhered to the paper so that a gilder working out of doors will be able to do gilding. This is easier for an amateur to work with. Tiny attached pieces can be easily handled and no waste occurs with this expensive material. Most leaf—real gold or otherwise—is twenty leaves to a book.

The metal leaf, though it is called "gold leaf," is easier to work with and much less expensive. In quantity purchases these 5½″ x 5½″ or larger sheets are inexpensive. Many paint stores carry the metal leaf and many also have "gold leaf" kits. The metal leaf is very susceptible to tarnish so sealer is used to prevent further tarnish. I have removed tarnish after a job was complete with a little diluted lemon juice, immediately neutralize with water, and dry. Then coat it with sealer.

This small chest can be used for practice when planning a full-sized piece. Here we see how the marbleizing is done, tapping across the surface to imitate marble. Last of all, the gold is applied to the edges.

The marbleizing on this Venetian shaped box was made by tapping gold accents on with a sponge. The turpentine-dampened sponge was dipped into Treasure Gold, and then applied to the box. The black center panel was painted on after the gold was dry. A print will be placed in the panel.

JAPAN GOLD SIZE

The mordant used varies. Mordant is the adhesive or varnish which is dried to the tacky stage and then receives the leaves of gold or other metal. Any gloss varnish could be used as a gold size. Any time you see the name "size"—this means adhesive. The name "Japan" on a gold size or drier means fast drying, and it really is. You may not be able to work fast enough to keep up with it. Apply a test patch, about 8″ x 8″, and time the drying. After twenty minutes it may be tacky enough to work well. Touch the surface ever so lightly; if there is a tacky click it is ready for applying the leaf. Continue to dry the test area. If it seems to have lost its tack after ten to fifteen minutes, that is all the time you have to work. If you have a fast drying gold size and it dries too rapidly, it can be removed with a rag dampened in turpentine. Then start again with another application of size. If you permit the gold size to dry twenty-four hours you can apply another coat and start again.

EIGHT HOUR MORDANT

Slow drying gold size may take four to eight hours to become tacky but you have one to two hours working time. If you use a fast size, cover a little at a time. Do as much as you can in twenty minutes, apply more size and wait until tacky and then place more leaf.

GOLD LEAF KITS

Gold leafing kits are abundant on the market now and generally work very well. One I have used seems very satisfactory. I don't like the disposable paste brushes that are included as you can't apply the adhesive evenly. The adhesive is rather like a thin latex and stays tacky a long time (twenty-four hours).

PREPARING THE GOLD LEAF

First, cut across the fold of the book of gold leaf so you have all single sheets. I handle the metal leaf sandwiched between two of the papers used in packaging. The leaf should be positioned so it extends one-half inch out of the papers; then lay this one-half inch of exposed leaf into the tacky surface and slip the leaf out of the papers easily onto the surface. After laying many leaves, I use a cotton ball and gently smooth down the leaf so it attaches evenly to the mordant. Go only in the direction of the grain as the gold leaf is so delicate it shows scratches if you smooth in circles. After the cotton polishing, collect the left-over scraps of gold leaf and save in a little jar. After much work you'll find these scraps handy fill-ins. Last, cover all metal leaf with découpage sealer, which is crystal clear.

Dissolve four empty gelatin capsules in a half cup of boiling water. Use this diluted gelatin mixture for a mordant on glass. (Most drug stores can supply you with the empty gelatin capsules.) The gelatin must dry only until tacky, then lay the leaf on the glass. Again, cotton is used to smooth the gold onto the surface. Silver or aluminum leaf will have the appearance of an old mirror, especially if your application is not perfect.

The Creil Technique

The original pieces were done during the 18th century. An invention of John Sadler, an English designer and engraver, is the basis of this exquisite ware. He discovered a method by which an engraved copper plate image could be transferred directly to white porcelain. He sought to guard his secret; however, he was imitated and the making of printed ware was soon widespread in England. There was a great demand for this beautiful ware, not only in his home land but throughout the entire European continent. Nowhere was there a livelier nor more enthusiastic demand than in France, where it became very serious competition for the domestic faience.

Therefore, the French potters began also to imitate the English work

The Creil technique of black and white on brilliant yellow is shown on this attractive two-deck card box. A very narrow gold border is used.

The chinoiserie cut-outs are used in the Creil technique on a yellow ground. Creil often features a border such as this.

in order to meet the competitor, and recapture their lost market. The first such factory was at Douai, which had arranged to have the Leech brothers from England oversee the manufacture of printed wares in France. They brought with them, also, experienced workers to train local potters in the craft.

In 1796 the Creil factory was established and soon was well known for the production of this type of transfer printed pottery. Their production was so well established that all French pottery of this type was known as Creil whether it was from this factory or not. The reason for their success was that they had been able to engage the service of Bagnall, an English engineer, and thirty workmen from the factory at Chantilly, who had been carefully trained by Bagnall.

The more important early factories making printed wares in France were Johnston, Montereau, Choisy, Sèvres, and Val-sous-Mendon. The Montereau factory was purchased by Creil in 1819. The Creil factory continued its production until 1895. The Choisy factory continued until 1914. By the time of Napoleon's Consulate, 1799–1804, there were twenty-nine factories and forty-six merchants in Paris alone. Napoleon himself ordered several services for different châteaux and the officers' mess.

Most of the Creil was painted in black on all white, some was done with black on white using yellow borders. A lesser amount was done by transferring black to all yellow. The rarest combination was a sepia on olive green. By the end of the 19th century many of these designs were done in multicolored decorations on a white ground. Many collectors of this beautiful ware consider the black on yellow to be the most flattering for "terre imprime." Varying from lemon yellow to earthy ochre, this coloring is most eagerly sought for today.

Many of the pottery shapes are typical of the English silver of the period of the Napoleonic Empire. There were certain French shapes developed from other forms and especially adapted for their own dinner services.

During the Empire period gelatin transfers were developed and for all practical purposes were a good replacement for the original method of direct transfer. This method soon replaced all others.

It is fairly accurate to assume the costume depicted is a key to the date of the piece. During the Directoire period pre-romantic designs were in vogue. Battles, processions and other great events were depicted. Madame Blanchard's balloon ascension was a frequent subject. Other favorite subjects were street vendors, marionette theatres, fables of La-Fontaine, the monuments of Paris, views of Venice and other Italian scenes, and provincial scenes. There were also drawing room settings, coach and horses, and favorite farm animals. There was little Chinese influence in the Creil designs.

The central designs were always accompanied by classic border material. Some of this was acanthus leaves, laurel wreaths, flower garlands, and other casual and formal accent motifs. Trophées were always popular in France. This subject called for a simple border selection.

The best Creil is characterized by delicately printed designs made with perfect transfers. Some pieces show hand retouching where a transfer had been mended. These pieces are not as collectible.

Toleware With Creil Designs

From the time the handsome idea of Creil was invented, a variety of imitations came into being. Many provincial pieces of tinware or tole were given a ground color of yellow (from pale yellow to mustard) and hand painted in delicate scrolls or garlands of laurel with the central motif of the trophy. This work was done largely on trays, lavabos, boxes, câche-pots, and planters. This tinware was largely for the provincial people. Since tin was more durable and could more readily be crafted by the tinsmith, the country people had their imitation of Creil. This particular interpretation of the original is a highly collectible commodity today. Much of the tole was handpainted to resemble closely the character of the pottery.

The original French provincial "tole" or tinware came into being as a suitable and available substitute for the very expensive porcelains and pottery. The free-hand painted tole motifs of field flowers, garlands, and borders are used on many of today's casual accessories.

I have mentioned these two techniques of decorating tin—or tole-ware—because it relates directly to the use of our Creil design cutouts for trays, tole lampshades, lamp bases and other metal ware. The soft yellow ground is a very good color to use in the home today. Like gold, it seems to enhance the setting in which it is used.

The prints for the Creil technique are to be used generally without coloring (sepia being an exception). The black and white is very smart on a yellow ground. Any simple ornament, trophy or figure surrounded by a border in the right scale mounted on yellow, white or olive green ground could be an interpretation of Creil. If you plan to use the olive green, color the print with #64 terra cotta and #54 Van Dyke brown pencils gently. It must be in the character of the Empire or Directoire period. The Creil designs should be on utility ware or accessories. Your selection of prints with which to do this could be based on costume or the aforementioned subject of soldiers, triumphal procession, transportation, ladies and gentlemen in Napoleonic costume or animals, particularly goats.

In most of our cities, large and small, it is possible to find ceramic hobbyists who have many shapes of boxes and trays available in bisque. This ware has been fired but not glazed. It is very suitable to use for découpage. You must seal the surface first, just as you do a wooden box, and apply two coats of flat or semi-gloss enamel for the ground on which to paste the découpage. Paste your cutouts in position, apply the borders, remove excess paste and allow to dry. Use many coats of varnish just as if you were working on wood. When a sufficient number of varnish layers are applied, sand the surface with wet or dry sandpaper. Next, use #0000 steel wool, polish over all to remove scratches. Last of all, wax the entire piece and polish to a gentle sheen.

Boulle

A French invention for the surface decoration of fine furniture was named after M. Boulle. He used tortoise shell and fine gauge brass laid together and cut out. When the assembly was finished and affixed to a surface, the brass scrolls were seen on a ground of tortoise shell. The beautiful warm reds of the shell were reversed for the companion piece, so no material was wasted.

Process: In order to make an effective scroll and not waste the inside pieces, this cutting will require a knife. The scrolls and motifs must fit the area to be done, if it is a small motif. They must fit in segments if it is larger. This handsome work should be done with gold tea chest paper and tortoise shell paper. Borders are used on all of this work.

Seal the tea chest paper on the back with sealer. Use a coat of gloss varnish on the front as sealer may remove gold color. Seal the front and back of the tortoise shell paper to make it stiffer and crisper to cut. Use very sharp blade. You can also cut out the tea chest paper only and lay it on the tortoise shell ground. In this instance, cut two gold layers at a time. Your work will be speeded along.

Marquetry

A popular French technique involving the use of light colored wood veneers inlaid on a ground of darker wood. The fruit and nut woods, as well as satinwood and boxwood, were used for the motifs. Mahogany,

Marquetry at its finest is seen in an 18th century example from the Civic Museum in Milan, Italy. It will provide design inspiration for use in découpage.

94

burl woods and crotch veneers were used as dark background. Flowers, birds and foliage in beautiful profusion were used to decorate furniture fronts, table tops, and drawer facings.

Process: Cut together wood veneer paper and the scroll print pattern. Paste on natural wood grain or simulated wood grain. Varnish.

Silhouette

Another Frenchman has his family name connected with a shadow detail technique of doing portraiture—and later applied to all flat black and white cutout work. This work was looked down on when it was introduced as it was done to obtain an inexpensive portrait likeness—avoiding the high cost of miniature paintings or porcelain portraits.

Process: Cut scrolls, flowers, people. Stain either side with india ink. Apply to white background. If reverse work is your plan, use the white prints on black background.

Intarsia (Inlaid marble)

This technique involves the use of marbleized papers to effect an inlaid appearance on furniture. Usually a wide flourish is established for a border and various colored marble tones are laid out in an effective front and top pattern.

Process: Cut designs from a main pattern. Paste onto the painted surface and sink under many layers of varnish.

Trompe l'oeil

Trompe l'oeil and découpage go together. The French word *tromper* means to fool or to deceive and *oeil* means eye. We now see a growing interest in this marvelous technique and there will be more and more in the future. The fruit or other objects which are used as cutout material depend upon the hand-painted shadows to complete the illusion.

In the color illustration opposite, the cutouts, all life-size, were applied to make-believe pigeonholes and drawers that had been blocked out in paint on the surface of the cabinet and shaded to trick the eye into seeing a third dimension. Actually the cabinet, 12 inches square by 18 inches high, has one door, no drawers. Book, wineglass, key, clock face and rose motifs were snipped from pages of magazines. Butterfly and apple were cut out of inexpensive prints. Playing cards and letters are real, but ribbon is a strip of paper that was pressed flat and pasted on. Each pigeonhole was charted first on paper.

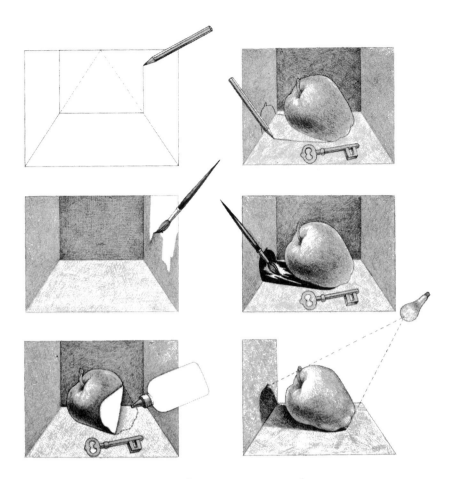

HOW TO PLOT AND PAINT TROMPE L'OEIL PIGEONHOLES[1]

1. Starting in center of top boundary for pigeonhole, draw diagonal lines to bottom corners. Join diagonals at mid points with line parallel to bottom. From same points, draw vertical lines to top. Erase lines indicated by dots.

2. Shade with paint each section of pigeonhole to give the effect of depth, varying darkness of shading to suggest direction of light source.

3. Glue cutouts on "floor" of pigeonhole.

4. To determine the realistic pattern of shadows cast by the cutouts, select a real apple, key, etc., place nearby and direct a light on them.

5. With soft pencil, copy the outlines of the real shadows around the objects in the pigeonhole.

6. Fill in shadows with shades of gray.

[1] Reprinted from House and Garden Magazine, Copyright © 1963 by the Condé Nast Publications, Inc.

Reproduction (with a few liberties) of a primitive painting in the Garbisch art collection. Background table and base are freehand painted and dishes are drawn and painted on heavy paper, then cut out. Prints used are antique and reproductions of old prints in full color. Old curly maple frame is used.

Repoussé

This very attractive technique involves filling the cavity of an embossed print with papier mâché or other hardening material. It is necessary to use a print on heavy paper. If the print was done in watercolor, be sure to apply two coats of sealer. Dry thoroughly. Soak the print in warm water twenty minutes to soften it so it will contour easily. The contour is created by pressing the print from the back side to stretch the paper into a convex shape.

Against a turkey-red grained background are placed three yellow-green finches on a pine bough. The side lighting helps set off the sculptured bodies in this handsome repoussé.

Yellow wild roses in repoussé shown on a cut-out panel of antique white. A green wooden wastebasket repeats the foliage color.

HOW TO DO A BIRD IN REPOUSSÉ

1. Hold the print to a window or other light, and trace the outline of the bird on the reverse side of the paper. This is done so you will know where to press the paper to create the bird's body shape.

2. Place the wet print on a piece of plastic foam, such as Oasis or styrofoam. With the burnishing tool or other rounded metal object begin to press on the area that you want the deepest. Continue pressing in gentle circles until you have come to the edge of the penciled outline. You are scooping out or hollowing a negative contour from the reverse side that will appear as a raised or embossed surface on the printed side.

3. When the shaping is complete, apply two coats of white glue and dry. Fill the cavity up to within one-eighth of an inch of the outline so the cutting will be easy, and the edge will flatten out when you glue. Use a ready mixed papier mâché or make a filling of wadded tissues and white glue. It is possible to use plastic wood or self-hardening clay, plaster, or spackling compound. On a cylindrical or other contoured surface, use a papier mâché filler as it will bend.

4. After the work is completely dried, cut out the bird, and glue to the surface with white glue. Begin the varnish finish. After ten coats you

98

are ready to sand. Use steel wool on the contoured bird and sandpaper (#400 wet or dry) on the flat areas.

The print can be cut out before stuffing, but for most people it is a little more difficult to handle this way.

QUESTIONS AND ANSWERS

Repoussé

1. Q. My print is on thin paper. What can I do to use it?

   A. Seal the print first, then glue or paste it to a heavier grade of paper, such as water color paper. Then proceed with the repoussé work.

2. Q. Where can you use repoussé birds when they are finished?

   A. They are beautiful on screens or boxes. An attractive wood stain can be a natural setting for birds. They are used on the top of basket purses and on wastebaskets.

3. Q. Can I combine repoussé flowers with Victorian découpage, and contour a gold paper braid basket for a container?

   A. Yes. That would be very attractive. It would be interesting to use a gold tea chest paper background for the flowers and gold basket.

4. Q. Should I stuff or contour a butterfly for use in a shadowbox picture?

   A. No. A butterfly's natural shape is flat except for the body.

5. Q. How many coats of varnish should I use if I plan to do flowers in repoussé in a shadow box?

   A. Two or three coats may be sufficient for a shadow box. If you need more, use more.

6. Q. Would it be permissible to glue gold cord or colored string when doing work in repoussé?

   A. Related materials such as gold cord, string, woven matting, grass cloth, and perhaps natural plant material such as twigs could be used. Fabrics can be used in repoussé.

7. Q. Are animals sometimes used as designs?

   A. Yes. There are no limits to the number of subjects that can be used.

8. Q. Can I use mother-of-pearl in the contours?

   A. Mother-of-pearl accent is beautiful and will contour on many surfaces.

Projects to Try

The following projects are easy to do if care is observed at each step. Read the instructions through completely and if you do not understand the procedure with the aid of the illustrations, go to the next project, and come back to this project later. (You will understand it.) Do not feel baffled if there are parts that seem to confuse you or that you do not understand. After all, you will find even in a class with the best instructor this situation arises. Relax, learn what you can, and upon returning to the project with a clear fresh mind, all will be clear and easy to understand.

Beginner Project: How to do a Metal Tray with Modern Prints

Prepare the tray. Wipe with alcohol if previously painted. If it is very glossy, use fine sandpaper to create a good surface for adhesion.

1. Choosing the background color is easy. You want the prints you choose to be against a color that will accent their beauty. This is a good place for an accent color you enjoy. Remember the varnish will mellow considerably, so use blue, green, red or soft yellow.

2. Apply two or three thin coats of paint. If your first coat has ridges, thin the paint with solvent and continue to apply a smooth coat. Sand very gently between coats.

3. Apply sealer to the front of the print. If the paper is heavy, you will need many extra coats of varnish to cover the edges. It is possible to taper these prints with sandpaper or wet it and roll off a layer of paper —this is hazardous for the beginner.

4. Cut out prints carefully, serrating the edges of the leaves by wiggling the paper back and forth to create a softer edge as you guide the paper into the scissors.

5. Apply paste to the tray and gently press the print into place. Roll out any excess paste, using a brayer (looks like a small rolling pin) or a wallpaper tool. A slightly damp cloth placed over the design prevents smearing paste as you roll.

6. Use gold paper braid as a narrow border—adhere with white glue. Apply sealer evenly over the entire surface before varnishing.

7. Now, begin the beautiful process which will make your tray permanently attractive and useful. Apply the varnish to the entire surface. Do not drag the brush across the edge of the container as this creates bubbles. Always pour the amount of varnish you will be using into a separate container, so you will not contaminate the entire can with dust and foreign matter. Keep the brush in turpentine from day to day.

The Basket Purse

The basket purse is a fashion accessory which is becoming increasingly popular all over the United States. Exquisite samples are seen in the smartest resort boutiques and specialty shops in many of our larger towns. The woman who appreciates these handmade, beautifully finished basket purses will part with a considerable sum of money in order to possess one. They are carried with casual clothes and street wear. They always attract attention! Some smaller basket models are made for dress-up and done with delicate prints and metallic coloring. Other small models are made for smaller women or little girls in this fashion-conscious world.

A white ground is used for the forget-me-not blue garland. A matching blue velvet ribbon is placed over wide pale green ribbon to trim the edge and handle. Sapphire and green amber are rubbed on the wood for a stunning effect. Blue and green berries are woven on the lining fabric.

The purse basket is an easy and popular fashion accessory. It is a distinguished piece to carry and easy enough to make. You may have a small basket which would be suitable. If not they are easy to find. It's best to buy one without a lid and have a separate lid cut to fit. Fine brass hinges give a professional touch. Now let's get started.

1. Sand the box and lid carefully with fine garnet sandpaper.

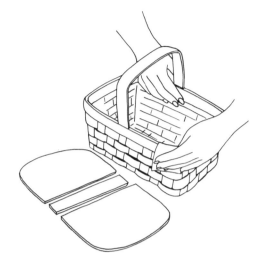

2. Stain the lid and basket with oil stain or Treasure Jewels thinned with turpentine.

3. Rub the stain color in wet with wet or dry emery paper. Do handle, lid and outside of the basket—not inside. This makes an incomparably smooth finish.

102

4. Seal prints, lid and basket. Cut out print for lid and under lid designs. Sealer makes the print easier to cut—prevents tearing when wet with paste.

5. Paste on motifs. Remove excess paste. Dry. Seal the surface of print and lid, top and underside. Also, seal the stain on the basket.

6. Begin the varnish finish. Apply ten coats. Then sand with wet or dry paper dipped in water. Apply six to ten more coats of varnish. Sand. Apply two coats wax.

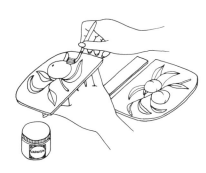

Fabric lining the basket purse:

7. Cut two sides and one bottom strip. Apply two coats acrylic spray to stiffen and protect lining.

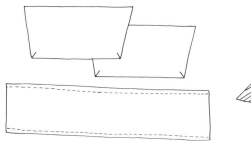

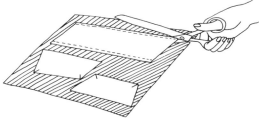

8. Glue lining. Glue in both sides first and center panel last. Glue on nylon ribbon or gimp braid available at upholstery shops. Make bow trim.

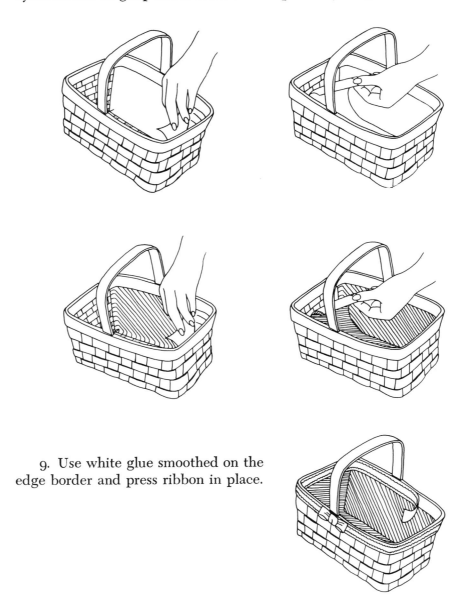

9. Use white glue smoothed on the edge border and press ribbon in place.

10. Place hinges ½″ from edge of lid. Slip under handle into place and install handle screw to secure center lid panel.

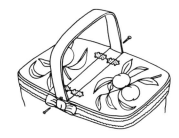

Finished basket

How to do a Shadowbox Picture

Assemble your materials:

    Frame
    Colored cutout prints: tiny ship or gondola
    Cement glue
    Paste
    Sponge
    Water
    Tiny matchbox
    Glass
    Gold Paper braid border

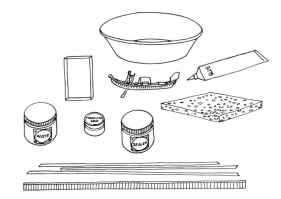

1. Wash glass with ½ and ½ vinegar water. Dry. Paste foreground prints onto the glass. Apply découpage paste over the area the print will cover. Press out excess paste. Remove with sponge. Set aside to dry. Clean all excess paste. Must be very clean.

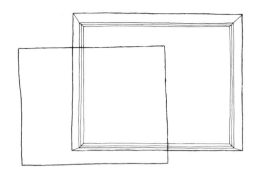

2. Place tiny print panels and people in the matchbox which will be the scene in the left foreground. Tiny people can be cut from découpage print catalogs showing prints in miniature.

3. Glue the matchbox to the back of the building so this setting can be seen through the open windows. Also, paste into place the canal panel.

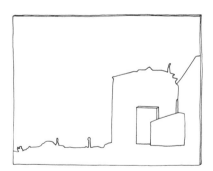

Seen from rear

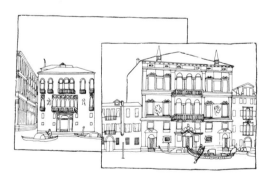

Canal panel

4. Paste gold tea chest paper to the back board (corrugated). Seal tea paper on both sides before using it. Allow pasted paper to dry thoroughly. Paste background print on gold tea paper. Use small gold paper braid

motifs inside open doors and windows to resemble grill work. Install small gondola or ship with glue or Plasti-Tak.

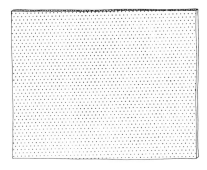

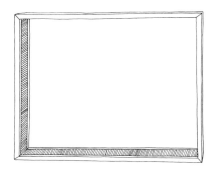

5. Paste in a strip of black cardboard allowing ¼″ for the back board (corrugated) to fit against. (Use shirtboard painted black with ink or paint.)

6. Use cement glue (Duco or other) to hold glass onto outside of the frame. Place glass immediately before glue sets. Cover edge with gold paper braid.

7. Nail backboard in place. Cover the back with dust paper and install a center pictured ring.

Venetian shadowbox showing placement of palazzos along the canal to give depth and create a vue d' optique. The building in the foreground has doors and windows opened into a matchbox scene.

The inside story is told when we see the matchbox attached to the print on the glass and the tiny silver filigree gondola in the canal on the back print. Hand-colored prints in pastel are framed in gold leaf shadowbox.

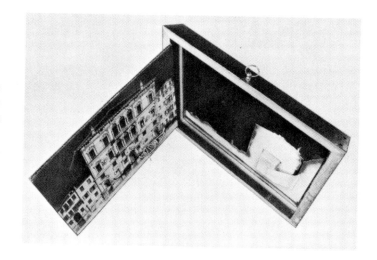

Chinoiserie shadowbox with a vue d' optique is colored in the 18th century palette and placed on a gold tea chest paper background. Three prints were used for this piece.

How to do Ribbon Découpage

This lovely antique technique was not called by this name traditionally, but ribbon découpage is a good name to use when you place ribbon or brocade behind the cutout print. Many of the varieties of cutout work did not have a standard name. Probably this is due to the fact each artist designing this work felt he had created something nobody else ever did. In so doing, he may or may not have given it a name. Many exquisite shadowbox cutouts were done as portraits of a favorite saint, usually performing a miracle.

1. Antique the print first. Moisten both sides of the print—lay on a flat table surface—drip tea or coffee to stain. Instant tea or coffee can be blown from the open hand to the print to create random age spots. Blot these if they are too intense and add more water or tea. Dry flat.

2. The print is not colored; however, if you wish to add subtle accents in pencil now is the time to do it. Seal the print back and front.

3. Cut out portions of the pattern that you wish to ornament with gold paper accents. Paste the gold paper in place on the back of the print—very carefully.

4. Cut the areas of the print where you wish to have the brocade showing through. It is not necessary to do anything to prepare the fabric if it lies flat. If you want to use a few spray coatings of acrylic plastic the fabric will be stiffer for smooth mounting; however, you might lose some of the color or alter the sheen. Spray-test first.

5. The print is somewhat wrinkly like an antique print. I do not think this is objectionable. You can dry mount the print flat with rubber cement or a photography shop can dry mount it to a board to be perfectly flat —this is your preference. I like the natural easy state of the print—wrinkly.

6. Cut a mat for the print or have the mat cut at the shop where you get your frame. Mount gold border strips and tortoise shell paper strips to make an inner border on the mat to make a French mat. Install in frame. Mount print on back board—set in place. Nail in the whole assembly. Paste dust paper and attach wire in screw eyes.

How to do a Lamp

Coordinating the size of the lamp base and the shade could be the most difficult part of this project. Be sure to have your lamp shade before you begin the découpage. Many electric repair companies have lamp parts and also the glass hurricane cylinder or chimney. If you buy all of your parts from a company they can also assemble your finished work. *Buy the shade before you begin.* Plan to use a related print border on the shade.

109

1. Assemble your materials.

2. Plan the design on the hurricane lamp base. Clean the inside and out with vinegar water to remove any oil or fingerprints. All work will be done inside the glass.

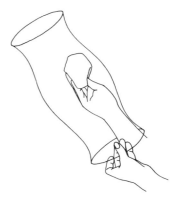

3. For work under glass do not seal the print. This is the secret of the perfectly clear paste job. If the print is very intricate you should seal very lightly on the back.

4. A china marking pencil or crayon can be used to indicate on the outside of the lamp the placement of motifs. Also, use a rubber band around the piece to make border indications. This can be moved up and down to the border edge. If you want an antiqued finish, this goes on before you paste, wipe or streak, or brush paint an antique glaze on.

5. Lightly apply paste on the *front* of the print which is to be used in the center area. Place the center motif first and the outer border last. Carefully press out excess paste and tap up with a damp sponge.

6. Follow the border rubber band and press your pasted border material into place. Do not overlap at the final piece; make it appear continuous.

7. If you want any gold accents, now is the time while the paste is still intact. Apply little pieces of bright gold foil behind openings, particularly areas which are reverse cut. *Lay lamp base on the side* in an airy place so the inside has an opportunity to get dry.

8. Dry overnight. Remove any excess paste when the individual motifs are dry underneath and will not move when touched with a slightly damp eversoft sponge. Set aside to dry again. You could use an electric fan now to dry quickly.

9. Use clear sealer over the entire design —this will prevent any paint from sneaking under the print. This is an important step so cautiously cover every little edge and especially where there might be an overlap. Dry thoroughly—use an electric fan.

111

10. Paint the inside of the lamp and the backside of the prints. I use a cloth pad—not a brush—inside, so I can easily pounce on a perfect layer of paint. Starting in the middle, pat the paint in an even layer in a wide spiral toward the outside edge. Turn over and do the same from the center to the outer edge. If you plan a contrasting band of Treasure Gold behind the border, now is the time to apply the gold with your finger. Tap it on at first, dry a little, and give a second coat to make the gold richer. You need a second coat of paint after twenty-four hours.

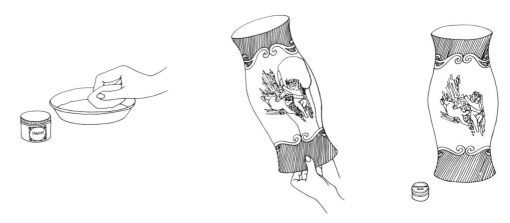

How to do a Lamp Shade

When doing the lamp base, you worked in reverse under glass. The traditional name for work under glass is reverse painting. Now, when you do the shade, the work will be the standard procedure. A plain ivory silk shade can be used or you can make the lamp more attractive by making a shade designed with the same prints as the base.

1. Assemble materials:
   Parchment shade
   Gold or silver spray paint
   Découpage paint and brush
   Clear spray
   Border cutouts
   Paste
   Sponge
   Water

2. Cut out the border material, either more of the lamp base prints or something related.

3. Paint the parchment paper shade with a silver or gold metallic spray to make it opaque. Do not get spray on the inside. This must be sealed with Treasure Sealer.

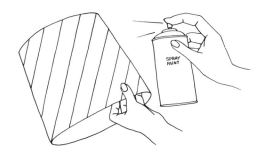

4. Paint the background with a pad dipped into the paint to imitate the texture of the base. You could use a small trim roller if you have one. Dry twenty-four hours. A second coat may be needed if the first coat wasn't even. Sand very lightly and wipe the dust away. Make measured *marks* on the edge for the border.

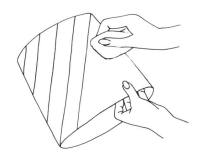

5. Apply paste to the area on which you intend to apply the border. Position prints and press on with a damp sponge. Do an area of about ten inches at a time, or whatever is near your border size. Repeat until you are finished. Allow paste to dry. Remove excess paste with a damp sponge.

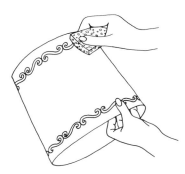

6. Paste any motifs on the lamp shade. Glue on narrow contrasting ribbon.

7. Dull plastic acrylic spray is used to fix the paint and protect the prints.

8. Have lamp assembled.

9. Which finial to use? Be sure to finish your shade (when it is assembled to the base) with an attractive finial. It could be painted the base color, but this is the finishing touch of a well-designed lamp.

Covering a Box With Paper

1. Apply paste evenly to sides and bottom of box. Place box in center of paper.
2. Smooth the paper across the bottom and up the sides of the box. press firmly to top edges and corners.
3. Cut off "loops" at corners, carefully so that edges of paper meet.
4. Fold paper over top edges of box, paste down firmly.
5. Miter top edge (shown in circle) by cutting through overlap at 45 degree angle.

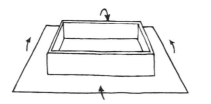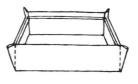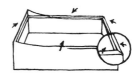

Lining Boxes

One of the special marks of a well done piece is choosing a related lining inside the box and finishing the underside of the box with great care.

Either use small brass feet on the bottom or a border design protected with varnish. On boxes which are heavy, you might prefer to use a felt or cork pad for the protection of furniture. It should not be glued on.

Each of us will devise a variation of his own on lining the box. I do believe a good lining is essential. There are at least three variations suitable for a box. An 18th century jewel box replica would surely have to be lined with a fine brocade, silk or velvet—either padded when using silk or flat when using the brocade or velvet.

The fabric lining is a bit tricky; with patience it will be a very successful lining, perhaps the easiest and most rapid of the three to do.

The découpage lining: a box to be used in the living room would be most intriguing if designs were carried out on the inside in the same manner as the outside.

The paper lining: the third type of lining is a solid lining of gold or silver tea paper, silver leaf, gold leaf or metal leaf—or a select marbleized book-binding paper for the tailored taste.

HOW TO DO LININGS

The fabric lining: cardboard from a dress box or shirt box or even a tablet will be quite suitable for the backing. Cut a piece to fit the bottom, minus ⅛″ all around the border. This seems terribly small, but wait till the fabric is glued on! Cut pieces now for the two ends and two sides, minus the ⅛″ border. It is easiest to do one side and an end together, so lay the cardboard on the back side of the fabric and cut it out allowing ½″ extra border. Cut V's at the crease and cut diagonally across ends. (Practice this on paper first if you are unsure. Fold the paper down all around and you will see how nicely the lining will fit.) Cut into your fabric and paste it down on the back side. Cut and paste both ends and sides. To make a final check on the fit, place the linings in the box, where they are to remain and slip the bottom piece (to which the fabric is pasted and ready) into place.

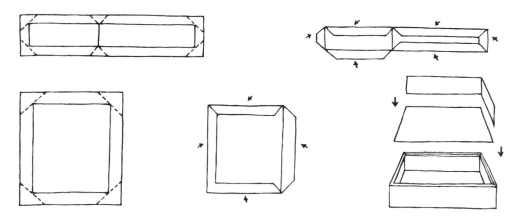

115

If you have no further alterations, paste the sides and bottom into position. The inside of the box was sealed and painted when the box was being prepared. This helps prevent warping of the box.

Go through the same procedure to line the top of the box. If the lid is too narrow for side pieces cover the cardboard for the inside top of the lid and glue in place a decorative cord around the edge to finish it. You may select a woven braid which would be in keeping and glue it in for the sides.

The découpage lining: this decorative lining is done using additional designs cut out for the inside. Two coats of paint are needed inside. This should be done when you are preparing the outside of the box. You may choose to make a contrasting color inside. At any rate, your basic preparation is just the same as the outside of the box. Plan the design, smooth paste over the section you are to apply the cutouts and arrange them, pressing as much paste from under the cutouts as is possible. A rolling pressure with thumb or index finger should accomplish this. After all the designs are in place, remove *excess* paste—picking it up with a *damp, but not wet,* sponge. Continue to tap up all the excess paste, then permit the work to dry—do not accelerate with heat at any time.

After twenty-four hours' drying, check to see that all the segments are tightly glued. A toothpick and a touch of white glue is used for any stragglers. Next, brush a thin coating of sealer and dry an hour. Now, apply the first coat of varnish, evenly but not generously. Follow the varnish label for drying interval—every twenty-four hours is safest. About four coats should do for the inside. Sand after the final coat of varnish—not between coats.

The paper lining: since the paste you use is a water base paste it would stretch and warp any lining paper, so be sure to use *sealer* on the front and back of your lining paper, dry thoroughly and cut the paper to fit the sides and the bottom. Paste in the section for the bottom first. Smooth paste evenly on the bottom of the box and press the paper into place. Using a wet finger and paste for lubrication press the paper down firmly and try to get any excess paste out at the edges. Apply paste to the sides and having the lining paper creased at the corners, lay it into place. Next, use the thumb or finger with a rolling movement to remove excess paste.

Use a damp sponge again to clean the excess paste from the inside surface of the box. Dry twenty-four hours and apply a coat of sealer. You do not need any further varnish as your paper now has two coats of sealer. There should be no bubbles or areas which did not stick. If a bubble or a blister should occur, slit through it with a razor blade and fill it with white glue applied with a toothpick or artist's tiny spatula and smooth into place.

Ideas for Accessories

All of these designs can be cut out by the amateur wordworker. The illustrations include: pencil and stationery box, book ends, key board, desk paper holder, either note size or business size, wooden shields, wooden clothes hanger, and special letter box with a drawer on each side and crest design.

Your First Découpage

Somewhere among your magazine clippings you have probably saved an idea you would love to try in découpage. You may have seen a lovely basket purse, a fabulous tray or stunning little box which you'd like to duplicate. You may have seen what you thought was a priceless antique accessory with mother-of-pearl inlay, only to be told that it was made just recently by a person who has no more training nor ability than you have. Right then and there you decide you can learn découpage, too!

You must start by deciding what project will be your first. Then get prints which will be suitable in scale and character. Assemble all your materials and begin. It is really about as uncomplicated as that! It is also important that you plan to work where and when you can find a time free from needless interruption. Only then, with materials set neatly for work in a light, airy and comfortable place, can you find freedom for creative expression and become absorbed in découpage—in such a setting fine work can be done.

In preparing to do découpage the following materials are necessary: print, pencils, paste, sealer, paint, brushes, sandpaper, steel wool, scissors, varnish and wax. There are other handy things to have but these are essential.

Prepare the piece to be done in découpage by painting and sanding very evenly and smoothly. Color a black and white print to coordinate with the background paint or use the print without coloring. In either case the print must be sealed. The cutout prints are placed in a pleasing arrangement and pasted down firmly. The final step is applying ten or more coats of varnish and sanding level. The varnish finish is complete when wax has been applied and polished to a sheen. Each step is relatively simple and when done with care the results are very pleasing.

Project Suggestions for a Beginner

Plan a group of three projects to learn working with wood, metal and glass. Relate the projects to bathroom, desk, vanity—such as
> Game accessories—cardbox, ashtray, bonbon dish
> Desk accessories—letter holder, ashtray, stamp box
> Entry hall—switchplate, serving tray, wastebasket
> Dressing room—vanity tray, switchplate, jewel box

Further Projects

For men—young and older:
> The crest box for jewelry or pocket items
> Organizer box—chest-top box
> Hobby box—boat box, model car box
> Stationery box—lap desk
> Good grooming kit—shoe polish, etc.

For young women:
> Curler box, sewing stand
> Vanity box, mirror
> Box purse

Basket purse
Stationery box
For the home:
    Candle table
    Small desk
    Mirror
    Tole planter
    Large tray
    China cabinet
    Lamp base and lamp shade
For special gifts—all ages:
    Bachelor's chest
    Doll bed, dresser
    Lap desk
    Picnic basket
    Courtin' basket
    Trinket box
    Poodle bed
    Shadowbox
    Découpage pictures

Panels, Screens, Pictures and Plaques

When working with only two dimensions, width and height, you have a different design problem than with three dimensions, width, height, and depth. When planning a composition for a picture, many prints will be used—either in a landscape, figure presentation, or flowers and fruit. The reason for a découpage picture is purely ornamental. "Beauty is its own excuse for being," Emerson says.

In planning a decorative panel or a useful screen your purpose may be to provide a subtle, but ornamental background. In this instance use less contrasting colors, a pale ground color and pastel colored or uncolored prints. This screen or panel will take its place quietly in a room setting. If your plan is to have the screen or panel a dominant design factor in the setting, it can be very ornamental and amount to a considerable factor in furnishing a room. This screen should show a sharp contrast in ground color as well as greater strength of design and color in the prints.

Plaques are used as beginner projects and test panels. They are quickly done and very good to do to learn découpage techniques. Usually a single print is cut out, applied and varnished.

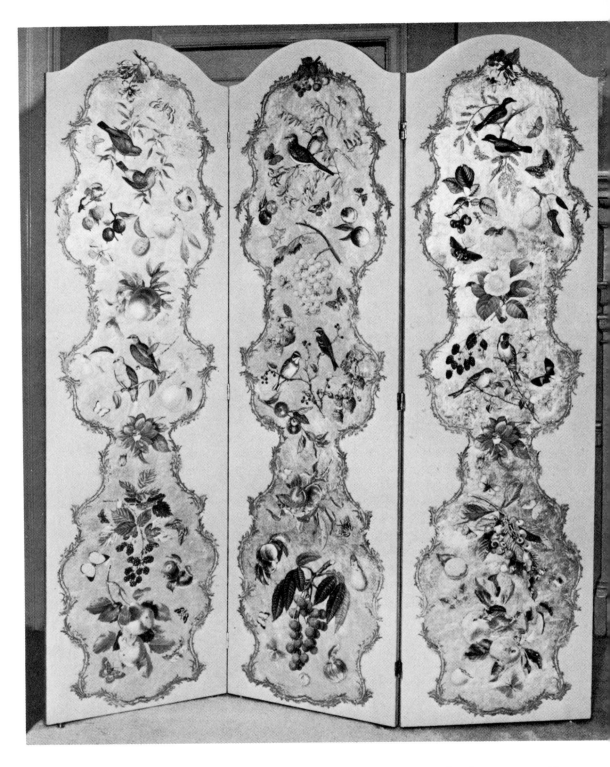

An outstanding example of a three panel screen. It is painted pale green outside with gold leaf background, enclosed in the cartouche border. Some prints are antique, some are Gould's tropical birds, Redouté's camellias and fruit reproductions. Only the cartouche is hand colored green and gold. This screen is one of the most arresting works in contemporary découpage.

Conclusion

The things you create are likely to weather the times—if they were basically good to start with. This is a reason many of the antique pieces of yesterday are desirable today. They were well thought out to start with and executed with great care. This, in essence, is the secret of a timeless piece, whether you buy it or make it.

The most enjoyable pastimes can be very rewarding cultural achievements as well. This description certainly fits découpage because it can be the beginning of a wonderful new art as well as an insight into the very interesting lives of people of the past. The current excitement about things antique is more than a passing fancy. These lovely things are part of an unhurried world, a world in which it was more important to be a fine craftsman than to produce something in a rush and get on with other urgent things.

People who are interested in découpage will experience a renaissance of the spirit, a dedication to the methods of the true craftsman and ultimately the deep satisfaction of looking upon beautiful works of découpage, which you have created. It is important to find a means of self-expression; however, the only way to become a member of the master craftsmen's group is through a continuous desire to improve and make this a reality. If you have ever complimented a friend or acquaintance who is very accomplished she will probably say, "I still have a lot to learn." This is especially true of découpage because the areas of knowledge are so broad. Once the search for information begins, you are off to an adventure of a greater dimension as one reference takes you to another. Your initial curiosity will lead you into a whole new world, a very satisfying experience.

You will find in learning to color prints that you gain a considerable understanding of color. In learning to cut the prints, you sense a great achievement in mastering the scissors. When you place your prints and plan the design, you have an exercise in two and three dimensional design. Each facet of a box must relate to the other sides and the top. The interrelation of design is a great puzzle on which to work. Solving this puzzle results in the best workable design as well as the most attractive piece. The first consideration must be to use related material in the same scale.

If you discipline yourself you have time for more enrichment. If you practice patience the rewards are limitless. Practice and discipline are also the secret of many other good things. They will be of ultimate value to you when you are learning découpage.

There will be changes of taste from decade to decade, but a beautiful piece of découpage is always desirable. If découpeurs produce lovely Victorian découpage I suspect there will be many people who see this and think Victorian is the only kind of découpage. If the use of 18th century reproductions becomes increasingly popular and lovely examples are seen, I'm sure the traditional work will be paramount. The use of old magazine pictures and cast off furniture will not always result in attractive work, and this can possibly cause the lovely art of découpage to deteriorate. I do hope to see the traditional materials used and preservation of the art carried to its highest form. Only then will découpage be recognized as a craft of merit in the decorative arts.

GLOSSARY

ABBÉ DE ST. NON 18th century artist designer of ornamental French trophées, who was a collector and a friend of Fragonard.

ALKYD-RESIN Basic ingredient for varnish, made from soya bean.

APPLIQUÉ Ornamental design motifs applied to a surface.

ARTE POVERO The poor man's art. Italian name for imitations of oriental lacquer furniture.

BANNISTER CUTTING Parallel line cutting done to resemble bannister rails, used in border cutouts and other decorative areas such as a basket.

BIEDERMEIER
(Bee-der-myer) Early 19th century German furniture style with solid geometric mass designs frequently incorporating pillars and claws, decorated with ormulu mounts.

BLEEDING PRINT A print in which the ink is alcohol soluble, causing a blurred appearance when sealer is applied.

BOMBÉ
(Bom bay) Furniture which is contoured with a vertical swell on the sides or front or both. This style prevailed in Europe during the 18th and 19th centuries.

BOUCHER, FRANÇOIS
(Boo-shay) 1703–1776. An outstanding artist and engraver, famed for his unusually charming cherubs and well drawn ladies of history and mythology.

BOULLE
(bool) A style of ornamental inlay for furniture. It was made of fine gauge brass which was tooled and laid in natural tortoise shell for a background.

123

BOULLE, ANDRÉ CHARLES (Bool)	1642–1732. Made fine furniture during reigns of Louis XIV, Louis XV and Louis XVI with various fine woods, tortoise shell and gilt bronze ornaments and mountings.
BURNISHER	A metal or agate tool used to compress paper and bevel the edge of a pasted print so the surface is smoother for applications of varnish.
CARTOUCHE (car-toosh)	A stylized scroll border used as a frame around 18th century subjects, to make a border of cutout material resembling the cartouche.
CERAMIC BISQUE	A piece of clay which has had a single firing to harden it, but no glaze applied to make a surface finish.
CHINOISERIE (Shin-wah-zer-ie)	A term used by the French to describe the Chinese influence or to express work done in the Chinese manner.
CREIL (Cray)	Ornamental designs transferred in black ink directly to the ware, originally copper plate engravings, later different designs applied to yellow or ochre colored ware.
DÉCOUPAGE (Day-coo-pahge)	The art of decorating surfaces with applied paper cutouts.
DRYBRUSH CUTTING	Découpage style of cutting showing an edge cut in the manner of a stroke from a nearly dry brush.
EMPIRE PALETTE	A selection of colors used together to express the taste in color used during the reign of the Emperor Napoleon Bonaparte.
ENGLEBRECHT, MARTIN	1684–1756. Made many copper plate engravings of prints for decorative purposes, designs to cut out for scrap books, peep shows and découpage.
FEATHER CUTTING, FEATHERING	Découpage technique of cutting to resemble feathers, especially outer motifs in intricate and graceful tufts. Feathering usually refers to the tufts of feather cutting in a print. It is also used in some regions to describe the serrated edge. It is referred to as feathered cutting or feathered edge.
FOREGROUND DETAIL CUTTING	Transforming a straight line at the bottom of the print into an interesting irregular line defining material or motifs on this edge or on either right or left side of the print.

FRAGONARD, JEAN HONORÉ (Frag-o-nar)	1732–1806. Artist, engraver, whose work was sought by collectors and royalty. His exquisite engraving is a graphic record of the opulent court life of the French Royalty.
FERRULE	A ring of metal put around a slender shaft to strengthen it or prevent splitting; the metal band which holds bristles of a brush in place.
GALBÉ (gal bay)	An elongated ogee curve used as a furniture contour similar to bombé.
GESSO (jes-oh) like the g in gesture	(Italian for gypsum)—A plaster prepared with glue for use in painting a smooth surface or making bas reliefs; a paste prepared from Spanish whiting and rabbit skin glue spread on a surface as a gilding base. Gesso-instant: Liquitex gesso, ready mixed.
GILDING	To overlay with or as if with a thin covering of gold—to give an attractive appearance to a surface.
GOLD LEAF	A sheet of gold ordinarily varying from four to five millionths of an inch in thickness that is used especially for gilding.
GOLD PAPER BRAID	Ornamental foil paper which is embossed with intricate designs and die-cut into delicate filigree. The designs are borders, scrolls, frames, corners, alphabets, and numerous other stylish motifs used in Victorian découpage.
GRISAILLE (gree-sail)	A decorative painting in gray monochrome; gray coloring used to resemble shadow and form of marble sculpture.
INCISED CUTTING	Découpage cutting in which the print is opened in contoured areas—not noticeable as a special pattern. The purpose is to prevent large areas without openings.
INTARSIA (in-tar-sha)	A mosaic usually of wood fitted and glued into a wooden support popular in 15th century Italy for decoration, later in the 18th century interpreted in marble and semiprecious stones used as rectangular inlays in furniture.
LADDER	Paper strips left uncut to hold delicate parts of the print together for further cutting and handling.
LADIES AMUSEMENT	"Ladies Amusement, or The Whole Art of Japan-

ning Made Easy": a book printed in London in 1760 for Robert Sayer containing some 1500 fascinating original drawings and designs, incorporating chinoiseries, birds, butterflies, flowers, landscapes and Oriental figures and a variety of borders and patterns. This book had an important effect on the designs of later Georgian craftsmen.

LATEX

A general group of water base enamel paints, originally made of rubber base resins, currently not made with rubber.

MARBLEIZED

The technique of creating a marbleized finish on furniture or other surfaces.

MARBLEIZED PAPER

Decorative papers of many designs and colors usually swirled in random patterns to resemble the effect of marble.

MARQUETRY
(mar-ket-ree)

A decorative process in which elaborate patterns are formed by the insertion of pieces of wood, shell or ivory into a wood veneer that is then applied to a piece of furniture.

MORDANT

An adhesive used to hold gold leaf or metal leaf onto a surface—it is usually a slow drying varnish.

OUTLINE DETAIL CUTTING

Narrow lines are cut into the print following the lines of the engraving. This may be done to accentuate birds' feathers, clouds, or straight lines of windows, building details or folds in fabrics.

OXYDIZE

To combine with oxygen; to dehydrogenate, especially by the action of oxygen.

PASTE

A preparation usually of flour or starch and water used as an adhesive or a vehicle for mordant or color.

PILLEMENT, JEAN
(Peel-mont)

1719–1808. French artist and designer during the reign of Louis XV and XVI. Much of his work was based on Oriental fantasies.

PLASTI-TAK

A plastic adhesive used for temporarily mounting prints or designs on surfaces.

POLYMERIZE
(plem-er-ize)

A chemical reaction in which two or more molecules change structure. A given material completely changes its identity.

POMPADOUR

Jeanne Antoinette Poisson, Marquise de Pompadour, 1721–1764; mistress of Louis XV of France.

PROVINCIAL GARDEN PALETTE	A group of colors consisting of lavenders and fragile blues, pinks and greens; used with a soft pastel background color on furniture or boxes.
REDOUTÉ, PIERRE-JOSEPH (Reh-doo-tay)	Botanical artist, who enjoyed the patronage of Marie Antoinette and Josephine Bonaparte. His fame rests in part upon the love dedicated to his favorite subject, the rose.
REPOUSSÉ (reh-pou-say)	A raised or embossed motif which has been shaped from the underside to give a sculptured appearance.
REVERSE CUTTING positive negative shadow	A découpage technique of cutting an area from a print to show a tuft of grass or other ornamental motif in either positive or negative according to whether you see a negative tuft of grass or a positive against the background. Shadow cutting repeats a reflection of the motif directly above.
SAYER, ROBERT	1725–1794. A print and map seller in London. Published "Ladies Amusement or Whole Art of Japanning Made Easy" in 1760.
SCISSORS, DÉCOUPAGE	Small sharp precision steel scissors with curved blades used for intricate cutting.
SCRIVAN	Italian name for secretary-desk. It is also spelled scriban in old French references.
SEALER	A coat (as of size) applied to prevent subsequent coats of paint or varnish from sinking in; used as a coating to prevent bleeding of inks or oil pencils.
SERRATED EDGE CUTTING	Notched or toothed on the edge. Cutting a serrated edge makes adhesion of print smoother, optically blends to background when pasted on.
SHADOWBOX	A shallow enclosing case usually with a glass front in which something is set for protection and display.
SHADOW CUTTING	See reverse cutting.
STENCIL CUTTING	A découpage technique of cutting crescent or S curves into the print as accent lines in the engraving. Usually done with a knife.
STRAIGHT CUTTING	Generally confined to border cutting and ladders.
SHELLAC	Purified lac resin usually prepared in thin orange or yellow flakes by heating or filtering and often

	bleached white; a preparation of lac dissolved usually in alcohol and used chiefly as a wood filler.
SILHOUETTE	From Etienne de Silhouette—controller of finances; a representation of the outlines of an object filled in with black or some other uniform color.
SIZE	A water-base gelatinous adhesive or paste.
TOILE DE JOUY (twal-duh-zwee)	An 18th century French scenic pattern usually printed on cotton, linen, or silk in one color on a light ground.
TREASURE GOLD	A wax metallic used in gilding.
TREASURE JEWELS	Wax metallics in color.
TREASURE SEALER	A water clear, alcohol soluble sealer, used on prints, and other porous surfaces. Also, used as a paint bonding adhesive on glass or metal.
TROMPE L'OEIL (tromp-loy-yah)	To fool the eye—a technique used in painting and découpage in which objects create an illusion of three dimensions.
TROPHÉES (tro faze)	An architectural ornament representing a group of military weapons; also, a drawing or etching of a group of articles related to a profession or trade.
VARNISH	A liquid preparation that when spread upon a surface dries forming a hard lustrous typically transparent coating.
VIGNETTE (Vin-yet)	To describe or sketch briefly; a running ornament (as of vine, leaves, tendrils, and grapes) put on or just before a page or at the beginning or end of a chapter; a picture that shades off gradually into the surrounding ground or the unprinted paper.
VUE D'OPTIQUE (view-dop-teek)	A three dimensional setting enclosed in a box or frame depicting a scene, or stage with figures in an elevated perspective.
WHITE GLUE	A polyvinyl resin adhesive—water soluble in liquid state but generally dries waterproof.
WATTEAU, JEAN ANTOINE	1684–1721. A French painter.
WAX, DÉCOUPAGE	A special white scented wax made for fine furniture and boxes. It does not distort color.
WAX GILT	A metallic wax used for gilding.

128

GUNS IN THE SKY

GUNS
IN THE SKY

The Air Gunners
of World War Two

Chaz Bowyer

Charles Scribner's Sons

New York

BY THE SAME AUTHOR

Calshot, 1913-61
The Flying Elephants
Mosquito at War
Hurricane at War
Airmen of World War One
Sunderland at War
Hampden Special
Beaufighter at War
Path Finders at War
Albert Ball, VC
History of the RAF, 1912-77
King of Combat – Sopwith Camel
For Valour – The Air VCs

Edited:
Bomber Pilot, 1916-18
Fighter Pilot on the Western Front
Wings over the Somme

Contents

Acknowlegments

Although the thought of attempting to compile a book about air gunners had flitted through my mind for several years, the real start to this book came from a remark made by Jack Edwards, erstwhile Chairman of the Manchester Branch of the Air Gunners' Association when introducing me to his members at an annual dinner and reunion, to which I had been most privileged to be invited. Faced with more than a hundred rugged, expectant faces, I promised to 'do something'. I have little doubt that the outcome of that off-the-cuff promise will disappoint many ex-AGs; I can only hope they will accept it at least as a *multum in parvo*, and no less than one man's sincere tribute to them, and especially their many comrades who 'failed to return'.

I am indebted to the following for permission to use certain material. My good friend Jack Bushby, not only for a direct extract from his *Gunner's Moon*, but also for his unfettered permission to use anything I might wish to steal from his unpublished manuscript *Air Gunners At War*, and several other unselfish kindnesses in assistance. Amy Howlett of William Kimber for A. J. Insall's account in *Observer*. Roy Benwell for an extract from his co-authored history of 158 Squadron, RAF, *In Brave Company*. Merle Olmsted for Ray Pritchard's account in *Aircraft Armament*. The USAF Aid Society for Beirne Lay Jr's vivid account of the notorious Regensburg mission. The RAF Escaping Society's records for the story of Cyril Copley's last operational sortie. Last, but never least, a long-time friend and fellow historian, Bruce Robertson, for authoritative and ever-ready practical help in many things.

For splendid help in unearthing suitable photographs I would thank particularly Mike Bailey, E. Beswick, 'Ted' Hine of the Imperial War Museum Photo Library, Ken Munson, John W. R. Taylor and the USAF Archives. And a special word of gratitude must be made to Dave Walker of Walkers Studios, Scarborough, whose superb skills produced unsurpassed reproductions of many original photos in a most suitable state for illustration.

Photo Credits

Prologue

The recorded history of military aviation is predominated by tales of the courage, daring, exploits – and sacrifices – of pilots. As captain of any aeroplane, of whatever type, this is perhaps as it should be. In the air a pilot had ultimate responsibility for all decisions. On his shoulders rested the considerable matters of safety of his crew, aircraft, passengers or freight, and – in any military context – the overall accomplishment of every given task. In multi-crew aircraft – the bomber was possibly the most obvious example – every pilot was backed by a crew of various skills and esoteric knowledge. Each had his vital, individual role to fulfil; a necessary segment of the whole team effort required to complete the job in hand. Yet of these crews only one role, other than the pilot's, could truly be called 'offensive', in the context of direct, personal action against the enemy – the aerial gunner.

Primarily regarded as defensive in character, air gunners were directly responsible for the survival of their aircraft and fellow crew members when under attack. Only the air gunner could hit back. Never content simply to ward off danger, air gunners were invariably eager to carry the war to the enemy.

From the moment of take-off on any operational sortie until the final return and touch-down at base, the air gunner maintained an unceasing vigilance, sweeping the surrounding skies continually, always alert for danger and ready to counter all onslaughts. Many air gunners during World War Two completed full operational tours without ever firing their guns 'in anger'; yet the strain on their nervous and physical systems was no less than on those who became embroiled in life-and-death battles against enemy antagonists. Even the briefest relaxation in vigilance while airborne might mean disaster for an air gunner's closest friends – death was always near in the swift arena of the air. In heavy bombers the loneliest role was that of a tail gunner – 'Arse-end Charlie' – be it in a Lancaster, Halifax, Stirling, Fortress or Liberator. The rear gunner was literally isolated from the reassuring physical proximity of other crew members, his only links being remote, spasmodic, distorted voices in his helmet earphones at intervals. His role called for special qualities of self-reliance, patience and courage. Incidentally, his was also the coldest job in any bomber crew, furthest removed from the comfort of any heating system.

For all the discomforts, dangers, and frightening casualty rates, at no time in aviation history was there ever any shortage of volunteers for air gunner duties. Men and boys, ranging in age from 16 to 70, eagerly applied to become aerial gunners; some going to extraordinary lengths to achieve that modest ambition. They came from every walk of life and filled the cockpits and gun turrets willingly, cheerfully accepting very short odds against eventual survival, yet ever determined to survive. Their material rewards were scanty in the contexts of pay, rank, or privileges. Indeed, such 'perks' were almost non-existent until the start of World War Two, and even thereafter air gunners remained low on the scales of fast or high promotion. To the layman the job of the air gunner was un-glamorous, 'third class' when compared with every other aircrew role. Though not entirely typical, the crass comments of one Australian ground officer at an Australian embarkation depot reflected too often the view of AGs by those totally ignorant of aircrew operations. 'Not enough guts for a pilot, not enough brains for an observer, and too lazy to do their wireless course. They're only air gunners.' Coming from one whose only possibility of danger in the war was death by suffocation amongst his paper files, such a remark was hardly encouraging for any would-be gunner.

The bulk of the text herein is deliberately descriptive of air gunners in the British, Allied and American air services. Such apparent bias is in no way indicative of any narrow-minded, nationalistic outlook on my part, but simply because the RAF and its sister services, USAF, RAAF *et al* have the longest and broadest history of employing aerial gunners and their appropriate equipment. While the story of aerial gunnery development *per se* is probably best illustrated and exemplified in progress and general operational usage in the RAF's history, I have emphasised other aspects equally by drawing upon the experiences of American, Australian and Canadian gunners, etc. The individual tales are illustrative of experiences undergone by many gunners in the air forces of all other countries and, it is hoped, serve as selected examples of the fraught and too often brief fighting careers of so many thousands of other men 'behind the guns'. True courage is not the prerogative of any particular section of the human race – self-sacrifice knows no barriers of race, class or creed.

Chaz Bowyer –
Norwich, 1978

'WE AIM NOT TO PLEASE'

– unofficial motto of the
  Air Gunners' Association

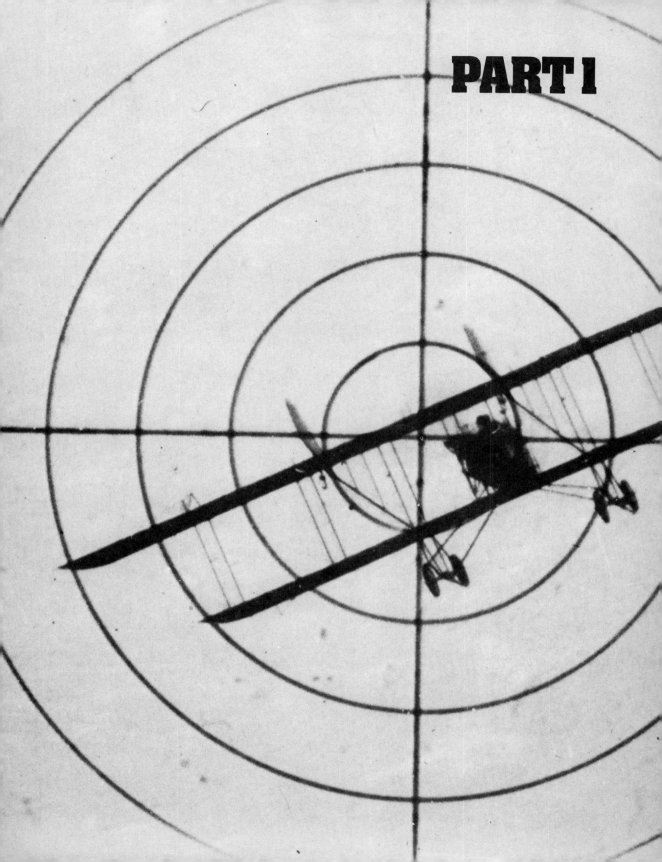

PART 1

1. Genesis

The birth of aerial gunnery came little more than eight years after the Wright brothers first paved a practical pathway to the clouds in 1903. It is perhaps a cynical commentary on man's priorities in evolution that, after many centuries of attempting to emulate the birds and gain entry to a new dimension of experience, flying, man should almost immediately apply his inventive genius to the possibilities of harnessing the new mode of locomotion to yet another means of destruction of his fellow being. Nevertheless, with man-controlled flight a practicable proposition, various military and naval minds throughout the world were quickly applied to the problems of airborne armament. In the United States of America, for example, the first experiment in aerial carriage of a Lewis machine gun was undertaken on 7 June 1912 by Captain Charles De F. Chandler who cradled the Lewis between his legs in a Wright Model B biplane, piloted by Lieutenant De Witt Milling. At a modest altitude Chandler fired a full drum of 47 bullets at a canvas sheet 300 feet below, registering roughly 12 per cent hits.

In Britain, on 27 November 1913, the noted civilian pilot, Marcus D. Manton, piloted a Grahame-White biplane over Bisley, carrying a Belgian officer, Lieutenant Stellingwerf, crouched on a crude wood-slat 'seat' immediately below Manton. With head bent forward, and both feet firmly braced against the spreader bar of the forward undercarriage wheels, the hapless Belgian clutched a Lewis machine gun between his knees and fired successfully at an eight metres-square sheet on the ground from a height of perhaps 300 yards. His first pass registered eleven hits out of a 25-rounds burst, while his second burst of 47 rounds included 15 hits on the sheet. The weapon used, a standard infantry Lewis .303-inch calibre machine gun, weighed some 26½ pounds, had a rate of fire of 560 rounds per minute, and its slim circular magazine held a total of 47 rounds of ammunition. With various minor modifications and an improved rate of fire, with reduced overall weight, the same Lewis machine gun design was to become a standard aerial weapon for many of the world's air services during the following three decades.

Similar experiments and trials with airborne guns were conducted in France and Germany in the immediate pre-1914 era, with varying degrees of success. By early 1913 most European nations involved in the development of aircraft for military purposes had recognized – at least, tacitly – the virtual inevitability of future

aerial warfare. If such vision was necessarily limited, even blinkered, in the higher military minds, this was excusable – despite the fashionable condemnation expressed by latter-day historians with the golden advantage of hindsight. Aeroplanes of the pre-1914 years were fragile vehicles in every sense; lightly constructed of wood, linen and wire bracing, woefully under-powered by inefficient internal combustion engines of thoroughly unreliable performance, and designed empirically. Barely capable of carrying a single pilot to any worthwhile height or range, such aeroplanes were heavily penalized by every additional pound weight of 'unnecessary' load, be it gun, bomb or person.

2 *Farman biplane, with mounted Colt Repeater rifle at Hendon, c. 1912.*

3 *Henry Farman of the RFC, mounting a Vickers gun in its forward cockpit, just prior to the 1914-18 war.*

In such circumstances it was fully justifiable for the various army chiefs to regard the aeroplane as basically a long arm of reconnaissance, an aerial 'scout' which extended the traditional role of the élite cavalryman of long, trusted experience. Such a role was at least a practicable one at the outbreak of war in August 1914. Thus at that date few aircraft in any of the European air services were either equipped or, indeed, designed to carry weapons. One of several notable exceptions was the British Vickers No 18 'Destroyer' (a predecessor of the Vickers FB5 'Gunbus') which was contracted for construction by the Admiralty in November 1912. The contract called for a 'fighting aeroplane', armed with a machine gun, and clearly intended the resulting aeroplane to have an offensive role. The inclusion of a machine gun in the terms of the contract necessitated production of a 'pusher' configuration, i.e. with the crew nacelle placed forward of the engine, due to the lack of any form of synchronization gun gear to permit firing of a machine gun through the normal tractor-design propeller arc.

This problem of fitting an effective gun to fire forward in the flight path in the absence of a synchronization gear persisted until 1915. It led to several later aircraft designs, such as the FE2b-series, which mounted one or more machine guns in the forward cockpit operated by hand by a second crew member. In the case of tractor aircraft designs – particularly those in use in 1914 and 1915 by the German Imperial Air Service – this second crew man, officially titled Observer from his original reconnaissance duties, was supplied

4 *Vickers FB5 'Gunbus' of 11 Squadron RFC on the Western Front, 1915, illustrating well the exposed position of the front observer/gunner.*

5

with a free-mounted machine gun attached to his cockpit by any one of a wide variety of pillar-type or early 'ring' mountings. Though unable to fire his gun directly forward along the aircraft's flight path, the Observer had a reasonably wide field of fire rearwards and on each side, and downwards. As such his job soon came to be one primarily of defence, but it could be one of offence when encountering an enemy aircraft.

The first few months of aerial activity above the battle lines in France in 1914 were chiefly concerned with tactical reconnaissance in support of ground forces, yet the crews showed immediate leanings towards a fighting role. Carrying aloft a heterogeneous collection of Service and sporting rifles and other weapons, the first 'Observers' quickly demonstrated a penchant for attacking any aerial opponent engaged on similar reconnaissance duties in the same patch of sky. The first acknowledged air-to-air combat victory of the war (air 'victories' occurred as early as August 1914, but not as a direct result of aerial gunnery) was credited to Corporal Louis Quenault, gunner in a Voisin III 'pusher' of Escadrille VB24 of the French Air Service piloted by Sergeant Joseph Frantz. During a bombing raid on Fort Brimont on 5 October 1914, Frantz spotted a German Aviatik two-seater and attacked, and Quenault's machine gun fire sent the Aviatik down in flames, killing both of its crew, Wilhelm Schlicting and Fritz von Zangen.

As the ground war in France became a stagnancy of fixed trench lines and immobile armies in 1915, with a dismal prospect of years of pure attrition ahead, the air war began to take rough shapes in patterns and equipment. Constantly seeking the offensive, Allied air crews made strenuous individual efforts to fit guns of all descriptions to their already-overloaded machines. A proliferation of highly amateur 'lash-up' gun mountings appeared in the front-line squadrons; usually without official sanction or approval. Meanwhile aircraft designers, bowing to the apparently inevitable, hastily sought the means and methods for providing reliable airborne weaponry on new designs of fighting aircraft. A significant landmark in military aviation annals occurred on 25 July 1915, when No. 11 Squadron, RFC, arrived in France to 'join the war'. Equipped throughout with one type of machine, the Vickers FB5 'Gunbus', it was the first-ever squadron of any national air service formed specifically for 'Fighting Duties' – and, indeed, the first such formation ever equipped with a single type of aeroplane.

With a maximum speed seldom exceeding 70 mph, and a Service ceiling of barely 9,000 feet, the FB5 mounted a single Lewis machine gun as standard armament in its forward cockpit, operated by hand by the Observer/Gunner. Even so 11 Squadron's gunners still contrived to pile on extra armament; usually an additional .303 SMLE Service rifle, but occasionally a second Lewis gun on a 'private' mounting for the use of the pilot. On operations over what had by then become termed the Western Front, FB5s gave sterling service, and the highly-exposed front gunners claimed a number of combat successes in clashes with their opposite numbers. The lot of the 'Gunbus' gunner was at its best a precarious one. Ensconced in a plywood cockpit little bigger than a baby's crib, sitting crouched behind the butt of his Lewis gun, with only a single leather lap strap to keep him 'secured' to his aircraft, the gunner was utterly exposed to wind and weather with only his flying clothing as protection against the icy outside air.

Lieutenant A. J. Insall, an Observer with 11 Squadron RFC when the unit first went to France, has recorded his own indelible impressions of a bomber escort patrol during the mid-1915 operations.

It was bitterly cold sitting there, huddled up and entirely passive, with scarcely more protection from the wind of our own making than that afforded to a ship's figurehead facing an Arctic gale, and my hands and my feet had some time ago lost all sense of feel, while my knees were just solid areas of bent leg. Elsewhere, circulation was normal and the mediocre amount of movement the confines of my cell allowed me was all I needed to make life bearable. No great effort was required to reach out and draw back the cocking handle of the Lewis gun as we passed over the German front-line trenches. It was only necessary to hook the gloved forefinger and jerk the handle back, and the trigger movement was nothing at all. The oil provided for machine gun mechanism at minus temperatures never ceased to rouse my admiration; in the coldest weather a gun would fire at once – dead slow, it is true, for the first two rounds, but after that at full speed, exhausting a full drum (of forty-seven rounds) in five seconds flat. For the loosening-up test a burst of at most three rounds was all that was necessary. It was a clear Notice of Intent that we invariably gave our friends across the way, whenever we prepared to invade their air, but it was better than a sluggish gun when it came to fisticuffs.

By the autumn of 1915 Allied two-seat reconnaissance aircraft were encountering a fresh menace in the skies, when the first examples of the single-seat monoplane (*Eindecker*) Fokker E.I and E.II commenced front-line operations. Agile, reasonably fast, and having a forward-firing synchronized machine gun, the Fokkers' reputation as deadly killers spread quickly along the Western Front. Though to some extent exaggerated, the *Eindeckers'* evil reputation was justified at that period, with a mounting toll of British and French two-seaters as witness to its efficiency. With no equivalent fighter in first-line service the Allied flying services could only rely on heavier escort formations for any vital recce sorties; while the RFC's BE2c crews manfully attempted to pile yet more armament onto their already burdened machines. Of necessity, local improvisation in extra armament became general amongst the BE squadrons; one BE2c of 4 Squadron RFC actually managing to festoon the forward Observer's cockpit with no less than four Lewis guns, each mounted on locally-manufactured pipe 'pillar' fitments and having a virtual all-round field of fire collectively. The weight penalty of such an arsenal on the BE's performance is not recorded, but can hardly have been less than near-disastrous.

In the German and French air services a proliferation of 'free' gun mountings had already begun to appear on two- and three-seat reconnaissance machines; primarily as defensive items, but also used effectively in occasional air-to-air combat. The 'art' of aerial gunnery was still regarded generally as a mere adjunct to the aeroplane's prime role, and training of Observers in specific gunnery was virtually non-existent by the close of 1915. The need for particular designs of ammunition, gun-sights, or other esoteric impedimenta was hardly appreciated as yet; gunnery was thought to be simply an extension of the traditional sporting gun or infantry machine-gunner's role. The ability to hit a fast-moving aeroplane in the air from another equally fast machine seemed no more of a problem than bagging a grouse or startled pheasant. Gun sighting still relied essentially on the ring and bead sightline of the infantry gun, with deflection allowances being a matter of instinctive experience by any individual gunner.

An illustration of the sketchiness of aerial gunner 'training' at that stage of the war is provided by the experience of John North.

I joined the Royal Flying Corps as a fitter in 1915 after being in the Territorials. I was posted to 57 Squadron then forming at Tadcaster, Yorkshire, and the commanding officer was delighted to hear that I had once done a course on the Maxim gun. He told me there was no one on the squadron who knew anything about air armament. I was forthwith posted to an 'air gunner's' course at Dymchurch, and after a few flights in an FE2b came back to the squadron as its Corporal armourer.

5 *Lewis machine gun instruction at the RFC School, Hythe, 1917.*

I was mad keen to fly but the CO said that as the only man who could service machine guns I was far too valuable. I only managed a few flights if there was a shortage of Observers. I am afraid that Observers came to us quite untrained in gunnery. On several occasions, in France, aircraft came back with the Observer dead, and the gun in pieces around him owing to his not knowing how to cure even a simple fault . . .

The need for training Observers for air operations became appreciated by RFC higher authority at the War Office in early 1915. Until then the 'back-seat' crews were largely comprised of infantry officers, usually with some experience in trench warfare, who volunteered for transfer to the air arm – if only to escape the primitive drudgery of a life amid mud, filth and squalor. Such 'training' as these received came from first-hand experience on operations across the lines in the main, though a minority recruited in Britain were given basic knowledge of, chiefly, wireless and camera work in the context of aerial warfare. In August 1915, however, the qualifications for an officer to be graded as a trained Observer were laid down by the GOC, RFC in the Field, and included:

a) Thorough knowledge of the Lewis gun
b) Skilled in the use of RFC cameras
c) Sending/receiving wireless at a rate of six words a minute, with 98 per cent accuracy
d) Thorough knowledge of aeroplane-artillery co-operation methods
e) Has carried out two reconnaissances, or has ranged artillery batteries successfully on two occasions

Immediately following this edict, a Machine Gun School, later called No. 1 School of Aerial Gunnery, and eventually No. 1 (Observers) School of Aerial Gunnery, was formed at Hythe in September 1915. Simultaneously a prerequisite course of instruction at the School of Wireless, Brooklands was instituted for embryo Observers.

In practice, especially in the fighting zones in France, would-be Observers were simply attached to particular RFC squadrons, and proceeded to accumulate a reasonably impressive number of operational flying hours over the lines before being officially recognized as Observers, and being permitted to sew the 'O' half-wing brevet on the left breast of their tunics. Many of the RFC's most prominent pilots were initiated into aerial warfare via an Observer's cockpit; notably Major J. T. B. McCudden, VC, DSO, MC, MM, Major W. A. Bishop, VC, DSO, MC, DFC, Major W. G. Barker, VC, DSO, MC, and many others of equal fighting repute. The proposed Observers' Wireless School at Brooklands only came into being in early 1917, but the Hythe School of Aerial Gunnery quickly established itself as the main air armament training centre for the RFC. In the latter part of 1916 a further, small School of Aerial Gunnery was established at Camiers on the French coast; charged with keeping Hythe fully up-dated on current fighting

tactics, to which Hythe reciprocated by informing Camiers of all latest equipment and apparatus. The Hythe course was of one month's duration, and concentrated almost wholly on gun instruction and air firing. In May 1917 a further school of aerial gunnery was formed in Egypt, and by August 1917 three more auxiliary schools were officially sanctioned in the United Kingdom.

By the summer of 1916 aerial activity above the Western Front had become greatly increased. Germany was about to introduce its *jagdstaffeln* – single-seat fighter units formed solely for air fighting roles; while on the Allied side huge preparations were in hand for the first Somme battle scheduled to commence on 1 July. On that date the RFC in France had a strength of 27 squadrons, including two Flights of 70 Squadron which was equipped with the new Sopwith $1\frac{1}{2}$ Strutter two-seater. The latter were equipped with a hand-operated Lewis gun on a French ring mounting, but when the third Flight of 70 Squadron arrived in France on July 30, its Sopwiths, being ex-RNAS, were fitted with a new gun ring mounting in the rear cockpit known as the Scarff No. 2 Ring Mounting. Brainchild of an RNAS Warrant Officer, this mounting was quickly to become the standard Observer-gunner's mounting on all two-seater aircraft throughout 1916–18, and indeed for more than 20 years after the war in the Royal Air Force.

One type of aircraft to equip RFC squadrons in early 1916 was the Farnborough-produced FE2b 'pusher' two-seater, and the first fully-equipped FE unit to join the war was No. 20, which arrived on 23 January 1916, and was joined on 20 February by a second FE unit, 25 Squadron. In the FE2b the Observer/gunner occupied the forward half of the plywood-skinned crew nacelle, and his position in many ways typified the plight of the early air gunners. Armed with a Lewis gun in the nose, on a simple tube 'ring' mounting, a second Lewis was normally placed at the rear of the gunner's cockpit, on a pillar mounting for rearward defence over the top wing. To operate this second Lewis gun, an FE gunner was forced to undo his solitary lap strap, climb onto his locker 'seat' facing the tail, and fire his Lewis gun standing precariously in a cockpit with sides which barely covered his ankles. His only 'security' was the grip he had on his Lewis gun, no matter what violent manoeuvring his pilot might choose to undertake during any combat. When it is realized that parachutes were never issued to RFC, RNAS or RAF aircrews during 1914–18, it can be appreciated that an FE gunner needed a special form of courage to accomplish any sortie into enemy territory.

Tales of the remarkable resolution and sheer bravery of the FE gunners are myriad, but two examples may serve to exemplify their fortitude and hazards. In September 1916, Corporal Burton Ankers was gunner in an FE of 18 Squadron piloted by Captain J. C. Callaghan. It was a contact patrol, i.e. low-level co-operation with forward infantry formations, and Ankers at one point lobbed over-board a message tin, with rag streamers attached, containing vital data for the ground commander. The tin's streamers became en-tangled with the FE's undercarriage. Coolly, Ankers climbed out of his 'bath-tub' cockpit and lowered himself down, then disengaged

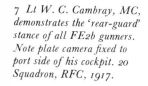

7 *Lt W. C. Cambray, MC, demonstrates the 'rear-guard' stance of all FE2b gunners. Note plate camera fixed to port side of his cockpit. 20 Squadron, RFC, 1917.*

the message tin – a feat which brought him the award of a Distinguished Conduct Medal (DCM). Ankers eventually achieved Wing Commander rank in the post-1918 RAF. Another 18 Squadron FE, piloted by Lieutenant Frank L. Barnard, became the target for a concentration of German fighters, and in the course of the combat Barnard's gunner, Lieutenant F. S. Rankin, was hit and fell onto the side of his forward cockpit. Barnard, ignoring the hail of bullets from his assailants, climbed out of his cockpit, pulled Rankin's inert body back, then resumed his seat, still holding onto Rankin, and flew back to base. (Barnard was afterwards admitted to hospital suffering from torn arm muscles – and was required by officialdom to justify his 'self-inflicted' injuries . . .!)

The complex roles for an RFC Observer/gunner continued to be increased during the 1916-18 years. Though patently an aerial gunner and his aircraft's first-line defence against enemy aerial attack, his duties remained equally important as pure Observer. The increasing use of wireless to guide ground artillery guns, a wide variety of tasks inherent with so-termed 'contact' patrols whereby aid and support were given to advance infantry formations, and daily photo-reconnaissance sorties, were often supplemented by pure bomb-aiming duties. And on many occasions Observers became extempore pilots when, with a pilot dead, wounded or otherwise incapacitated, the 'passenger' was faced with a grim choice; inevitable death in a subsequent crash, or a hair-thin prospect of survival if he could somehow fly his aircraft back to safety in Allied territory. Untrained in pilotage, with no dual controls in his own cockpit to manoeuvre, any Observer in such perilous circumstances was forced to climb into the pilot's cockpit and manage as best he could. Official records are liberally dotted with stories of Observers who thus cheated death and brought their machine, and pilot, back.

By early 1917 the trend in Allied aeroplane designs favoured the tractor type of machine, though the doughty FE-series soldiered on

until the 1918 Armistice in other roles. Epitomising the two-seat tractor type of that era was the Bristol F2b Fighter, which first entered squadron service in France in March 1917. Aptly nicknamed 'King of Two-seaters' by its crews, the F2b exemplified the traditional two-man, back-to-back fighting team of pilot and Observer. Ostensibly designed initially as a 'Fighter Reconnaissance' machine, the Bristol F2b quickly made a huge reputation as a pure-fighter, and its crews established fighting tallies second to none. Both pilot and gunner in an F2b quickly became indivisible halves of a

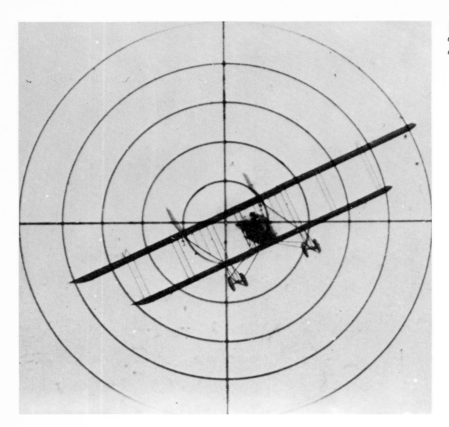

fighting 'twin' combination, reaching a peak of instinctive understanding in combat that gave each man the most effective
opportunities for victory over any opponent.

Other fresh multi-seat designs to join the RFC's operations included the De Havilland 4 day bomber-recce aircraft, and, by
night, the Handley Page o/100 behemoth, with its 100-feet wing
span, and front and mid-fuselage gunners' cockpits. In the latter
the front gunner usually doubled in role as the chief bomb-aimer,
having a bomb sight affixed to the nose of his cockpit. A third major
design brought into use was the De Havilland 9 day bomber which,
in 1918, was to form the bulk of two-seater units in the RAF's
Independent Force. Due to its relatively poor performance, the
DH9 was never popular with its crews, who faced grim odds in
enemy fighter opposition on virtually the whole of every bombing
sortie undertaken by day over Germany. Outclassed in every facet of
performance by the fleet Fokkers, and usually vastly outnumbered,
DH9 crews had only one faint salvation; a tight formation in
which all rear gunners could combine their fire in a lattice-work
of deadly crossfire. In formations totalling, usually, at most 12 DH9s,
the handful of rear gunners frequently faced determined and con-
tinual attacks by packs of 40 or 50 German fighters, resulting in

casualty rates which might have disheartened lesser men. Nevertheless, in the five months' existence of the Independent Force, with an overall total of 246 Observer/gunners missing, killed, wounded or injured, they claimed a total of 157 enemy aircraft destroyed or shot down out of control.

The whole question of aerial victories – 'scores' as such tallies are usually called by aviation writers – was something of a thorny one when relating to the combat successes of aerial gunners throughout 1914-18. A mountain of latter-day books, features and magazine articles have almost exclusively concentrated on the combat victories claimed by the pilots of each nation participating in that war. Little if any publicity has been expounded on the prodigious successes achieved by the 'back-seat' man. Though seldom officially sanctioned, many gunners' victories were simply credited, or at least 'shared' officially with the pilot of the particular aircraft. At least one well-known American 'ace' pilot, credited with six 'victories', had no direct part in five of his credited 'score'; these had been destroyed solely by his front gunner.

The contemporary feelings of aerial gunners in regard to such matters is probably accurately reflected in a popular ditty composed at that period (1918) by an anonymous RAF wit. Titled 'The PBO's Lament', and sung to the music of 'A Bachelor Gay' (from the musical comedy 'Maid of the Mountains'), its verses exemplified

11 Observer-gunners of 149 Squadron, RFC, checking out their Lewis guns in the unit armoury, St. Omer, 19 July 1918, prior to a war sortie. The fur-lined Sidcot flying overall-suit, plus thigh-length fur 'fug' boots were their only protection against the freezing upper air temperatures.

13 *Twins – a pair of yoked Lewis guns on an RE8 of 15 Squadron, RFC, on 25 March 1918. Twin-gun rear defence was not uncommon in 1917-18, and was colloquially dubbed 'Huntley & Palmer' by the gunners of the period. Far left can be seen the pilot's forward-firing Vickers gun.*

the traditional part-cynical, part-fatalistic brand of Service humour – with a 'bite' of stark truth when read between the lines. One verse ran;

> When you're doing an escort stunt
> And the Huns get on your tail
> You start the fight with a cheerful sight
> And the beggars go down like hail;
> Alas, the pilot's jealous scorn
> Is a thing we learn to know;
> You may get umpteen Huns in flames
> Don't think that they'll believe your claims
> You're only a PBO, you're only a PBO.[1]

CHORUS: At seventeen he's firing rather badly
> At a Hun of tender blue
> At fifteen thou' you see him point out sadly
> Some Huns of a different hue
> At ten or twelve you find him shooting madly
> With six or eight or more;
> When he fancies he is past hope
> Fires a long burst as a last hope
> And a Tripe[2] spins down on fire to the floor.

[1] PBO – Poor Bloody Observer
[2] Fokker Dr1 Triplane

15 *Up front. Lt Cooke of
214 Squadron, RAF, in the
forward gunner's cockpit of a
Handley Page 0/400 heavy
bomber, late 1918. On the
nose is his drift bomb-sight.*

Another minor (?) bone of contention amongst 1914-18 gunners
was the general question of rank and, therefore, official status. In
the German Imperial Air Service observers were almost invariably
commissioned officers and, indeed, 'in charge' of any two-seat
aircraft, while pilots included a very large proportion of non-
commissioned officers, often of quite lowly military rank. In the
Allied services, however, the reverse tended to be true. In the RFC,
for example, especially in the early years of the war, pilots were
seldom non-commissioned, whereas gunners (as opposed to trained
Observers) were almost invariably air mechanics or junior NCOs
who volunteered for the job. By 1918, NCOs still formed a large
proportion of RAF gunners, though by then commissioned
Observers were in roughly equal numbers. Thus, to take again an

16 *'PBO' – the front
gunner of a Handley Page
0/400 bomber at Cressy,
France, on 25 September
1918; epitomising all 'Poor
Bloody Observers' both in
dress and fighting stance.
Note empty cartridge-case
canvas bag attached to
Lewis gun.*

example of a reasonably typical RFC two-seater crew in 1916-17; the pilot might be a Captain, with all appropriate rates of pay, privileges and status, while his fighting partner in combat could often be an air mechanic, with rock-bottom pay and status. And, after any operational sortie, the latter simply reverted to his daily routine of mundane duties and discipline.

In the post-1918 RAF, as will be seen, this tendency to treat air gunners as part-time aircrew men was to become almost official policy; yet – such was the spirit of air gunners in every era – there was never a lack of volunteers among the 'other ranks'. Merely to fly was each man's prime ambition, and it mattered little in which capacity this was achieved. Such modest ambition often led to eventual acceptance as 'true' aircrew, being trained as a pilot or, later, navigator.

In terms of pure equipment, the air gunners of 1918, in all air services, were little progressed from their 1916 state. In the main, multi-seat aircraft gunners' cockpits were still open structures of barest utility, with no protection from slipstream or icy air temperatures at height. Parachutes were almost totally non-existent, oxygen for high-level sorties a rarity and only then in experimental and crude form. Heated clothing had been attempted in a variety of – mainly – unsuccessful forms. The air gunner (like his pilot) perforce relied upon a swaddling of leather, fur and canvas clothing for body protection from the cruel elements, and, not least, a sturdy, healthy body. His 'hardware', too, had made little progress. The basic weapon was still a rifle-calibre machine gun of infantry origin, lightened of unnecessary framework or water-cooling apparatus; though twin-gun installations had become relatively common. Sighting had improved only marginally, from the simple ring and bead arrangement, with additional deflection-calculating fitments.

Guns of heavier calibre had indeed been tried in solitary experiments, usually on the larger designs of aircraft, such as the German Gotha and Friedrichshafen bombers and British Felixstowe flying boats; while as early as 1913 a French Voisin had a 37 mm cannon fixed in its forward cockpit. In general operational use, however, the modified infantry Lewis, Maxim, or Parabellum gun was standard; fitted on a fixed ring around the cockpit coaming, with a traversing capability and vertical adjustment. Gunners literally stood to their guns in combat, braced by legs and feet inside a fragile wood and fabric nacelle, often without any security belt or strap to keep them inside the fuselage during combat manoeuvring. Wielding his gun in every direction against a howling slipstream, and exposed in body from the waist up, the gunner was also – either in a 'pusher' or a tractor aircraft – a human shield against enemy fire directed at his pilot from front or rear respectively. (In either case a pilot was basically protected on his other face by the aircraft engine.)

Not all of a gunner's problems in the air were associated with enemy activity; there were occasions when it was a case of 'Protect me from my friends'. As on 6 January 1918 when Captain J. H. Hedley was flying as rear gunner to Lieutenant Makepeace of 20 Squadron, in a Bristol F2b at some 15,000 feet. During the course of a brief combat, Makepeace suddenly stood the F2b on its nose in a quick dive; then as he recovered at the bottom of his short descent he felt a distinct thump behind him. Glancing back over his shoulder, he was astonished to see his gunner, Hedley, clinging by fingers and boots to the top of the rear fuselage. It transpired that when the F2b first dived, the sudden whip of the fuselage had literally thrown Hedley clear out of his cockpit – the gunner had unstrapped himself in preparation for the coming combat – and by the sheerest coincidence Hedley's falling body had arrived at exactly the same point in space as the F2b as it pulled out of its dive. Hedley remained in his precarious position until the F2b had landed back at base – only to be mildly rebuked for 'endangering the machine's structure'. Yet another extract from the 'PBO's Lament' was perhaps appropriate:

> We all of us know the case
> When the pilot came home alone
> No doubt it was only a slight mistake
> But his attitude's clearly shown;
> He shoved his joystick suddenly down
> As far as it would go;
> 'Hullo, you seem to have gone,' he said,
> 'I fear you must be somewhat dead';
> 'But you're only a PBO, yes, you're only a PBO'.

2. The Locust Years

The immediate impact on the world's aerial services of the cessation of hostilities in Europe in November 1918 was a rigorous reduction in sheer numerical strength of each country's air arm. Germany and her allies of the Central Powers suffered a rigid ban on all military aircraft design or production; while the Royal Air Force – the world's first independent (of Army or Navy control) air service, and at that time, the world's largest air service – was literally decimated in strength within eighteen months of the armistice. Each nation's relief at the end of the years of carnage was, naturally, channelled into a widespread revulsion against anything connected with war. Popular opinion was more concerned with resuming a peaceful existence than with any form of military might.

Only a relative handful of far-sighted individuals could envisage a need for strong military and naval defence forces; even fewer could be found to justify the existence of a separate, third service. The crippling costs of four years of war had to be retrenched; industry and commerce held priority in any national purse. In the USA the air arm was still subordinated to the Army, and was to remain very much a 'minor' formation of the US Army until the middle of World War Two; while the French air service made little progress in the 1920s and '30s. Germany, forbidden by international treaties imposed by the 'victors', had to wait until 1935 before its new leader, Adolf Hitler, considered it propitious to announce to the world the existence of a new Luftwaffe.

In Britain the infant Royal Air Force began its 'peace years' as the target not only for near-disastrous reduction in strength and financial support, but also as a bone of contention between Army, Admiralty and Air Ministry. Chief guardian of the RAF's independence was Sir Hugh Trenchard, Chief of Air Staff, who fought a long, wearisome battle with other Service chiefs, politicians and faceless bureaucrats for a decade before handing over his 'reins' to a younger CAS. Bedevilled throughout his tenure of office by constant demands for dissolution of the RAF into fragmented sections of both Army and Navy, Trenchard's prime torment was the miserly annual budget allotted to the RAF. On less money than it cost Britain for any one day's war effort in 1914-18, he was expected to reconstitute the skeleton RAF, build it up to a reasonable strength and quality, and perform all the various commitments allotted to the air arm in an empire still spread across the whole globe.

18 Ninak – *the De Havilland 9A, which first saw service in 1918 and soldiered on for another ten years on operations with the post-war RAF. This particular 'Ninak' was H3510, 'L' of 8 Squadron, over Baghdad, 1926, with Flt Lt A. G. Jones-Williams as pilot and Flight Sgt Benson wielding the rear Lewis gun.*

In practical terms, Trenchard's immediate post-1918 RAF was wholly equipped with aircraft and armament designed in 1916-17 or before. Yet his peacetime budget was too small for serious attempts to contract newer, more modern machines and hardware generally. Thus, for the next ten years, virtually all RAF units were forced to carry on with obsolete aircraft, having a minimum of technical back-up support, and still to fulfil an almost non-stop operational role in many quarters. In regard to personnel Trenchard was more fortunate. Restricted by pure finance, he could at least be highly selective in recruiting from the vast mass of experienced wartime men available and eager to make a career in the RAF. Even so, the pay rates and conditions of service Trenchard could offer were by no means totally attractive; any man joining, re-enlisting, or simply 'signing on' towards a pensionable period of service knew from the outset that RAF life would be hard, with few luxuries and little incentive in any material context. Only a sense of vocation would justify contemplation of a career in RAF 'blue' uniform.

Using Britain's many overseas empire and mandatory commitments as his main operational priority, Trenchard proceeded to base the bulk of RAF squadrons abroad; in Mesopotamia (later retitled Iraq), Palestine, Egypt, Malta, the Persian Gulf, and the vast sub-continent of India. Such a deployment was not only logical but necessary to ensure Britain's sea trade routes unfettered access to the outermost posts of empire. Here, at least, 'his' air force was out of reach of the Whitehall protagonists, while their daily watch and ward role provided a *raison d'être* for the very existence of the RAF. For the air and ground crews of overseas units the prospect had mixed blessings. By the mid-1920s an overseas tour of duty meant a five years' stint away from Britain, either wholly in one area, such as India, or split into a two years' spell in the near East followed by three years in India. With little, if any, money to spare for such 'non-priority' items as married quarters or official hirings, such a duty tour all too often meant a full five years' separation for husbands from their families in Britain; while bachelor airmen had little recreation beyond that which they created by their own efforts.

Aircrew members of the RAF were in just two categories; pilots or Observers. Aircraft were a motley array of ex-wartime designs, but the first-line units abroad were mainly equipped with either the two-seat De Havilland 9A, or 'Ninak' as it was universally dubbed, or the sturdy Bristol F2b. Though the Observer's tasks were similar to his 1918 roles, in fact the bulk of 'back-seat' jobs were undertaken by volunteer ground tradesmen, eager to fly and quickly competent in their dual role as air gunner and, on occasion, bomb aimer. Armament continued to be of 1918 vintage until well into the late 1930s; with a Scarff Ring-mounted Lewis gun in the rear cockpit, and bombs of up to 230lbs carried on under-wing or under-fuselage racks, hand-released via Bowden Cable lanyards and toggles. Precision in bombing came by dint of sheer experience and constant operational practice in a majority of cases; while effective use of the rear Lewis gun was easily learned against land targets.

A glimpse of the conditions under which most airmen gunners operated is given by Air Commodore Tyndall-Carill-Worsley, a pilot with 20 Squadron in the early 1930s serving on the North-West Frontier Province of India (now Pakistan):

In the Bristol Fighters and Westland Wapitis which we flew, the Lewis guns were on Scarff mountings and consequently, particularly in the 'Brisfit' (F2b), the aircraftman in the back seat was particularly un-comfortable and had many long, boring, monotonous hours on recon-naissance flights, just hoping the pilot might have a message to pass which would at least break the tedium and keep him in practice. The accepted method of passing the time was to play noughts-and-crosses by wireless with the duty operator back at squadron headquarters.

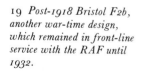

19 *Post-1918 Bristol F2b, another war-time design, which remained in front-line service with the RAF until 1932.*

This was carried on in a sort of W/T shorthand code which all wireless-operators knew, but which few pilots could ever understand. On one of my first flights, at the end of a long artillery-spotting exercise, I was mystified to be handed a chit from the rear cockpit which was a message from base, consisting entirely of four letters 'PUFO'. It had to be explained to me that this was the traditional way for base to pass permission to return, and was simply an abbreviation for 'Pack Up and —— Off!'

In between times, when one had permission to bomb, the poor air gunner just had to sit there and take it whilst one went through all the violent manoeuvres involved in a good beat-up. One occupational hazard for pilots in those times, especially new ones, was the danger of getting a good wallop on the head from the Lewis gun as the gunner decided to move it from one side to the other, via a forward arc instead of towards the rear. When doing high-level, as opposed to dive-bombing, the AG did the bomb-aiming, using the high altitude drift sight clamped outside the fuselage. To do this he had to lean over the side and, since there was no inter-com, he 'requested' alterations of course by reaching over and thumping the pilot on the appropriate shoulder.

In October 1928 the first post-1918 designed aircraft to reach the RAF in India was the Westland Wapiti; a two-seat biplane basically to replace the ageing 'Ninak' though incorporating various DH9A components in its construction. First units to operate the Wapiti in India were Nos. 11 and 39 Squadrons, and it was in an 11 Squadron Wapiti on 17 May 1930 that an air gunner exemplified the close bond between pilot and 'back-seat passenger' of that era. Piloted by Flying Officer Stroud, with AC1 S. Wiltshire as gunner, the aircraft was engaged in some low-level bombing and strafing of rebel tribesmen during the notorious 'Red Shirts' uprising, when, at approximately 600 feet altitude, Stroud was hit in the neck by an Afridi marksman's rifle bullet. Stroud immediately signalled to Wiltshire to take over controls – the Wapiti incorporated dual flying controls in the back seat – then collapsed in his cockpit. Wiltshire was faced with a dilemma. He could take to his parachute, but was uncertain whether his pilot was dead or

20 *Bomber defence. Vickers Virginia Mk VII, J6856, with its 'fighting tops' upper wing gunner cockpits; supplementing the normal nose and tail guns.*

simply unconscious. He decided to stay with the aircraft and, despite virtual total ignorance of how to fly an aeroplane, managed to guide the Wapiti back to the squadron base. Tragically, Wiltshire, with no knowledge of landing technique, crashed on his final approach and died in the attempt. Wiltshire's courage was honoured by a posthumous promotion to the rank of Corporal.

The esteem in which the 'spare-time' gunners were held is perhaps illustrated by the remark of one senior Flight commander to his latest officer-pilot, fresh from training school in Britain and about to make his first 'practice' flight over the wild North-West Frontier Province. Told in no uncertain terms that his passenger would not be any of the squadron's experienced gunners, the young Pilot Officer resentfully queried this decision. The cynical reply quickly disillusioned him. 'Pilots we can always get, but good fitters are bloody hard to find. Until you know what the hell you're doing out here, I'm not risking precious airmen's lives on you!' With few exceptions, pilots of all ranks quickly came to appreciate the sterling work undertaken by the flying ground crew, and a bond of mutual respect and friendship grew into a lasting tradition; a 'partnership' which in no way corroded discipline but produced a peak of effort and efficiency seldom surpassed in any other era of RAF history.

If such respect and recognition were manifest on the 'sharp end' operational squadrons, they were little reflected in the material bene-fits thought appropriate by the Air Ministry masters in Whitehall. Aerial gunnery carried no advancement in promotion, while financially an airman regularly flying hazardous sorties over hostile territory gained a minimum of sixpence per day added to his pay as a ground tradesman, plus (occasionally) a further eighteen pence per day when employed 'on operations'. This latter qualification caused many wry smiles among the aircrews of squadrons based in both the Near East and India. From the cessation of hostilities in

Europe in 1918, the overseas units had known virtually no period of peaceful service. Constantly airborne in support of the garrison armies attempting to quell and control seemingly endless uprisings and revolts instigated by dissident tribesmen, the airmen also faced no little hazard when on 'routine' sorties. In India operations were flown over bald mountain and desert landscapes, where a forced landing due to any cause almost invariably meant a disastrous crash. Survival of such a crash merely placed a crew at the mercy of primitive tribes whose concept of mercy fell far short of Western ideals. All crews carried leaflets, printed in several local dialects, guaranteeing a financial reward for the return of any RAF crew unharmed; but the practical value of these 'ghooli chits' was questionable in countries where illiteracy ran as high as 98 per cent amongst local populations.

Although faced with no air opposition, RAF crews on operations had no sinecure when engaged in necessarily low-level bombing sorties against rebellious tribal forces. The desert Arab and mountain Pathan were raised from infancy with a rifle in their hands; it was the badge of manhood, and a deadly weapon against any target within range. Just one example of such effective opposition to air attack occurred during the widespread Arab revolt in 1919-20. The British Army employed 120,000 troops against an estimated force of 200,000 Arabs, and suffered casualties of 876 men killed and a further 1,000 wounded. The RAF in support flew some 4,000 hours

22 *Scarff Ring and Lewis gun on a Westland Wapiti IIa of 27 Squadron, India, 1938; operational armament which had not changed in type for more than 20 years by then. Note side 'holster' for a signal pistol.*

of operations, expending over 180,000 machine gun bullets in the process. Air casualties from ground fire amounted to eleven aircraft shot down, and a further 57 aircraft rendered unfit to fly by serious bullet damage. Added to any operational risk was the constant danger of unreliable engines which might result in a forced landing in the desert wastelands – parachutes did not become a general issue item for India crews until December 1928 – apart from any one of a hundred other possible mechanical failures when airborne. The 'operational two-bob bonus' was worthily earned by all air gunners of the period, while the parsimonious purse-guardians of the Treasury seldom, if ever, obtained such value for their largesse. Cost-effectiveness was the watch-word of the RAF's 'adolescence', yet the Whitehall 'Shylocks' could hardly have obtained a better bargain for their money.

While the RAF's front-line squadrons manfully coped with an almost daily operational commitment throughout the 1920s and early 1930s, flying obsolete aircraft armed with 1918 armament, progressive improvement in airborne guns and gunnery was slow and minimal. Basic aircraft designs of the period remained tied to the biplane configuration, with a somewhat blinkered adherence to 1918 conceptions of the role of the multi-cockpit aeroplane for warlike purposes. Ring-mounted machine guns remained hand-operated, but by the 1930s the gradual increase in aircraft speeds began to produce purely physical problems for the air gunner. Slipstream forces inhibited the freely-swinging operation of any hand-manipulated gun, and the clear need for power assistance for the gun, and protection for the gun operator, became urgent.

Attempts to solve these main problems came in a variety of forms. Aircraft of the era could be classified roughly in three main types of design relevant to the carriage of air gunners. Primarily there was the two-seat fighter-bomber of 1916 concept, with a pilot and rear gunner, back-to-back. Next in importance came the 'heavy' bomber, with several gunner cockpits for (mainly) self-defence; and lastly, the more general reconnaissance and army co-operation types of machine. Of these the most significant were the fighter and the bomber; though the degree of priority here depended largely on individual national conceptions of air strategy and tactical employment. Of the major air forces then existing, the USA tended to concentrate on fighters initially, though by the 1930s the legendary Boeing 'Fortress' long-range bomber was in embryo. The RAF, however, paid much more attention to the bomber, in spite of its obvious need for an effective metropolitan defence fighter force. France, though possessing possibly the largest air service in numerical terms, stagnated in its approach to progressive development of aircraft design. In Germany the secretly-assembling Luftwaffe, in the main, concentrated on fighters, dive-bombers in the *Stuka* category, for direct tactical support of ground forces, and the fast though medium-range twin-engined bomber, exemplified by the Heinkel HeIII, Dornier Do17 and, later, Junkers Ju88.

In the context of aerial gunnery, possibly the most interesting lines of development were those taken (or not taken) by the RAF and Air Ministry. Having fought one air war with machine guns designed specifically for ground use, by 1919 a number of hard lessons had been learned. Though still content to continue using the infantry .303 Lewis gun as a standard gunner's weapon, it had been realized at an early stage of the aerial fighting that the Lewis's designated 500 rounds-per-minute (rpm) rate of fire was much too slow when attempting to hit a moving target at speeds in excess of 100 mph. Target acquisition – the time an enemy aircraft actually remained in a gunner's sightline – was in mere seconds; hence it was essential to hit it with as many bullets as possible within those fleeting moments. By 1918, therefore, successive modification – usually undertaken locally by squadron armourers – had both lightened the weight of the Lewis (by removing unnecessary water-cooling jackets from barrels *et al*), and improved the rate of fire to approximately 800 rpm or even more. The basic mounting for the air gunner remained a Scarff Ring, if slightly improved in minor details, until the outbreak of World War Two; though in that heyday of the private aircraft industries in Britain several individual aircraft manufacturers tried out privately-designed equivalent mountings for their own designs of aeroplanes.

Ammunition for aerial machine guns remained standard Army-issue rimmed cartridges – a decision based simply on economic grounds of cost and supply. Types of .303-inch ammunition also remained basic, with Ball and Armour Piercing (AP) rounds as the

23 *Corporal air gunner in a Hawker Demon of 23 Squadron, RAF receiving Lewis gun ammunition drums from ground staff, late 1930s.*

24 *Hawker Hart J9933, which became the prototype Hawker Demon, fitted with a 'wind-shield' for both pilot and gunner experimentally.*

25 *Birdcage. Bristol Type 120, experimentally fitted with a gunner's cupola, at Filton, January 1932. Later taken over by the RAF as K3587, the design provided much useful information on the effect of a gun 'turret' on aircraft performance.*

two main types of bullet used. When it is recalled that until the late 1930s virtually all first-line aircraft were still of 1918 concept in construction and configuration – wood, alloy metal-framed, fabric-skinned biplanes – the retention of these two major types of bullet is logical. Only with the beginning of World War Two did armour plate begin to be used widely in the new metal monoplanes, necessitating the use of ammunition specifically designed to penetrate or destroy this increased protection for crews, engines, and fuel tanks. Gun sighting on the hand-operated Lewis gun also remained merely a slightly improved version of the 1917-18 Norman Vane Sight; requiring deflection angles and trajectory problems to be solved by the individual gunner.

It was not until 1930 that thoughts were first turned to the possibility of replacing the Lewis gun with a more effective, truly aerial machine gun, designed to cope with the problems peculiar to air combat as opposed to those of the infantry gunner. Several gun designs were mooted and considered, but two emerged as the most significant. The first was, ironically, a machine gun originally designed in 1918 by the French general Berthier for ground use. Adopted by the Vickers Company of Britain, the Berthier gun was extensively redesigned and, after extended trials and tribulations, lasting from 1930 to 1935, the resulting gun emerged as the VGO – Vickers Gas-Operated – or, as it was more usually titled, the Vickers 'K' Gun. It was a magazine-fed machine gun, much the same as the Lewis; having a spring-tensioned drum capacity of 100 rounds initially (though in service this was discreetly reduced to a maximum content of 96 rounds or less – depending on the armourer's individual experience of bloodied knuckles and broken finger nails when attempting to pre-tension the clockwork-like drum spring. . . !). The VGO's chief claims to fame were, primarily, an rpm of 1,000, and a much longer service 'life' for its components (when compared with the Lewis) which was welcomed by the armament staff. Easier to maintain and overtly more efficient than the trusty Lewis, by 1939 all hand-operated machine guns in first-line RAF aircraft were VGOs – at least, officially – and the gun remained in operational service until well into 1943.

Even as the VGO was being initially considered by the RAF, however, its death knell was being developed – the gun turret. The increasing problem of protecting an air gunner from the effects of higher speeds and higher altitudes in succeeding aircraft types coming into RAF use was of prime importance. Imposed physical parameters on any air gunner quite patently reduced his fighting capacity and, therefore, the defence of his aircraft. Slipstream effect on any gun attempting to fire on a beam was first tackled by the provision of back windshields, then partially enclosed triplex cupolas, or 'glasshouses'. These cumbrous structures, while pointing the way to the eventual solution, were totally impractical for any firstline operations, and were regarded solely as experimental stages in the evolution of the true gun turret.

The first totally-enclosed, power-operated, rotating gun turret to be put into RAF squadron use was a Boulton Paul design, the brainchild of J. D. North and H. A. Hughes of that firm, fitted in the nose of a new bomber design, the Boulton Paul Sidestrand, J9186. A cylindrical cupola turret, semi-operated by power-assisted controls, its 'power' came from a compressed air bottle (120 psi), and the turret could only be power-operated in rotation (a full 360 degrees when its Lewis gun was elevated to 70 degrees). Such movement came from an engine-driven compressor feeding the air system to turret controls via a rotating service joint in the turret base. Elevation and depression of its solitary Lewis gun produced a compensating, balancing movement of the gunner's seat. One RAF Staff officer who expressed a wish to try it for himself commenced rotation – and was so astonished at the turret's relative

26 *Boulton Paul Overstrand bomber, with power-operated gun turret in the nose, 1936. The front vertical opening for the single machine gun was closed by a zip fastener when not in use.*

speed that he remained inside, whirling like a top until both he and the air system were exhausted.

Although simply a test vehicle for the BP turret, Sidestrand J9186 reached 101 Squadron on 22 February 1934 for Service trials, and was an immediate success. Whereas previous target hits averaged 15 per cent, with the new turret gunners registered as high as 85 per cent strikes. In March 1934 J9186 was returned to its makers, and on 24 January 1935, retitled BP Overstrand, the first example of an operational Overstrand, J9185, joined 101 Squadron for service. Full re-equipment of the unit with Overstrands was complete by the summer of 1935, and, in the event, it was the only RAF squadron to be fully equipped with the type – hence the motif of a round tower which is 101 Squadron's official badge, commemorating their pioneering turreted aircraft. Apart from its nose turret, however, the Overstrand carried two other Lewis gunners; one in the traditional 'mid-upper' cockpit in the rear fuselage, and a second position immediately below him in a ventral, rear-facing, belly gun location. The latter was not a new conception – Gotha bombers and others had employed a variety of tunnels and 'under-

gun' devices in 1916-18 in attempts to obviate the under blind spots of defence.

Attempts to eliminate all defensive blind areas on the heavier bombers occupied many years of thought in most of the world's air services of the period. The main danger lay in attack from below (and, indeed, remained so throughout the 1939-45 aerial conflict). Prone position under-guns partially solved this dilemma, but hardly eliminated the hazard. In flying boats, additional extreme tail cock-pits, with Scarff Ring-mounted Lewis guns, provided one answer; but in more conventional bomber aircraft attempts were made to provide a form of retractable cupola belly turret. This style of gun turret is best illustrated by the British Handley Page Heyford bomber and the Luftwaffe's Junkers Ju52 equivalent. Known in-variably as the 'dustbin turret', it comprised a cramped, cylindrical, metal can, tightly containing one gunner and one hand-operated machine gun. The late F. D. Bradbrooke's experiences in a Heyford 'dustbin' during the 1936 Annual Air Exercises give an intimate indication of the under-gunner's plight;

> It has some comfort, not because there is an inch clearance for back, knees or feet, but because it is tailored accurately to fit. If a can-opener had been handy I might, in fact, have eased mine slightly at the arm-pits. The rim of the little balcony reaches barely to the knees as one sits, and a re-entrant bulge between them adds to the field of fire that little extra something which we hope the others haven't got. When the opening faces dead aft there is an eddy which calls for goggles, but when turned abeam there is no wind draught. The sensation when winding this pill box round is at least novel . . .

The overall question of suitable machine guns for air use – part-solved, if only temporarily, by the eventual introduction of the VGO 'K' – brought consideration of an American-designed gun into the

27 *Upstairs, downstairs. Handley Page Heyford II, demonstrating its normal nose and dorsal gun cockpits, and the fully extended ventral 'dustbin' gun turret for belly defence.*

armament picture; the .300 Browning machine gun. Originally produced pre-1914 as an infantry gun by the Colt Firearms Company, the Browning had first seen RAF trials in 1918, when an example had been installed and tested in a Bristol F2b. Adopted by the post-1918 US Army Air Corps as a standard weapon for both pilot and Observer weapons, the British manufacturing rights were acquired by Armstrong Whitworth, who received an order from the British Government for six examples in 1926. These six, adapted to the British .303-inch calibre, were delivered in 1929, and tested with great success. An improved '1930-pattern' version followed, and after much adaptation and prolonged testing and modification to British aircraft requirements, came into wide RAF service in late 1936. By July 1939, some 20,000 Brownings were on RAF charge, and by mid-1941 these were rolling off factory production lines at a rate of almost 2,000 per week.

The advantages of the Browning over the Vickers belt-fed pilot's gun and the air gunner's VGO 'K' gun lay in its belt feed, as opposed to magazine or drum, its ease of maintenance, and – most important, its adaptability for multiple gun turret mountings in the new generation of totally enclosed, power-operated gun turrets which began to appear on the latest British bomber designs of the late 1930s. The same basic Browning also provided the eight-gun wing armament of the Hawker Hurricane and Supermarine Spitfire of 1936-40 era. The Browning's technical simplicity (in Service terms of operation and in-the-field maintenance) and reliability led to its adoption as the standard RAF bomber's defensive gun throughout World War Two.

Heavier calibre guns and cannons were mooted for bomber turrets as early as 1938, by Boulton Paul, but in mid-1940 Lord Beaverbrook, then responsible for all British aircraft production, vetoed all further development. When, in mid-1941, the 20mm cannon turret idea was resumed, the opportunity had been too long delayed; no such turret ever reached operational status with the RAF before the close of hostilities in Europe in 1945. An interim measure for heavier calibre guns was a partial use of the American .50 calibre machine gun; though its possible adoption by the RAF had been turned down originally in 1928 in favour of the .303 Browning.

Exponents and opponents of the large calibre gun for bomber defence remain fairly evenly divided in the hindsight of experience. After facing longer-range cannons from the Luftwaffe fighter opposition in the latter years of the war, an air gunner's views tended to depend on the type of bombing operations he had been engaged in – by day or by night. By day the obvious advantages of longer range guns were apparent – earlier engagement and, therefore, possibly, avoidance of any surprise onslaught. By night the air war was different. Fighter versus bomber combat was essentially a close quarter affair, savagely brief for the most part, and mainly fought well within the effective range of a .303-inch

Browning. Thus a battery of four Brownings could be more efficient – and deadly – than a single or (at best) twin heavy calibre cannons. Undoubtedly the foregoing remarks are an over-simplification, and are offered with distinct reservations, knowing that the basic controversy will continue until the last ancient air gunner finally hangs up his cocking toggle.

The advent of the 'new' generation of bombers in the RAF in the mid-1930s led to the first regular inclusion of 'straight' air gunners in each bomber crew; hitherto the back-seat man was all too often simply regarded as a mere passenger, or even pure ballast to balance an aeroplane's centre of gravity. Air Gunner, as a distinct aircrew category or 'trade', was not fully recognized until the beginning of 1939 in the RAF; when Air Ministry Order (AMO) A.17/1939 dated 19 January 1939 finally laid down official policy and conditions of service *et al* for 'Aircraft Crews (other than Pilots)' [*sic*]. Until the issue of this AMO, gunners in the RAF were virtually in two categories – air gunners and wireless operators. Qualification as an aerial gunner previously had been 'rewarded' solely by a special arm badge, in gilding metal, officially termed Winged Bullet, and worn on the upper arm of the right sleeve of the airman's tunic. Employment as an aerial gunner was only on a part-time basis, with a nominal daily few pence added to an airman's pay when he was actually engaged in official flying duties in that capacity.

The January 1939 AMO placed all air gunners on a full-time employment basis, albeit in the aircrew category of wireless operator on satisfactory completion of a gunnery course of instruction. At the same time existing aerial gunners (except those in flying boat

28 *Rear gunner in a Fairey Battle bomber, 1939. Note that the airman-gunner is wearing the winged brass bullet badge on his tunic sleeve – badge of the pre-1940 air gunner in the RAF. His headwear is part of his anti-gas clothing.*

squadrons) were expected to take the wireless operators' training course. Prospects of further upgrading in aircrew status, and rank, were restricted by the same AMO to the possibility of selection, after about three years' crew service, for training as an Air Observer. If selected, the airman underwent a 16-weeks' course in navigation and bombing, on successful completion of which he would receive acting rank as a Sergeant; and after six months duty as 'Acting Observer' would be confirmed in rank and crew category, and authorized to wear the winged 'O' flying badge of an Air Observer above his left tunic pocket. His daily rate of pay, incidentally, went up from nine shillings to 12 shillings and sixpence on such confirmation. Eventual rise to commissioned rank was envisaged but only on a very limited scale.

On 12 December 1939 another AMO, A.552, finally introduced the now-familiar AG cloth badge for wear by air gunners. All air gunners, when qualified, were in future to be of at least the rank of Sergeant; while commissioned ranks were provided for, though only in rough proportion of one-to-three to navigators or pilots. The Winged Bullet badge, originally introduced by AMO A.204/23, was declared obsolescent on the inauguration of the new, cloth AG brevet. The chief instigator of this new aircrew flying badge was Air Chief Marshal Sir Edgar Ludlow-Hewitt, at that time AOC-in-C, Bomber Command. His views were endorsed by the Air Council, and within three weeks a possible badge had been designed and circulated for comment internally prior to submitting the design for royal approval. When the design reached the Chief of Air Staff, MRAF Sir Cyril Newall, he noticed that the wing comprised 13 feathers. His reaction is recorded as, 'Agree, but I suggest in the interests of those who may be superstitious either 12 or 14 feathers, not 13.'

Group Captain E. H. Hooper, CBE, then a Wing Commander in the Directorate of Personal Services, who had designed the badge originally, cut away the smaller root wing with a pair of nail scissors, thereby reducing the total feathers to twelve. Royal approval followed quickly, and the general design was later adopted by all Dominion air forces.

The introduction into RAF first-line service of the Handley Page Hampden, Bristol Blenheim, Armstrong Whitworth Whitley and Vickers Wellington twin-engined, all-metal construction, monoplane bombers brought a vital need for specific gunnery and gun turret training for all air gunners. The Hampden relied on hand-operated VGO 'K' guns in its defensive locations, but the remaining three incorporated power-operated gun turrets, either in nose, mid-upper and/or tail positions. Each of these aircraft employed a different design of turret; a reflection of the continuing freedom permitted to individual aircraft manufacturers when providing aircraft for the national air services. A need for at least semi-standardization in gun turret design had yet to be fully appreciated.

In its pursuit of an efficient power-operated gun turret design for RAF bombers, the British aircraft industry was nevertheless years ahead of virtually every other major power. In France, America and Germany the outbreak of war in 1939 found each country's air service still relying in the main on hand-swivelled defensive guns, despite possessing bombers with top speeds well in excess of 200 mph. Only in Italy had any genuine attempts been made to up-date an air gunner's equipment in this context. The US Army Air Corps, by then equipped only with three obsolete bomber types and the first examples of the Boeing B-17 'Flying Fortress', had shown minimal interest in the question of turrets; preferring to rely on integral waist and nose locations for hand-fired .50 calibre machine guns. Indeed when offered a gun turret design several years before the war, the Chief of the aviation armament section rejected it as 'too heavy and too complicated', adding the rider, 'and because it is power-operated, which seems unnecessary in a device to carry a machine gun for defensive purposes.'

Thus, in September 1939, the only major power whose bomber force possessed first-line aircraft fitted with power-operated gun turrets as a norm was Britain. It is true that most such turrets were armed with only a single .303 calibre machine gun, or twin guns, but multi-gun turrets were already in service with the first Short Sunderland flying boat units in RAF Coastal Command, and the coming generation of truly heavy, four-engined bombers, mainly still in prototype or drawing board form, were all to incorporate multi-gun installations. The inadequacy of single, hand-triggered guns was to become manifest when the early daylight bombing and reconnaissance sorties over Germany's coastal areas met initial opposition from the fast, cannon-armed Luftwaffe fighters. An exception was the Boulton Paul Defiant fighter – an anachronistic design which perpetuated the 1918 concept of a two-seat fighter. In the Defiant its sole offensive armament was a four-gun, Boulton Paul-designed turret behind the pilot's cockpit. Despite the optimistic early combat claims by the Defiant crews in early 1940, such a concept was fore-doomed, and the lesson was learned by the RAF abruptly and at a bloody cost in valuable aircrew lives.

3. The Valiant Years

The years 1939 to 1945 can truly be regarded as the 'golden era' of the air gunner. Never before, or since, were gunners employed in such large numbers, or given the official recognition and status befitting their onerous responsibilities. Until 1939, as has been related, the air gunner had been regarded in the main as little better than a 'useful passenger', rather than a full-time aircrew member of equal standing with other crew members. Conversely, as the potential of aerial bombing began to be realized in practical terms, and particularly by 1943 as the awesome strength and striking power of the true heavy bomber emerged, air gunners had established for themselves vital roles in several contexts – indeed, were virtually indispensable. Such a state of affairs continued until the cessation of hostilities in 1945, but in the immediate post-war years, especially with the advent of the jet-engined bomber, the gunner's role became – necessarily and logically – obsolete. Indeed, the aircrew category of Air Gunner became officially redundant in the RAF with effect from 1 January 1955, and thereafter air signallers undertook the few remaining gunnery duties in existing aircraft requiring any such role.

To trace the general development and progress of aerial gunnery, and *per se* air gunners, throughout the 1939-45 war, the RAF may be taken as possibly the best yardstick. The German Luftwaffe employed few bombers fitted with gun turrets; the French air arm played, relatively, a small part in operations while the USAAF's massive contribution to Allied aerial might is dealt with separately in later chapters. At the outbreak of war RAF bomber strength was comprised wholly of single- or twin-engined aircraft. Of these only the Whitley and Wellington were regarded as in any sense 'heavy' bombers; the remainder – Hampdens, Blenheims and Fairey Battles – were essentially medium-range 'light' bombers. Both the Whitley and the Wellington incorporated nose and tail gun turrets, power-operated; while the remainder – with the exception of the Blenheim's mid-upper Bristol turret – relied on hand-operated machine guns. In some early Marks of Wellington an additional under-belly, retractable 'dustbin' turret was fitted, though these quickly became redundant and were removed.

The lot of the air gunner in each case was not an enviable one. Though issued with the full contemporary flying clothing for air-crews, he (like every other crew member) had little, if any, provision

31 *Sergeant air gunner and his VGO 'K' gun, c. 1940.*

for heating in any form to combat the freezing temperatures of the upper night air. Nor were his 'tools of the trade' – his guns and ammunition supplies – protected from the effects of severe icing. The inevitable result became apparent during the RAF's initial night forays over Germany, with guns, turrets, and gunners reduced to a semi-efficient state by the physical restrictions of icing and frostbite. Attempts to solve this general problem of crew comfort throughout the war were seldom fully successful; while the air gunner's job remained the coldest one in every bomber crew until the end. The medical standards required of any potential aircrew in the RAF had always been exceptionally high at any period, but it must be remarked that sheer stamina and fortitude were needed in particular by air gunners, especially those who served in the four-engined heavy bombers from 1941 onwards. Sitting almost immobile in the cramped panoply of a metal and perspex cupola for six, eight, ten or even more hours, constantly vigilant, yet unable to relieve cramped legs, arms and back, called for frequent extraordinary feats of physical endurance.

Nor was the question of temperature the gunner's only problem. At high altitude, when oxygen became a necessity, much depended on the type of aircraft in which he flew. For example, in a Hampden with an endurance of approximately ten hours, the oxygen supply sufficed for only four and a quarter hours at a mere 15,000 feet. Lack of oxygen resulted in anoxia and, quickly, euphoria, as

witnessed by the experience of a rear gunner in a Halifax on the night of 28 April 1942. The after-raid report recorded that the gunner, while approaching the target area, began to 'feel queer', a feeling which gradually increased until he started to gasp and wondered whether he'd been wounded without realizing it. Then the thought occurred to him dimly that his state might be due to lack of oxygen, so he reported this to his skipper. The pilot ordered the flight engineer to take a portable oxygen bottle back, but the gunner refused this, saying that they were over the target and he had to watch for nightfighters. The gunner later recalled getting very angry with the flight engineer, and on leaving the target area at some 20,000 feet, was heard on the intercom saying in no uncertain terms that he was 'not worried about night fighters'. The whole situation had been brought about by a leak in the main oxygen pipeline. On several occasions, however, lack of oxygen literally killed some rear air gunners before the fault was realized and remedied by other crew members. The physical isolation in the extreme tail exacerbated such circumstances.

The problem of extreme cold suffered by all air gunners – whether inside gun turrets or, as in the case of the USAAF's Fortress and Liberator crews, waist gunners – was never satisfactorily resolved during the war. In the RAF during the first two years of operations, most gunners resorted to layer upon layer of woollen and silk clothing to protect hands, feet and trunk; while exposed faces were liberally coated in some form of lanolin-based grease to ward off frostbite. At the beginning of 1942 electrically-heated flying clothing

33 Rear turret of Armstrong Whitworth Whitley K8942 at an air gunnery school, c. 1941–2; fitted here with a single camera gun. Pupil (?) is wearing the two-piece, fur-lined, leather Irvin suit and parachute harness.

34 One-Off! Westland P.12 'Duo-Mono' experimental anti-invasion design, based on the Westland Lysander first prototype (K6127) with a mock-up Nash & Thompson four .303-gun turret at rear. Tested in 1940-1, it remained a one-off experiment, despite very successful flight trials.

began to be issued, though the early suits suffered spasmodic failures due partially to electrical faults, and to no little extent by careless stowage and use of these suits by the crews. Frostbite was a particular nightmare amongst USAAF waist gunners during 1942-43, until better protection measures were introduced, including the fitting of a plexiglas waist window which still allowed flexible movement of the waist .50 machine guns.

Undoubtedly the greatest hazard (apart from direct wounding by enemy aircraft or flak guns), and certainly the most feared, was fire in an aircraft. Though this fear – and it was *the* prime fear – was felt by all aircrews, the turret gunner had if anything extra reason for his apprehension. Surrounded by alloy metal framework and perspex only inches away from every part of his body, he was in the midst of a conglomeration of highly explosive ammunition, hydraulic pipelines, and electrical wiring. Behind him (in the case of the tail gunner) was the hollow tunnel of the fuselage stretching forward to the nose compartment. In the event of any damage to almost

35 *TAG. Telegraphist Air Gunner of the Fleet Air Arm base,* HMS Sparrowhawk, *in full flying gear, with VGO 'K' gun. Over 1,000 TAGs saw operational service, of whom nearly 400 were killed on active service around the globe.*

any section of that fuselage, with any consequent outbreak of fuel fire, he was at the receiving end of a slipstream-driven furnace promoted by venturi effect through the fuselage 'tube'. Normally, too, the tail gunner's parachute pack was stowed inside the fuselage, behind his turret doors. Any damage or heat-buckling to his turret doors meant that he was automatically cut off from his only safe means of abandoning a stricken aircraft.

For gunners in the other types of bomber – the Blenheims, Bostons, Mitchells, Venturas, Baltimore *et al* – the situation was, to some extent, even more immediate if any fire broke out. With relatively less fuselage space in which to 'manoeuvre', the gunner – usually in a mid-upper or possibly prone ventral location – *had* to act immediately if he was to avoid being 'fried'. Baling out by parachute from such twin-engined 'medium' bombers was never an easy prospect; indeed, the various Marks of Blenheim held something of an evil reputation amongst air crews in this context. Like every military aircraft, such bombers were, objectively viewed, potential death traps in the event of any one of a hundred mishaps. For example, a fully loaded Lancaster bomber, on take-off for a sortie over Germany, was in essence a metal container for more than 2,000 gallons of pure petrol, plus another 150 gallons of oil; miles of pipeline containing highly inflammable hydraulic oil for controls and flaps, gun turrets, etc. In its belly might be between eight and ten tons of lethal high explosive and/or pyrotechnic stores; while threaded through most of the internal fuselage ran some 14,000 rounds of ammunition in extended alloy tracks guiding the belted ammunition to the gunners' turrets; interlaced with oxygen lines, electrical wiring, intercommunication cables, and host of fittings which would need relatively little heat to be converted into molten metal. Inside such a 'flying bomb' were seven or eight human beings, merely clothed in apparel designed to keep out the cold, but in no way fire-proof or bullet-proof. And such men took off night after night for an eight or ten hours' stint inside such a 'metal box', facing enemy opposition from flak guns, night fighters and, not least, hostile weather conditions – each intent on destroying or at least crippling their aircraft.

That young men, from all walks of life and widely varying backgrounds, cheerfully accepted such built-in odds against ultimate

37 *Swordfish offices. The rear TAG's cockpit in a Fairey Swordfish II, looking aft, with single VGO 'K' gun on its Fairey mounting.*

survival night after night – and be it remembered always, each man was a volunteer – is a measure of the quality and courage of the bomber crews of all nations during those fateful years. Only the unimaginative failed to know fear before each take-off; while each succeeding sortie or mission merely accentuated that inner terror as experience taught early recognition of every potentially deadly circumstance. By 1942 every member of an operational aircrew was initially expected to undertake a tour of approximately 30 sorties, after which he was usually 'rested' in some non-operational sphere such as instructional duties at an OTU within the Command. He could still be ordered to undertake a second tour of operations, on completion of which it was a matter of voluntary choice whether he wished to carry on with a third tour.[1] In practice it was not uncommon for a complete crew on finishing their first tour immediately to volunteer for a second spell, such was the community spirit of the bomber crews. Many individual air gunners remained on operations well beyond the second tour 'cut-off' point, by voluntarily tagging on to any crew short of a gunner. Various statistics have been published in the past to illustrate the hair-thin chances of any individual actually surviving a first tour, and then a second or even third period. Marshal of the RAF Sir Arthur Harris – 'Butch' to the thousands of bomber men he commanded from 1942 until the end of the war – calculated a man's chances of achieving a full first tour of operations as 'scarcely one in three'. To tempt providence by volunteering for further tours could only reduce such thin odds.

For the air gunners (and other aircrew) of the RAF during the period 1939-41, however, there was no set 'tour'; operations continued to be flown until local commanders considered it propitious to 'rest' any man, or RAF Records Office – that mysterious human-cum-computer complex which was a constant source of ironic or cynical amusement to all members of the RAF throughout the war, and indeed since – deemed it necessary to promote or post a man to other duties. The psychological advantages of giving a man a 'set target' of sorties to achieve became recognized early by the RAF and, later, the USAAF. In complete contrast it should be noted here that aircrews in the Luftwaffe were never given a stipulated 'tour' on operational flying during the war, ceasing flying only when severe injuries or death 'finished' them, or, being subordinated to either the Army or Navy, they were switched to the role of infantryman or sailor as the occasion demanded.

In terms of his 'ironmongery' the RAF gunner of 1939-41 was ill-served for the purposes of a modern air war. Though protected to some extent from the elements by some form of cupola or gun turret, his personal discomfort was hardly assuaged. Lack of adequate heating, life-saving oxygen equipment, and protective clothing

[1]In the USAAF a tour of operations ('missions') in the ETO was normally 25 sorties, after which the individual was 'rotated Stateside' – sent home to the USA. However, as in the RAF, many crew men voluntarily stayed on operations.

38 *Threading in the ammunition belts to rear turret of a 214 Squadron Vickers Wellington (Z8900), Stradishall, 1942.*

against bullet or shell damage often eroded the 100 per cent concentration so necessary for his role. While the numbing effect of squatting on a small metal seat for hours might be ignored by the more stoic, the prospect of permanent crippling of fingers and feet as a result of agonizing frostbite hardly enhanced efficiency. Armour plating to resist attacks from German fighters was unknown, except for individual fitments near the pilot in certain aircraft, but a number of veterans of the French campaign of May-June 1940 are on record as preferring to carry the ordinary issue infantryman's steel helmet with them on operations over occupied Europe in the following year. Though usually worn on the head, no small number of these were placed under a gunner's *derrière* – a question of individual priorities!

In the case of gunners who operated single or twin hand-operated machine guns, sighting remained only a modification of the decades-old ring and bead sight; leaving the gunner to calculate deflection angles when firing at a moving target. Tracer ammunition, though useful as a very rough guide to the trajectory of his bullets, was not accurate enough visually to verify aim. Where gunners had the benefit of a power-operated battery of two or four .303 Browning guns, however, sighting was by means of the early Marks of Reflector Sight. This provided an illuminated circle via optical lenses directly in line with the gunner's eye-line. Adjustment, by a range knob, of the circle's diameter gave the gunner automatic deflection angle in proportion to the target's known wing span. The same basic sight was also used in RAF fighters of that period; while a slightly adapted version replaced the fixed ring and bead on free gun installations. Thus a gunner could keep an opponent within his sight-circle and estimate reasonably accurately that opponent's range from him – always providing he had kept his aircraft recognition training up to date.

39 *The lonely rear turret of an Armstrong Whitworth Whitley bomber, c. 1940.*

40 *Waist gunner in an RAF Coastal Command Liberator. Twin .303 Brownings, fed from ammunition boxes immediately below. The AG sat to the right of his guns to sight and operate them.*

With the general advent of radar airborne devices by early 1943 the air gunner's war by night entered a new and deadlier phase. The rapidly escalating might of the RAF's bombing offensive, complemented by day by the USAAF, had led to greatly increased, even desperate, up-grading of German ground and air opposition. Luftwaffe night fighters – the air gunner's constant *bête noire* – totalled (in January 1943) some 600, mostly Messerschmitt Bf 110s, the majority of which carried *Lichtenstein* radar in their nose compartments. With this the Messerschmitts could detect Allied bombers up to a maximum range of two and a half miles, and in co-ordination with ground defence radar control centres, could intercept with precision. Backed by hundreds of flak batteries, many radar-guided, and mushrooming belts of searchlight installations, the night defence of Hitler's Reich was now receiving highest priority. In the following years the nightly battles over Germany became a highly technical 'game' of cat and mouse, as each opponent discovered and countered the other's latest move in the race for superior radar defence and offence.

One of the first defensive measures introduced to RAF bombers to counter the Luftwaffe's advantage of *Lichtenstein* 'cat's eyes' detection equipment was *Monica* – a rear-facing, searching radar transmitter and receiver, tuned to the same wavelength and acting as a pre-warning of the approach of any Luftwaffe fighter by emitting a series of 'pips' fed into the bomber intercomm. In practice the

41 *Opposition.*
Messerschmitt Bf 110G-4b
night fighter, fitted with S.N-2
radar aerial proboscis array,
and ventral gun pack.

42 *B-25J Mitchell 'light' bomber with rear, upper and side gun locations.*

disadvantage of *Monica* was a matter of identification – too often the set merely indicated the presence of other bombers in the stream, thereby keeping gunners on the *qui vive* for long, unnecessary periods of strain. First used operationally on 16/17 June 1943, *Monica* was quickly replaced by an off-shoot of the *H2S* navigational radar device. Code-named *Mousetrap* originally, but changed to *Fishpond*, the new warning set eliminated the sound 'pip' warning and replaced it with a blip on a cathode ray screen display. The main advantages of *Fishpond* were its ability to cover all aircraft in proximity both below and on the same level as the bomber, while actual bearing and range of any nearby or approaching aircraft could be 'read' off the screen with accuracy. Before 1943 was out, however, the Luftwaffe had found two answers to the RAF's tail-warning radar. Utilizing the known wavelengths of both *H2S* and its associated *Fishpond*, Messerschmitt Bf 110s and Junkers 88s were being fitted with *Naxos* and *SN-2* nose radar sets; both of which homed in on the transmissions of the RAF bombers' own defence radar. On 19 February 1944, for an example of the effectiveness of these fresh devices, the RAF lost 78 of the 823 bombers despatched to destroy Leipzig; losses almost entirely attributed by the Luftwaffe to its *SN2*-equipped fighters.

By the close of 1943 further measures to counter the RAF's bomber assaults were introduced by the Luftwaffe. One did not rely on radar, simply concentration of night fighters in a relatively small area of the night sky directly in touch with any bomber stream. This was the so-called 'Wild Boar' system, where specified 'levels' of altitude were 'allotted' to the flak guns and searchlight batteries, above which the night fighters could roam at will. The second, more pernicious, tactic was to introduce radar-equipped fighters into the actual bomber stream. 'Wild Boar' fighters were first used against the force attacking the German rocket station, Peenemunde, on the night of 17 August 1943; resulting in the loss to the RAF of 41 bombers. Just six nights later, over Berlin, 56 bombers were brought down, of which at least 33 fell to the 'Wild Boar' pilots. The efficacy of the night fighter which hunted its victims within the bomber stream can be illustrated by the high scores claimed (rightly) by many Luftwaffe fighter pilots; some of these accounting for five, six or even more British bombers in the course of one night's patrols. Even more of a testimony to their successes is the stark fact that of all such victims, up to 80 per cent were destroyed without even offering return fire. The main tactic responsible for such utter surprise of a bomber's ever-alert gunners was the use of the upward-slanting twin 20 mm cannon *Schrägemusik* installation in many Luftwaffe machines. By approaching from well below, unheralded, a German crew could fly underneath the bomber to a position slightly ahead of it, then pull up the nose of their fighter and blast the bomber as it flew through the consequent burst.

All the radar 'black boxes' installed in RAF aircraft for defence against surprise attack, however, could not surpass the 'Eyeball, Mk I' – a gunner's natural keen eyesight. Increasingly during the latter years 1943-5, bomber captains, irrespective of rank or position, relied implicitly on their air gunners to warn them, not only of the presence and location of fighters, but also of precise evasion manoeuvres to take. A sudden order over the intercomm from either gunner to 'Corkscrew port down, Go, Go, Go! . . .' (as appropriate) was obeyed by a skipper instantly – delay by only seconds invited disaster. Just as his course was dictated by his navigator, and his final bombing run-up by the bomb aimer, so the defence of the aircraft was in the eyes and hands of his gunners. Many bomber crews, alert to the realistic possibilities of damage to the inter-communication lines, installed a simple electrical signalling system, whereby each gunner could indicate action by using the Morse Code in a series of tiny electric lights in the pilot's cockpit. By 'blipping' his light button to send a visual Morse Code single letter, a gunner could call for specific evasion tactics, without any voice contact.

Captains, usually individuals of the pre-war regular RAF, with old-fashioned notions of discipline, who insisted on pedantic authority in all matters of rank and precedence in decision, seldom lived to exercise such authority for long. Tragically, those very few who did attempt to carry parade-ground discipline into the cockpit of an operational aircraft too often dragged a faithful crew into oblivion with them. The attitude of the more experienced senior officer to such matters is perhaps exemplified in the case (on official record) of an Australian Flight Sergeant tail gunner. Having returned to base in a shattered Lancaster, after surviving a series of fighter attacks, the Aussie, in colourful invective, proceeded to berate his skipper in loud and no uncertain terms for over-riding his (the gunner's) evasion orders during the various attacks. All this was in the hearing of both his own crew and the nearby ground crews, and the recipient, a Squadron Leader new to operations, immediately placed his gunner under close arrest and charged him with gross insubordination. The charge was immediately 'Dismissed' by the Station commander next day, on hearing the full circumstances; while the bureaucratic Squadron Leader was quietly posted within twenty-four hours to a backwater, non-operational post. Aircrew discipline was always of the highest, but it was the willing discipline of survival, and not a slavish adherence to 'the book'; only by 100 per cent cohesive teamwork could any crew even hope to be still living at the end of its tour.

The constantly changing radar war in the air increased the dangers to both bombers and their fighter and flak opponents, and probably reached its peak during the latter part of 1944. Yet little real improvement to the RAF air gunners' equipment was introduced during the latter phases of the war. In late 1943 a specification was issued for a rear turret, carrying twin .50 Browning machine guns, and resulted in a roomy turret designed by the Rose Brothers' firm of Gainsborough, Lincolnshire. The Rose turret incorporated several novel features for the period. In existing hydraulically-operated gun turrets there was always a tendency for a certain amount of 'back-lash' when elevating or traversing, i.e. a slight over-shooting of any specific point aimed at, requiring delicate adjustment pressure being applied to the controls to align accurately with the target. In the Rose turret this 'creep' was eliminated, and alignment was always positive to control. Internal space was such that initial trials included the installation of a second seat. With two gunners inside, one would aim and fire the guns, while his 'partner' fed target data into a computer-box of the gyro gunsight, which employed the infra-red principle. In practice the two-gunner idea was not used.

Yet another aspect of the Rose turret was the extensive cut-out of perspex immediately in front of the gunner. This modification was the direct result of operational experience. Even on standard Boulton Paul or Nash turrets in the tail location, many gunners had already sacrificed the illusory 'protection' of totally enclosed perspex cupolas for locally modified cut-out 'clear vision' panels. With outside air temperatures in the night skies plummeting to minus 30 or 40 degrees centigrade, it might be thought that the risk of frostbite was increased considerably for the turret occupant. Yet comparative air tests showed that the difference between outside and

inside temperatures at altitude varied by a mere four degrees at most – an indication, too, of the 'normal' turret air temperatures borne by most gunners! In the Rose turret this large aperture was sufficiently wide enough to offer an additional emergency exit for the gunner, whereby the gunner could slide forward and take a 'header' dive directly out of his turret. The Rose turret went into limited operational use by the end of 1944 and, generally, was well received by its occupants.

Another attempt to improve a gunner's chances of survival was the AGLT ('Air Gun Layer Turret'), developed in 1943-44 by Dr Alan Hodgkin, a member of the scientific research team headed by Dr (later, Professor) P. I. Dee. Incorporating radar control, giving automatic gun aiming and firing at any detected approaching enemy fighter, the AGLT, known by the RAF as 'Village Inn,' was eventually fitted in a few Lancasters during the last weeks of the

war, almost too late to be of any significant impact on the operational scene. Another improved form of turret, incorporating twin 20 mm cannons, for the mid-upper position, was developed and tested before the cessation of hostilities, yet never saw operational use. Originally conceived, in principle, as early as 1940, its development had been curtailed by the (then) Minister of Aircraft Production, Lord Beaverbrook. By the time this embargo had been lifted too much time had been wasted for the cannon-turret to have any chance of introduction at squadron level. After the war the twin 20 mm cannon turret, designated Bristol B.17, became standard mid-upper equipment in the Lancaster's successors, the Avro Lincoln bomber and Avro Shackleton maritime reconnaissance aircraft.

In May 1945, when a totally ruined and defeated Nazi Germany finally surrendered, the tally of sacrifices by the Allied aircrews were totted up. The particular statistics for air gunners alone are

45 *The first Bristol B.17 twin 20 mm cannon mid-upper turret, fitted here in 1944 in Avro Lancaster JB456 for trials. It came too late for wartime operational use.*

unknown precisely (at least, by the author, despite exhaustive research); yet an idea of the effort and cost of the Allied bomber war can be scaled, to a great degree, by considering in isolation the grim toll of RAF Bomber Command. From 3 September 1939 until 8 May 1945, Bomber Command aircraft flew a total of 364,514 individual sorties by day and night. In the same period the command lost a total of 8,325 aircraft to direct enemy action. In human terms these losses represented a total of 47,268 men killed on operations, apart from a further 4,200 wounded or crippled, and another 8,300 killed or dead in 'non-operational' spheres of the command's activities. It is therefore a reasonable deduction – though it is emphasized that it *is* merely reasonable speculation by this author – that some 8,000 or more RAF air gunners were killed in Bomber Command alone. A proportion of other gunners must be added from the grim totals of those air crews killed, wounded or injured in so-called 'non-operational' spheres of flying.

The objective historian may well relate such figures to the several millions of dead resulting from the global war of 1939-45, and count such a cost relatively small in sheer statistical context. A much more accurate evaluation of the air gunners' sacrifices, however, should be made in direct relation to bomber aircrew casualties – illustrating that air gunners killed represent virtually 20 per cent of the casualty figure – almost one in every five men lost. Add to these figures the many gunners lost in other commands, both in Europe and the myriad 'overseas' theatres of operations, and an inkling of the air gunners' war can be estimated. Almost always of relatively low rank, with few 'privileges' in status, pay and conditions of promotion – very few indeed ever rose to even mildly senior commissioned rank – the lot of the air gunner was not an attractive one. In many ways too – though most gunners would deny this, in deference to the other members of their crews – the gunner's task was one of the most hazardous in any aircrew flying on operations. While every member of a bomber team played a vital part in the successes of his crew, the gunners were not only the prime target for any opposing fighter, but were the crew's foremost defenders. It was an awesome responsibility to place on youthful shoulders – they seldom failed to uphold this duty to their comrades.

PART 2

4. First Op

Like every other aircrew member, if any particular sortie stands out clearly in an air gunner's memory, apart from any particularly 'dicey' trip, it is his first operational flight. Here was the culmination of many months, even years, of hopes, ambitions – and fears. Now he was going to be put to the supreme test, not only of his skill but also of his nerve, courage, 'guts' – call it what you will. This was the real thing – 'out there' were a myriad of unknown dangers and hazards perpetrated by people who had only one object – to kill him. All the theories expounded in classrooms, all the hints, tips and anecdotes garnered from veteran gunners, all the imagined terrors – all these were now to be tested and tried in the only possible way; by climbing into a turret in a fully-loaded bomber and flying over enemy-occupied lands. It was the moment when all pretences were ruthlessly stripped away, when the true character of a man emerged; the acid test.

Jack Bushby describes himself as a 'second generation' aviation 'nut', born in 1920 and totally immersed in aviation from his schooldays through the medium of the pulp magazines and Hollywood air epics of the early 1930s. Before the outbreak of

46 *Avro Manchester R5833, OL–N, of B Flight, 83 Squadron, Scampton on 8 April 1942. Crew (l-r): Sgt Jack Bushby; Plt Off Billings, RNZAF (Nav); Sgt Dodsworth (Wop/AG); Sgt Baines (Wop/AG); Sgt Williams (2/P); WO Whitehead, DFM (captain). Motto on nose was in Welsh,* Ar Hyd Y Nos *('All through the night') appropriately.*

World War Two while employed in a Fleet Street advertising agency, he made his first move towards achieving his ambition to fly when he became a 'week-end airman'; joining 601 Squadron of the Auxiliary Air Force (AAF) as an Aircraftman 2nd Class (AC2), the 'lowest and most dejected thing of fortune', as Shakespeare had it. The start of hostilities with Nazi Germany saw Bushby remustered after suitable training to the 'trade' of parachute packer, still in RAF Trade Group V, the 'great unskilled' aircrafthand, general duties (ACH/GD) branch. Shortly after he volunteered for 'straight' air gunner duties, was examined and tested, and accepted for aircrew training. It was, however, to be a further 18 months before the RAF Record Office, in its mysterious wisdom, thought it propitious to add one Bushby, J., to the long queue of potential aircrew U/t (under training); that vast breed of young hopefuls marked apart from their fellow airmen by virtue of the tiny piece of triangular white linen tucked in the front of their side-cap, or 'fore-and-aft' Service hat.

Progressing through Armament School and OTU, Bushby finally reached the 'sharp end' in early 1942, with a posting to 83 Squadron, based at Scampton, just north of Lincoln city. Then on 28 January, came his initiation into ops.

We foregathered after breakfast to see what was ordered for the day. 'Ops tonight. Night flying tests as soon as your aircraft are serviceable. Briefing four o'clock'. This was it! This was the moment the score or so of us who had come from the OTU and scores more like us, no doubt, at other bomber stations had thought about for months. This was the moment we had trained, flown, studied and sweated, 'Ops tonight'. The second-tour veterans were unruffled. They had seen it all before. For we initiates it was best summed up in Dick's (second pilot) sardonic comment, 'Feel like King Canute. Bags of confidence, but I'd like to know just what the hell's going to happen.'

On the short, half-hour test flight before lunch never was an aircraft given such meticulous inspection. I polished and repolished the perspex of the rear turret and spent extra time on the ground cleaning the gun barrels far more than they needed. At lunch we were subdued, each busy with his own thoughts. Afterwards I borrowed a bicycle and pedalled round the perimeter track to where our (Manchester) aircraft stood at dispersal, fitters busy on the wing, their heads buried in the engines and – novel and awe-inspiring sight – a train of linked bomb trolleys stationary beneath the fuselage and the armourers already busy winching up the long, sinister 1000lb bombs into the belly.

I went inside and crawled through to the turret looking for something to do, wondering if there was something vital, something important they had told me about in training which I had been stupid enough to forget. The ground crew were good-tempered, although I must have been in their way, elbowing me politely aside and busy with their tasks. Quite honestly I might just as well have been up in the Mess, but something kept me out there on the cold airfield. Subconsciously I felt that close attention to one's equipment before an operation was something one had to do, and this really was the only reason for my presence

47 *Mid-upper and rear gun turrets of an Avro Manchester (ZN-J, 106 Sqn) — Fraser Nash FN7 and FN20 respectively.*

there. Anyway I seemed to have been the only one affected so because none of the rest of my crew put in an appearance. Finally the Sergeant armourer, who had seen many crews come and go, and who may well have guessed at what was in my mind, waved at me and I went over and accepted his offer of a cigarette. 'Everything OK?' he asked. It was more of a statement than a question. 'Er, yes, far as I can see.' 'Don't worry, cock. They'll go all right if you need 'em', and he jerked his head at the four guns protruding from the turret. I got the message and, mounting my bicycle, pedalled back to the Mess. I was in time for a cup of tea, and joined Whitey (skipper) and Dick, sprawled comfortably in armchairs before the fire. 'Where've you been?' asked Whitey. 'Thought you'd chickened out' said Dick, always ready with a wisecrack. 'Just been down to the aircraft, looking around'. Whitey shot me a keen glance. 'That's the stuff', was all he said but to me it was a medal!

There was one more thing to be done in preparation. This was a letter to my parents. It was the sort of letter one might expect to be written at the time and under those conditions, and as I sealed it, I wondered what to do with it. In the crew room, carefully emptying pockets of every scrap of paper which might be useful to an enemy for identification, I got an idea. Bundled up in heavy flying suit with helmet and mask, and carrying a parachute, I wandered into Chiefy's office. 'Chiefy,' I said with what I hoped was nonchalance, 'Forgot to post this and I don't want to trail back to the crew room. Hang on to it for me, will you? I'll collect it in the morning.' 'All right mate,' he said, 'They all leave 'em with me.' He pulled open his battle dress blouse and I saw that my letter was only one of several tucked in there. He winked and turned away to answer someone's call. This made me feel a lot better. It was something I had wanted to do, yet felt afraid of embarrassment if anyone noticed it. Here was I, thinking I was the only sentimental fool on the squadron, yet it seemed that many more had the same thought. Later Chiefy told me how many times, after distributing the letters back to their owners next day, he had to keep one or two back and send them on, swearing at the war with each one.

The greatest surprise about my first briefing was that it was all exactly as I had imagined it from the training films and the cinema. On the wall, at the end of the large room, was a map of Europe; and a ribbon had been pinned with one end located at Scampton and the other somewhere on the French coast. I peered forward with everyone else. 'Boulogne' said someone, and there was an audible sigh as fifty men sat back. Whitey was almost smiling. 'Piece of cake' he whispered to Dick out of the corner of his mouth. Then the squadron commander climbed up to the dais and raised his hand for silence. He had it in an instant. 'Well, chaps, your target for tonight is Boulogne.' It flashed across my mind as remarkable that he actually used the exact words just as they did in the films. 'This, as the second-tour bods among you will realise, is an easy one. It is 83's first op with Manchesters, and Command just daren't trust you lot any farther than that'. This got him the intended laugh. Then followed target details, photographs of the docks and harbour at Boulogne, anti-aircraft defences – 'Nothing to speak of, chaps. Most of it has been withdrawn lately for the Eastern front'. There was a discussion on weather from the meteorological officer whose appearance was greeted with groans and ironic cheers, which he smilingly acknowledged as part of the ritual pattern.

Then came what I thought one of the most interesting parts of the briefing, and something very few persons apart from those present have ever known about. This was an announcement of what the German Very-Light recognition colours were for that night. I still marvel today that for months on end bomber crews operating over Germany were able to learn the secret German code signals on every night they

48 *FN7 mid-upper turret, known usually as the 'Botha' from the type of aircraft (as here) in which it was first used. Evacuation from this type of turret was, to say the very least, not easy, even for a small man.*

operated. Somewhere in Germany or occupied Europe, in hourly fear
of detection and death, working in some obscure niche where he had
access to this vital, secret intelligence, an individual was able to
transmit it to England within an hour or two. For a time during
1942 the 'service' ceased to operate, and this fact did not go unmarked
amongst crews. Ironic and seemingly callous remarks were made
quietly at briefing. 'Poor bastard, reckon he's got the chop'. Despite this
the 'service' began again later in the year. Whoever he – or maybe she –
was – British agent, French sympathiser and resistance worker, or
dedicated German anti-Nazi – the grateful thanks of hundreds of ex-
Bomber Command aircrews will always be his.

Last of all came the issue of escape kits. These were small canvas
packages containing French money, a map of northern Europe printed
on a silk handkerchief, matches, a tiny compass, and other small items
judged useful for survivors from a shot-down aircraft endeavouring to
avoid capture. We had seen escape and evasion training films. We had
been given lectures by those who had escaped or evaded capture. It had
all been thrilling and mysterious, but now, as I weighed this little packet
in my hand, I realised that it was no longer celluloid melodrama or
blackboard imagery. This little packet was for *me* to use in case *I* was to
find myself suddenly alone at night in hostile Europe! It was a sobering

49 *Waiting to go. 83
Squadron crews at Scampton,
early 1942, waiting outside
their hangar for
transportation to their
aircraft dispersals prior to
an operational sortie. Jack
Bushby is part-hidden
behind the sapling in the
foreground.*

thought. I already had a pencil in my pocket whose clip was magnetized and would serve as a rudimentary compass needle. Two of the buttons on my flies of my battle dress trousers were also polarized to act in the same way if torn off and one balanced on the other. This was really spy stuff, exciting, fascinating, and not a little terrifying.

Every detail of that first operation is as clear as if it happened last night. The tension of anticipation, the take-off, the flight over a darkened England, snow-covered fields glistening in the moonlight. Then the silver sheen of the Channel and a few minutes later, over to one side, a darkening border to the sheen that was France and enemy territory. So far we might have been alone in the sky. Not a thing stirred on the ground, not a light shone nor anything to show that this was war and we were penetrating a hostile frontier. I listened to the brief exchanges over the intercomm between Whitey, Dick and Bill at his navigation table. Routine passing of terse information. Checking of course and airspeed. Then, from Whitey, 'Five minutes to go. Think that's it ahead'. Then as I turned the turret to starboard I saw against the black land mass a brief twinkle in the sky. Then another, and another. Half a dozen then nothing more. I knew what it was. This was the flak, the anti-aircraft shells bursting against the night sky. So often had I watched it from the ground, but now I saw it from above and aimed, if not at us, then at others of our kind.

'Target in sight, port a bit!' This in an excited crackle over the intercomm from Bill. 'OK, I see it. Gunners keep your eyes peeled!' Unconsciously I had twirled the turret to one side, trying to see round the tail of the aircraft. Whitey's sharp reminder jerked me back into a recollection of my job, and I slowly rotated the turret from side to side, peering up at the star-sprinkled sky, striving for the first glimpse of a blackness against the black which might be a prowling night fighter.

'Bomb doors open!' The aircraft lurched as the drag of the opening bomb doors came in.

'OK Whitey, starboard now and straight in. I can see the docks'.

'Leave it a minute!' Whitey's voice was terse.

Then he saw what he had been waiting for. A searchlight stabbed up from the ground, its sword-like brilliance wavering and then settling on one spot in the sky. Instantly another and another lanced up, all converging on the same spot, and I caught the dull glint of perspex. Even as we watched, streams of anti-aircraft fire came curling up from the ground to converge on the apex of the searchlight cone. Coloured balls of tracer, at first seeming to rise slowly, hesitatingly, and then as they came to our height shooting up to the sky and bursting in a myriad of twinkling reds, blues, greens, blossoming as a lethal night flower. 'Right, they're busy with that poor sod. In we go!' (Whitey's first-tour experience paying off).

The aircraft lurched as Whitey swung it round sharply to port. Below I could see the blackness of the town divided into a dull silver checkerboard of water in the docks area. Bill began his bombing-run monologue, 'Left, left . . . right . . . steady at that . . . right a bit . . . OK . . . Bombs gone!' Immediately he said the words the nose went down as Whitey pushed the stick forward. The dive was sudden and vicious and I wondered, in a momentary panic, if we had been hit. Then, as he flattened out, the sky behind me exploded in a twinkling, blazing

blossom of flak. I could even see the puffs of black smoke against the stars. 'Flak astern' – this was what I was supposed to report. Whitey's reply had a chuckle in it, 'An' that's the right place for it'. He had known all the time what would happen. Whilst the defences concentrated on the aircraft coned in the searchlights he had begun his run-in. Then, as they switched their attention to us, he had made that sudden, speed-boosting dive and the consequent hail of flak had burst precisely where we would have been if we had carried on flying straight and level after releasing the bombs. 'You cunning old sod', remarked Dick in admiration. 'Got to be in this game, mate' . . .

On the flight home I felt dry and drained of energy. I still kept the turret dutifully rotating side to side and assiduously searched the sky, but so tensed had I been on that target run-up that it would have been an effort to have sounded an alarm even if I had seen anything. I realized I was freezing cold and wished we were getting nearer to base. We landed two hours later and as the Manchester swung round on the dispersal point and the engines were switched off I yawned and stretched. Then I went to clear the guns of the live round which was always up the breech of each gun on operational flying. Then it was that I made an awful discovery! In my raw inexperience I had flown the entire operation with the safety catches 'on' all four guns! If we had been attacked it would have been up to me to defend the others, and by the time I discovered that the guns were not firing, and searched about for a reason, it would have been too late. I felt humbled and bitterly ashamed of my stupidity. Nevertheless it was a lesson, and ever after that I always made sure on that point at least. I went farther, and every time I flew after that got the skipper's permission to fire a short burst into the air once we were over the sea. Then I knew the guns would be ready to fire at an instant.

Afterwards came the debriefing. Every crew crowded into the room in station headquarters, in battle dress, roll-neck sweaters and flying

50 *The 'Off'. Lancaster R5620, OL-H (nearest) leads the 'taxi-rank' out for take-off for the third 1,000-bomber raid, against Bremen on 25 June 1942. This particular Lancaster did not return.*

boots, dirty around the eyes from helmets and oxygen masks, and eyes glinting with excitement. The mug of hot sweet tea handed to each as he entered – Oh, that post-operational tea! Never in my life before or since have I tasted such nectar! Then the call to one of the tables where a frantically scribbling intelligence officer shot his sharp pre-formed questions at us and noted the answers. Did you find the target? How do you know? Could you identify the point your bombs fell? Did you get a photograph? (A swift anxious glance here between Dick and Whitey. The one in his inexperience had forgotten to remind the other who had overlooked it in preoccupation.) We each gave our version of events, and probably exaggerated them in the novelty of it all. So much so that on the way to the Mess for bacon and eggs Whitey gave us a little lecture. 'Don't ever tell them anything unless you're absolutely certain', he advised. 'It's dead easy to think you were smack on target and then, when the photograph comes out, find you were miles away. It gets you a reputation as a line-shooter and they just don't believe you after that.'

It was good advice and we remembered it. He then went on to read the riot act about our having forgotten to release the photo-flash and take the picture. 'Look', he said, 'It's Bill's job to get the picture but he's hellish busy and so am I when the bombs are just away. I don't care if the whole bleeding lot of you scream out a reminder; just so long as we don't forget it again!' We never did, but in doing so we all learned to hate and detest those paralysing few moments flying straight and level over the target after the bombs were released, whilst the million-candlepower photographic flash dropped away beneath and shed its momentary glare over the scene to be recorded on the camera film. Every instinct urged us to dive, twist, duck, weave, anything to avoid the deadly gun batteries below us, predicting our path with menacing accuracy.

Next night no ops. Down in the pubs and dance halls of Lincoln, chests were out a little bit farther and gas masks and caps swung a fraction jauntier. At last we had 'got some in'. Only one, admittedly, but we were the only ones that knew that . . .

5. Behind the Guns

Charlie Driver was on the tall side for an air gunner, an inch short of six feet, in fact. Nevertheless, it was December 1939, and higher authority had yet to get out the slide rule and calculate the 'correct' parameters of height, weight and shape of the ideal aircrew candidate. In truth, according to his Service Record, the 18-year-old AC2 was not a 'proper' air gunner, being classified as a ground tradesman, a fitter/rigger under training, who had contrived to be accepted as temporary aircrew, with the extra few pence per day given to flying personnel. A pre-war RAF regular since November 1938, Driver joined 9 Squadron at Honington, Suffolk two weeks after the outbreak of war with Germany, flying in Wellington bombers as a front turret gunner. Unrestricted bombing of German targets was forbidden at that early stage of Bomber Command's campaign, and the *modus operandi* was mainly in the form of so-called 'armed reconnaissances' over enemy coastal installations, photographing and reconnoitring German naval bases and harbours.

On the morning of 18 December 1939, Driver was in the nose turret of Wellington N2983, one of nine bombers from 9 Squadron participating in a 24-bomber formation reconnaissance of the Wilhelmshaven area. Other Wellingtons from 37 and 149 Squadrons soon joined up and all set out across the North Sea for their objective, in four small tight formations. Two Wellingtons quickly aborted the sortie with engine troubles, but the remainder flew steadily on in perfect blue skies. Contemporary Air Ministry opinion was still entrenched in the complacent belief that armed bombers required no fighter escort; a tight formation, concentrating all gunners' fire, was sufficient to ward off any air assault. This comfortable chairborne theory was about to be cruelly shattered.

As the Wellingtons neared the enemy coast, well-alerted anti-aircraft batteries put up a fierce barrage of flak surrounding the tightly-packed bombers. At some 18,000 feet altitude, against a brilliant unclouded blue sky, the bombers were a perfect target. Flying serenely on the Wellingtons wheeled and approached Wilhelmshaven, and within seconds were swamped in a succession of slashing attacks by Messerschmitt Bf 110 two-seat fighters from I/ZG 76 (Staffel 1 of Zerstörgruppe 76). Boring in from every angle the Messerschmitt crews had a field day of destruction. Within minutes six of the bombers had been sent down flaming into the sea, and all had suffered bullet and cannon shell damage.

In Driver's aircraft, his pilot, Sergeant John Ramshaw, an ex-Halton aircraft apprentice, stuck grimly to his pre-briefed plan, holding the Wellington rock-steady in formation in order to give his gunners every chance of success. In the rear turret LAC Walter Lilley repeatedly warded off a seemingly endless stream of Messerschmitts attempting to cripple the bomber from the rear. Lilley's crisp shooting sent at least two of his assailants down in severely damaged condition before a particularly savage burst of cannon shells smashed the bomber's intercommunication system,

52 *Vickers Wellington 1a bomber.*

wrecked its wireless, and tore great chunks out of the geodetic fuselage. At that moment Lilley's guns jammed, but with great coolness the rear gunner set about unjamming his weapons in order to continue the fight – and died as yet another *Zerstörer* raked his turret.

In the nose turret, Driver had his hands full, firing at every fighter to come within range. Then two Messerschmitts attacked simultaneously, one from above and the other from below. The latter's cannons struck home, ripping out the side of Driver's turret and gouging the bottom out beneath Driver's dangling feet. 'The first thing I knew was that I felt pretty cold around my feet and legs. I looked down and saw water below me', said Driver later. Then his guns refused to fire – a shell had literally sheared off half of both barrels – and a second burst shattered the perspex cupola around Driver's head, leaving him exposed. Swinging round on his seat Driver could see that his turret was on fire just behind him, so he removed one of his leather flying gauntlets and beat out the flames quickly. This done he wriggled his way back into the fuselage where he found his skipper, Ramshaw, calmly whistling a tune as he continued to evade the continuing fighter attacks.

With the second pilot, Driver made his way to the rear turret, and between them they extricated the body of Lilley, laid him on the fuselage floor and covered him over. The second pilot was then hit in the arm by a stray bullet, but reassured Driver that he was okay and went forward again to help Ramshaw. Looking out of the astro-dome, Driver could see that virtually the whole of the wings' fabric was stripped back, and the engines' cowlings were battered and torn from shell strikes. At that moment the last Messerschmitt swung away and headed for Germany, leaving the crippled Wellington to its fate. It was then discovered that the main petrol tanks had been holed, leaving at most 30 minutes' flying time on the reserve tanks. It meant a ditching in the North Sea. As his engines died, starved of fuel, and Ramshaw prepared to bring the tattered Wellington down as safely as possible, he spotted a Grimsby fishing trawler ahead of him. By sheer skill he ditched his aircraft about 400 yards from the trawler, though the impact with the water slammed him forward, banging his head and leaving him semi-dazed. Driver helped to release the aircraft dinghy and assisted his friends as they climbed into it; then made his own exit through the astro-dome. Ramshaw, still dazed, exited through his own escape hatch but fell into the sea. Immediately Driver went to his pilot's assistance and managed to get him aboard the dinghy. Fifteen minutes later the crew survivors were taken aboard the trawler, which promptly set course for Grimsby. The sea trip proved too much for Charlie Driver – he was sea-sick all the way back to port.

When they totted up the results of that day's disaster a total of 12 Wellingtons had been shot down, while a further three were wrecked on reaching the English coast. German claims from the so-termed 'Battle of Heligoland Bight' were extremely optimistic, a total of 34 victories (although this score was later reduced by Berlin to 27). German losses – despite the contemporary RAF claims and Air Ministry propaganda – amounted to two Messerschmitts shot down, with several others suffering damage in some degree. For his part in the operation Charlie Driver was awarded a Distinguished Flying Medal (DFM) – only the second such award to be made in the war. He remained a ground tradesman until the end of 1941, being eventually remustered as a fitter II (airframe) in the interim. Then, in early 1942, they made Charlie an air gunner . . . officially.

William Gray Lillie – 'Bill' to his friends – hailed from Sudbury in Suffolk, and was a carpenter's assistant when, aged 18, he decided to join the RAF in 1937. Nearly three years later, he was Corporal Lillie, on the strength of 204 Squadron, a Short Sunderland unit in Coastal Command. Like most boys of his era flying was his chief ambition, and by early 1940 Bill was regularly flying as an air gunner in the squadron's huge flying boats. On 2 April he was one of Flight Lieutenant Frank Phillips' crew in Sunderland N9046, KG-F, when Phillips flew from Pembroke Dock to Invergordon in Scotland, from where they were to operate on convoy patrols out over the Northern waters. No time was lost in 'going to war', and next morning Phillips was airborne, heading towards the Norwegian coastal waters for an escort cover patrol over an Allied shipping convoy. As second pilot he had Flying Officer Armitstead, while manning the three guns' positions were Leading Aircraftman (LAC) Frame in the two-gun front turret, LAC Dixon amidships on the beam VGO, and in the far tail Bill Lillie, squatting behind a quartet of .303 Browning machine guns in his Frazer Nash FN13 power-operated turret.

Rendezvous with the convoy was made on time and the Sunderland crew settled down for a ten-hours' watch-and-ward monotony,

quartering the sea for U-boats ahead and to beam of the convoy's path, while Lillie and his colleagues gently scanned the surrounding sky methodically in every direction looking for possible Luftwaffe interference. Until that day Sunderlands in general had never clashed with any German aircraft, but Bill Lillie and his fellow-gunners were taking no chances on being surprised. At 3.30 pm, while searching some 20 miles off the starboard flank of the convoy, their vigilance was rewarded when they spotted two twin-engined aircraft coming fast towards them, beating low across the sea from the direction of Norway. As the pair of Junkers Ju88s came within range of the Sunderland they circled for two minutes, then made up their minds and bore in from the beam singly. As the Junkers opened fire, all three Sunderland gunners replied at a range of 800 yards. The clash was brief and both Junkers withdrew and made off.

An hour later four more Junkers appeared, to be met with an anti-aircraft barrage from the convoy, causing the Germans to break formation before flying high over the shipping and attempting to bomb. Having released their bomb loads all four Junkers flew eastwards and out of sight. Obviously the Germans now had the convoy well marked – more attacks must follow. Shortly afterwards, one Sunderland gunner spotted yet another formation of Junkers coming in, six in number. Frank Phillips had no illusions about the Sunderland's capacity for air fighting, and promptly took the flying boat down low in order to protect the aircraft's weak spot, its vulnerable under-belly hull. Lillie, Frame and Dixon calmly waited for the Germans' first moves.

Two Junkers split off from their formation and headed straight at the Sunderland, cannons firing in a swift attack. Lillie and Dixon responded with a crossfire of brief, accurate bursts and the two attackers climbed away, out of range. Perhaps three minutes passed before the second attack, this time by the remaining four Ju88s, which came in from the rear of the Sunderland in single succession, apparently intent on destroying the tail turret gunner first. Lillie waited patiently as a terrifying stream of cannon shells and tracers whipped by each side of him; then when the first Ju88 was about 100 yards away he fired all four guns in a fierce burst. The German skidded sideways, flicked erratically, erupted in flames and plunged straight into the sea. Switching his sight to the second Ju88, Lillie slammed another four-gun burst into this one's port engine. The Junkers banked away shakily, smoke pluming from the shattered engine, and slowly cleared eastwards, flashing 'Help' signals.

At the same moment Armitstead, standing in the astro-dome acting as a fire-controller, yelled to Phillips to take evasive action; two of the Junkers high above were attempting to drop their bombs on the Sunderland. Phillips pulled the lumbering Sunderland into a bank and the bombs whistled past harmlessly. It was the last gesture from the Germans, who next flew off in the path of

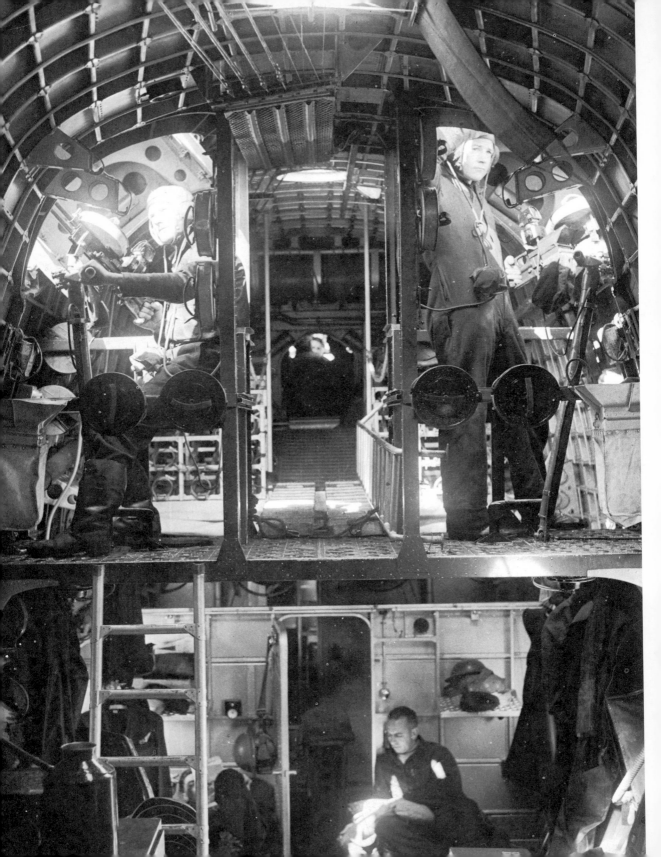

their damaged companion towards Norway. Phillips took stock of his battle damage. Three main fuel tanks had been badly perforated by bullets, trimming gear was out of action while the Sunderland generally bore dozens of holes and gashes from cannon shell damage. Phillips himself had suffered a slashed eye-lid from flying splinters, and his second pilot and navigator (Godwin) had also been cut by shell splinters. Heading back to Invergordon, the Sunderland lost some 500 gallons of fuel before reaching base two hours later, where Phillips brought the flying boat in for a good landing. Confirmation that Lillie's second Junkers eventually crashed in Norway came through to the squadron, and on 13 April Phillips was awarded a Distinguished Flying Cross (DFC), while Bill Lillie received a well-earned DFM for his part in the first-ever Sunderland air-to-air battle with the Luftwaffe.

6. The Long, Long Road

Leslie Sidwell's only ambition in the RAF was to become an air gunner. An uncomplicated ambition, and one which might have been thought relatively simple to attain, given normal circumstances and no undue diversions or accidents of fate. True, Leslie, over 30 years of age, was older than most aircrew aspirants when war with Germany was declared in September 1939. Yet he was fit, and, most important, unwavering in his ultimate goal. This last aspect he put rather forcibly to the recruiting officer, telling him quite categorically that it was straight air gunner or nothing for him. The officer's response was equally simple – impossible for a brand new recruit. So Leslie and the RAF parted company immediately.

By May 1940, still a civilian, Leslie was spending a day walking in his beloved Cotswolds, strolling through Chedworth, when he chanced upon a group of tired, battle-weary soldiers, survivors of Dunkirk. Leslie stopped and spoke with them. On the train taking him back to Coventry that day realization came to Leslie that there really was a war on, it wasn't simply headlines in the newspaper, relating to some other world. First thing next morning he went straight to his nearest recruiting office – he knew he would feel better in a uniform, any uniform. Accepted by the RAF, Leslie Sidwell's subsequent trials and tribulations to achieve his continuing determined aim to be an air gunner reflect a myriad of similar experiences by other would-be air crews, if in varying degrees of individual frustration. Within weeks of enlisting Sidwell found himself classified as a U/t (Under Training) Service Policeman – a 'Snoop' – and soon discovered that he was not exactly in the most popular trade in the Service! For several months he carried out all such duties allotted to him, but meanwhile commenced a campaign of regular applications to his Commanding Officer for permission to remuster to air gunner. As a trainee, however, he was listed as 'Supernumerary' on establishment – a solid Service excuse for ignoring any administrative decisions on Sidwell's career.

A further police training course at Uxbridge followed which merely stiffened, if possible, Sidwell's ultimate aim. From here he was posted to the rarified cloistered atmosphere of Oxford. It was, in Service terminology, a 'cushy' number; civilian billets with all mod cons, good fishing in the river, even 'sleeping' night duties. Cushy or not, it was anathema to Sidwell, still seeking action in the air. Pure chance finally gave him the opening he craved; a private chat

56 *Air gunners at an OTU having the intricacies of a turret's innards explained.*

with a senior officer on an informal occasion. Impressed with Sidwell's eagerness, the officer evidently pulled a few influential strings, because within a week Sidwell was sent to 10 OTU, Abingdon, for an air crew medical, which he passed without trouble. Finally, in October 1941, his posting was notified, to 14 Initial Training Wing (ITW) at Hastings, for a six-weeks' ITW basic training prior to actual gunnery instruction.

Headquarters for the would-be gunners was the Marine Court, a large, white, super-luxury hotel – at least, it would have been super-luxury had not the war intervened. Sidwell's ITW AG course was the first formed there and – not unexpectedly – the place was a shambles. A maze of long passages, stairs, lifts which were permanently out of action, dead and lifeless lights and power points. No heating or chairs or tables – and at first, no instructors. Billeted on the sixth floor, with 14 flights of stairs to scale several times every day, life was at least energetic. Bare hotel rooms were their classrooms, unheated and usually with icy winds howling through broken windows.

The syllabus covered not only basic armament, gunnery and the Morse Code, but also navigation, mathematics (an unpleasant surprise to all), RAF Law, administration, and several other subjects which embryo gunners found great difficulty in associating with their eventual trade. There was also the usual Service rumour of both intermediate and final examinations, failure of either entailing immediate return to unit without argument. No guns were in evidence for demonstration, no charts available for navigation, and one solitary copy of the Manual of Air Force Law per class. One thing was in abundance – Physical Training Instructors (PTIs), abounding in rude health and even ruder language from every crevice. Mathematics was the worst obstacle to most – how many values of x did one need to shoot down a Messerschmitt? – but interesting gems of RAF wisdom were also integrated with the algebraic equations. Such vital facets as the construction of field latrines, purification of drinking water, curing snake-bites and scorpion stings, calculation of camel loads, and what to do about bilharzia – fascinating lore derived from the *Airman's Pocket Book*, 1926 edition.

Finally, in December, Sidwell's course was sent on to the next phase, at Manby. Here, they imagined, they would be able to see aeroplanes and real guns. Hopes were crushed upon arrival when they were told that they were merely in transit until another gunnery school, somewhere, could be found to take them. For the next month Sidwell and his colleagues were subjected to the whims and crusty temper of a station commander whose private ideas on Service discipline might have found favour with Kipling's Soldiers Three, but hardly accorded with the new, willing discipline of potential air crews; culminating in a 100 per cent Station parade on Boxing Day, 1941, followed immediately by all 3,000 officers, airmen and WAAFs being sent on a gruelling route march as 'punishment' for a single, minor misdemeanour. Sidwell was more than usually relieved to obtain his 'release' from Manby on 1 January. Placed

57 *Embryo gunners try their hand at tackling a moving target.*

58 *Would-be TAG of the Fleet Air Arm sighting a camera gun at* HMS Kestrel, *1939.*

in charge of a party of 40 disgruntled airmen (and 80 kitbags), Sidwell was charged with delivering all safe and sound to No. 9 Air Gunnery School, Llandwrog, in Wales.

After a nervous day's journey across Britain – including seven changes of trains, and arguments with indignant aged RTO's en route who resented not being informed beforehand of the course's travel arrangements – Sidwell arrived at Llandwrog with his entourage all present. The new school was in direct contrast to Manby's Victorian regime; transport was sent to bring the course from the railway station and, without prior notice, and at 0100 hours, a splendid hot meal was cheerfully served up. The course's morale took a decided up-swing. Llandwrog proved to be a new, barely-completed airfield. Air gunner pupils flew in tired Whitley bombers, practising their trade by shooting at canvas drogues towed by ancient Westland Lysanders. For much of that winter the sea, normally in its proper place just beyond the main runway, spread itself all over the camp, with an unavoidable effect on normal aircraft maintenance. On one of the first mornings of the new course, two Whitleys collided over the airfield and all 20 men inside were

59 *On the butts. Harmonization and live firing practice – note raised red flag to warn passers-by – on the station stop butt.*

killed. Sidwell, on his first gunnery exercise over the sea, heard both of his Whitley's engines cut out completely, leaving the pilot to accomplish a shaky forced landing – just – on the Morfa Nevin golf course. In spite of these vicissitudes morale remained high and flying continued apace. Then, after almost three years of dogged determination and no little patience, Leslie Sidwell became a qualified Air Gunner, was commissioned, and posted to 23 OTU, Pershore, for final operational training and crewing-up.

At Pershore Sidwell had his first taste of 'ops' on the second and third 'thousand-bomber' raids of June 1942, when OTU crews were hastily roped in to make up the desired total of bombers. From here he joined 7 Squadron at Oakington, flying the giant Short Stirling bombers on first-line operations. His 'sharp-end' career was relatively brief; on only his tenth sortie, over Hamburg, his Stirling was hit and became an inferno of fire. Sidwell baled out, along with only two other crew members. Later, as a 'Kriegie'[1]

[1] From Kriegsgefangener – Prisoner of War.

76

60 *End result. An operational gunner of 206 Squadron, Coastal Command, with his twin VGO guns.*

Sidwell was ensconsed in the East compound of the notorious Stalag Luft III, Sagan, and reflected philosophically on his RAF 'career'. He would have liked to have completed a full tour of ops, naturally, but then ten ops wasn't a bad total – too many of his friends had never even reached that tally. The early years of frustration, boredom, and obstacles had been well worth it; he was still alive – and he had been an Air Gunner.

7. The Long, Short & the Tall

Air gunners came in all shapes and sizes – and ages. In an era when anyone in the United Kingdom less than the arbitrary age of 21 years was legally termed an 'Infant', and was not allowed to vote in any parliamentary election, 'boys' in their late 'teens completed scores of operations over enemy territory – and were then challenged to produce evidence of being 'over 18' before being served with an innocuous pint of ale in a local pub. At the other end of the time scale, however, many men with entitlement to wear 1914-18 campaign medal ribbons could occasionally be found hiding quietly behind the Browning guns in a World War Two bomber's turret. The doyen of these 're-treads', as they were affectionately dubbed by their fellow aircrews, was an old-age pensioner – Lionel Frederick William Cohen, DSO, MC, DFC, with a row of ribbons dating back to pre-Boer War years, and known to all from childhood as 'Sos'.

Born in 1874, in the next 70 years 'Sos' Cohen packed more adventure and hazard into one man's life than any 20 men picked at random from any crowd. The long pathway to an air gunner's seat started in Cohen's adolescence. The son of a Newcastle-upon-Tyne ship-owner, he was raised in London and on leaving school took ship to South Africa where, in 1893, he enlisted as a trooper and fought in the Matabele wars. An inveterate 'hobo', Sos travelled around the African continent extensively until the advent of the Boer War, when he promptly re-enlisted as a sort of Intelligence commando. In this, his second war, he hunted Boers – who put a high price on his head, dead or alive – in the raw country bordering Mozambique. After the war Sos stayed in South Africa, as one of the first owners of the Rand Daily Mail. Just one of his chores here was to dismiss an English journalist then employed by the paper – named Edgar Wallace. His fortunes prospered on the Johannesburg Stock Exchange, and in his spare time Sos tasted new adventure by taking up ballooning. Then came a financial crash, Sos lost his fortune, and was duly 'hammered' by the Exchange.[1] Refusing all offers of help, Sos went to work in a gold mine, escaped death by a hairsbreadth when a rooffall nearly buried him alive but left him with

---

[1] Many years later Sos returned, paid off every debt, re-applied for membership of the Exchange, was accepted – then, with great pleasure promptly resigned his membership.

nothing more serious than a sprained ankle, and within a week heard that England was at war again, with Germany.

Without hesitation Sos re-enlisted, again as a trooper, alongside the very men he had fought only a dozen years before, and in 1915 was commissioned in the 1st South Africa Horse. After a year of action against German forces, Sos heard that the tiny detachment of Royal Naval Air Service assisting Smuts' armies needed observers with intimate knowledge of the African bush, and promptly volunteered. For much of 1916 he flew on reconnaissance patrols in the RNAS's ancient BE2cs, Voisins and Farmans, gathering information; while other 'air' duties included construction of usable landing strips for the fragile aircraft in the untamed, red dust country. The latter years of the war were spent on the ground, as part of an armed Intelligence formation, 'Co-Force', and when peace was eventually declared, Sos had collected a DSO, MC and three 'Mentioned in Despatches' awards for his services.

The 'peace' years for Sos were filled with more mining activities, interspersed with big-game safaris, but he finally returned to England in 1926 to take up an appointment on the London Stock Exchange. In 1937 Sos, and some ex-RAF contemporaries, originated the idea of a voluntary reserve of older aircrews which would be immediately available for service in the event of any European war embroiling Britain; thus, when war did erupt in September 1939, Sos immediately reminded the Air Ministry of his existing commission in the RAFVR and, despite his age of 64, insisted on his 'right' to join up again. He was accepted and appointed to a staff job with Coastal Command Headquarters.

61 *Wing Commander Lionel 'Sos' Cohen, DSO, MC, DFC – the oldest operational air gunner.*

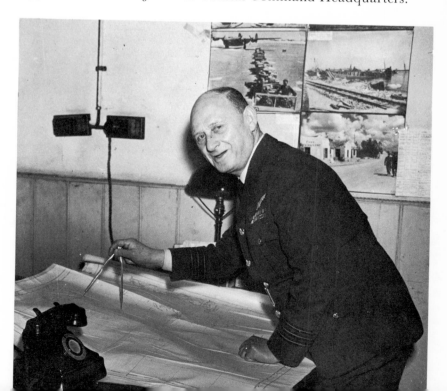

If higher authority had any thoughts of patronising Sos by permitting an old-age pensioner, however much bemedalled, to sit out his fourth war behind a 'mahogany bomber' (RAF parlance for a desk), it was sadly mistaken. Wangling an appointment as 'Liaison Officer', Sos then proceeded to argue that the only authentic method of gaining real knowledge of Coastal Command's aircrews' problems was to join with them on the operational scene, and see for himself, first-hand, how to overcome any obstacles to ultimate efficiency. Thus, for nearly four years, Sos Cohen 'tagged on' to a variety of operational crews, flying in Lockheed Hudsons, Catalinas, Liberators and Halifaxes; enduring the long hours of squatting behind his guns, cramped near-frozen on many occasions. On one Liberator sortie well up into the Arctic Circle, around Bear Island, the aircraft heating system went 'on the blink', but Sos insisted on doing his full stint in his turret, and on landing back at Reykjavik it took two other crew members to prise his stiffened bones out from his seat. He flew in a Sunderland which attacked a U-Boat repeatedly and finally claimed it sunk; endured a 21-hours Catalina patrol; was wounded by flak during a close attack on the German battleship *Lutzow*. And his penultimate sortie was as rear gunner in a Halifax which was hit by flak during an attack on an enemy convoy and had its hydraulics shot out and one engine set afire. He walked away from the subsequent crash-landing unscathed, and shortly after flew his last – sixty-ninth – operational sortie.

On 1 February 1944 the London Gazette announced the award of a DFC to Wing Commander L. F. W. Cohen, DSO, MC, and its citation diplomatically referred to his age as 58. A few days later Sos celebrated the award – and his seventieth birthday . . . In August 1960 Sos died peacefully at the age of 86 – it had been a 'very full life.'

If Sos Cohen was the oldest air gunner in the world, he was not the only 'old man' to swivel a gun turret in hostile skies during 1939-45. Ex-Royal Flying Corps and Royal Naval Air Service aircrews of the pre-1918 vintage were in abundance at recruiting offices in late 1939, seeking to join the latest war in the air. Sidney Carlin, MC, DCM was one. Yorkshire-born, Carlin had fought on the ground in the early years of the 'Great War', losing a leg in action. Discharged from active service officially, Carlin had a wooden leg fitted, then bullied his way into the RFC for pilot training. In May 1918 he joined the famed 74 Squadron RAF, flying SE5As under the inspiring leadership of the New Zealander Major Keith 'Grid' Caldwell, MC, DFC, and ran up a useful tally of combat victories. Emigrating to Rhodesia between the wars, Carlin returned to England when war erupted again. His application for flying duties as a pilot was firmly denied, but Carlin insisted, and was eventually permitted to become an air gunner. As such he flew in Defiant two-seaters, but in his 'off-duty' and leave periods scrounged rides as gunner to Wing Commander Percy Pickard, DSO, DFC, then commanding 311 (Czech) Squadron, and flying several bombing sorties over Germany. Then, on 12 May 1941, Carlin was on his airfield when it was subjected to a low-level sneak hit-and-run strafe by Luftwaffe fighters. Hobbling as fast as he could, and loudly cursing his attackers, Sidney 'Timbertoes' Carlin was heading towards his aircraft when a swathe of German bullets killed him.

A contemporary of Carlin's was W. S. Fielding-Johnson, a pilot with 56 Squadron during the Kaiser's war, flying SE5As and being awarded a triple Military Cross for his prowess, and at least eight combat victories. Rejoining the RAF, he became an air gunner on bombers and was awarded a DFC; matching the war effort of his twenty-three-year-old son who was flying DH Mosquito bombers in the same RAF Group as his very active fifty-two-year-old father. Yet another 're-tread' was Flight Sergeant A. H. Bolton, a 1914-18 veteran who gained a DFM at the age of 48 for air gunner operations. That men of such relatively advanced years could endure the long hours of vigilance, discomfort and hazard implicit in an air gunner's role might be thought, by a layman, to illustrate the 'non-active' nature of the job. Nothing could be further from the truth. The unceasing, nerve-stretching alertness required of an air-gunner on operations took a heavy toll of a young man's physical limits; it needed virtually an abnormal effort for a man decades past his physical peak to combat the fatigue, stress and pure physical limitations of an ageing body, and still be relied upon to fulfil his duties. And it speaks volumes for the esoteric camaradie of all air crews that the occasional 'old gentlemen' were absorbed into any crew of youngsters less than half their age; accepted wholly as 'one of the boys', if good-humouredly chaffed in off-duty moments as 'ancient mariners'.

If age brought experience and, very occasionally, even wisdom, a lack of years was never the criterion for simple courage. Most operational aircrew during 1939-45 were in their early twenties, quite a number of them having yet to celebrate their twenty-first birthday. It might be put down to the boundless optimism, self-confidence and seemingly unconquerable resilience of all youth that such mere 'boys' could – and did – triumph over circumstances and situations which would give pause to an older, wiser man. In the context of unadulterated valour, however, age has always been relative. Daily and nightly witness to the death and maiming of close friends and companions 'aged' every young boy into manhood swiftly. The leisurely transition from adolescent to mature manhood in any peaceful civilian existence was crystallized abruptly, even savagely, into mere days or weeks for so many young aircrew members during wartime.

Of the 51 airmen ever awarded a Victoria Cross during 1914-18 and 1939-45, the youngest air VC was an air gunner, John

62 *Flight Sergeant John Hannah, VC – the youngest-ever air VC – behind the twin VGOs of an 83 Squadron Hampden's mid-upper cockpit. Note the early form of gun travel interrupter to prevent firing at the tail section.*

Hannah, an eighteen-year-old Scot who on the night of 15 September 1940 was the wireless operator/air gunner in a Hampden of 83 Squadron RAF sent to bomb a concentration of reported invasion barges in the port of Antwerp. Hit by flak in its open bomb bay above the target, Hannah's aircraft burst into flames in the mid-fuselage. The furnace literally melted away the under-gunner's compartment and its occupant, George James, had no option but to fling himself out into the night and trust to his parachute. Just above him in the upper gunner's compartment young Hannah was in the centre of a raging cauldron of wind-driven flames. Instinctively he fought the fire, with his extinguisher, then his log book, and finally his hands. Near to suffocation in the dense fumes, he also had to deal with exploding pans of ammunition racked beside his twin VGO guns.

The internal width of a Hampden fuselage was almost exactly three feet, and in such a confined space, hampered by his bulky flying clothing and a myriad of metal obstacles, the young Scot fought a terrifying holocaust of fire – and won. The fire was subdued, and Hannah was then able to crawl forward and report to his skipper, Pilot Officer Connor, that the fire was out. Here Hannah found that the navigator, Doug Hayhurst, had also baled out, so he gathered such maps as he could find and helped Connor to navigate their battered bomber back to Scampton and an eventual safe landing. On 10 October 1940 both men attended an investiture at Buckingham Palace, where Connor received a DFC, and John Hannah had his bronze cross pinned below his AG's brevet by HM King George VI.

A second VC went to another air gunner, a Canadian of Polish extraction called Andrew Charles Mynarski. Joining the RCAF in

September 1941, Mynarski was trained as a WAG (Wireless Air Gunner 'S'), and eventually in April 1944 joined 419 Squadron at Middleton St George. On his twelfth operational sortie, on 12 June, Mynarski was mid-upper gunner in Lancaster KB726, 'A-Apple,' detailed as one of the force despatched to attack the marshalling yards at Cambrai. It was a low-level raid, briefed to bomb from 2,000 feet. The run-in to the target was made through a veritable hail of flak; then before reaching the objective Mynarski's Lancaster was jumped by a Junkers Ju88 nightfighter, which bore in from the port beam, raking the bomber with cannon shells, and following up with an equally devastating attack from below and astern.

Both port engines failed and a roaring fire erupted in the rear fuselage of the stricken Lancaster just to the rear of Mynarski's turret, which spread almost instantly along the port wing, threatening to explode the wing petrol tanks. In the rear turret Flying Officer George Brophy had taken the brunt of the Junkers' onslaught, having his turret's hydraulic lines shattered, leaving him with only his manual winding handle with which to rotate the turret. His skipper, Art de Breyne, having checked the uselessness of his controls, and realizing the dangers of the burning wing, ordered his crew to bale out. Brophy wound his turret towards the beam – then his winding mechanism handle sheared; he was trapped, helpless without outside aid.

Mynarski, obeying his pilot's last order, climbed down from his turret and was about to go forward to the escape hatch, when he glanced to the rear of the fuselage and realized Brophy was still in his turret, despite the raging fire. Unhesitating, Mynarski scrambled through the flames and began beating against the jammed turret's doors in an attempt to get it moving. His flying clothing

63 (Below left) *Pilot Officer Andrew Charles Mynarski, VC, of 419 (Moose) Squadron, RCAF.*

64 (Bottom right) *Wing Commander (later, Group Captain) Arthur E. Lowe, MBE, DFC, an ex-Halton aircraft apprentice who became the first-ever AG to command an operational bomber squadron (77).*

already saturated in hydraulic oil from the ruptured system's pipe-lines, burst into flames, but he continued to hammer against the turret doors. Brophy could see Mynarski's burning clothing and yelled to him to get out of the bomber before it was too late. Reluctantly Mynarski left his friend and made his way along the fuselage to the escape hatch. Before diving through the open hatchway, Mynarski straightened up, facing the rear turret, and saluted Brophy as a sincere gesture of farewell; then, with his clothing and parachute a mass of flames, Andy Mynarski jumped. At such low altitude, and in his parlous physical state, Mynarski stood no chance of survival, and he plunged to the earth, where his body was discovered shortly after by local Frenchmen.

The crippled Lancaster exploded on impact with the ground; yet by some near-miracle Brophy's turret was flung clear of the burning wreckage, and he survived, along with the remaining members of the crew. Only after the war, when the crew was repatriated to England from prisoner camps, was Mynarski's story put before higher authority. On 11 October 1946 Andrew Mynarski was awarded a posthumous Victoria Cross – in attempting to succour a fellow gunner, he had jeopardized his only hope of personal survival, and his utterly selfless action had cost him his life.

65 *Dorsal gunner in a Lockheed Hudson's mid-upper 'egg' turret.*

8. They Pressed On

They called them 'Press-on types' in the RAF; men who stayed at their allotted posts disdaining all attempts by the enemy to prevent them completing their given tasks. The official phrase was 'Devotion to duty', though such praise was usually loudly derided by the men concerned. Call it determination, obstinacy, or sheer bloody-mindedness if you will, but such men stayed to fight theoretically impossible odds against personal survival – and often won through. It was a trait found amongst all aircrew categories, yet particularly exemplified by the air gunners. Theirs was a double responsibility in a way. Primarily they were there for just that purpose – to ward off anything thrown at them by the enemy and thus protect their aircraft and crew. Any gunner leaving his post during action would automatically place the lives of his crew in jeopardy. Add to this direct responsibility a natural human desire to hit back when attacked, and one begins to comprehend the spirit which held such men in their seats when instinct and common sense dictated escape.

Norman Francis Williams would be the first to scoff at any suggestion of being a 'Press-on type'. An Australian from Leeton, New South Wales, in early 1943 he was a Sergeant air gunner serving with 10 Squadron, flying in Halifax bombers from Melbourne, Yorkshire. The bombing offensive against Germany was at an intensive period, and in just two months' operations Williams's skill and courage brought him the awards of a DFM and Bar – a rare medal combination. Volunteering for further operations with Don Bennett's elite Path Finder Force (PFF), he was transferred to 35 Squadron, another Halifax unit based, in June 1943, at Gravely, in Huntingdonshire. That same month Williams was in the rear turret of his Halifax bound for a raid on Dusseldorf. It was a bright moonlit night, though with thin haze distorting visibility, as he methodically quartered the sky searching for enemy nightfighters. Then, as his crew began their bombing run into the target, Williams saw the red winking flashes of a fighter's guns looming larger from the port quarter, slightly above him. Swinging his guns towards the attacker, Williams loosed several brief bursts – then 'the world fell on top of me.'; a second fighter had curved in from below as the Halifax began its evasion turn, raking the bomber with a stream of cannon shells and tracer bullets.

Williams was hit in the stomach by one cannon shell, and his

66 *Warrant Officer N. F. Williams, CGM, DFM & Bar, RAAF.*

legs and thighs riddled with bullets. Then a further burst, almost simultaneously from the first fighter slashed through the port side of Williams' turret, knocking out one gun and rendering the turret temporarily out of action. Other damage to the bomber included wounding the mid-upper gunner in the head, and rupturing a main petrol tank. Burning fuel spilled along the wing, illuminating the Halifax as a perfect target for any German fighter within range. In great pain, and with his body paralysed below his waist, Williams

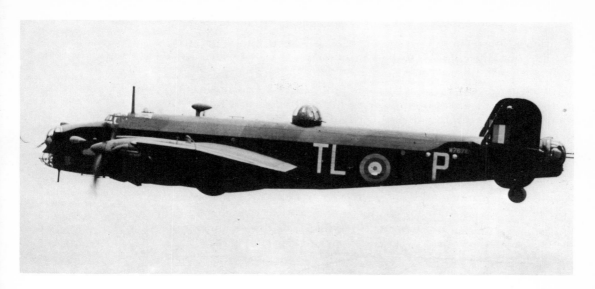

67 Handley Page Halifax W7676, TL-P of 35 Squadron, illustrating the three turrets – nose, tail & mid-upper – fitted to the early versions of this bomber. This particular Halifax was lost over Nuremburg on the night of 28/29 August 1942, when with the Path Finder Force.

continued to give his skipper evasion directions while keeping a lookout for the two fighters. Both Germans returned to the attack in a prolonged series of lightning assaults, and Williams continued directing his skipper; at the same time requesting the bomb aimer to take the place of the wounded mid-upper gunner. As the bomb aimer settled into the upper turret the pair of fighters bore in together from the port beam. Williams told the pilot to go into a steep bank, then as the nearest fighter came into his sight line, gave it a full burst from his guns. The fighter exploded in mid-air, and fell earthwards in a cascade of burning debris.

For the next few minutes the burning Halifax was unmolested so the bomb aimer climbed out of the mid-upper turret and went forward to complete his own job of releasing the bomb load on target. Williams in his part-shattered rear turret began to regain feeling down one thigh and leg, when yet another fighter attack came roaring in from a variety of angles. Eventually the German lined up dead astern for its latest move, bringing it dead into Williams's sights. He waited coolly until the fighter filled his vision, then let it have a full burst. The German passed underneath the tail with Williams's fire following, then fell away shedding chunks of metal until it passed out of vision. At that point the Halifax had been subjected to a total of nearly 40 separate fighter attacks.

As the crew realized the danger had now passed – the wing fire had died down, so the pilot extinguished it in a short dive – they prepared for the return journey. Williams refused to leave his turret until they were well out of enemy-occupied territorial skies, but when he finally agreed to be extricated the turret doors were found to be jammed. Reaching base again the pilot brought the bomber in for a skilful crash-landing, and they had to chop Williams out of the shambles of his turret. Taken immediately to hospital, where he remained for the next two months, Norman Williams was later awarded a Conspicuous Gallantry Medal (CGM) to add to his DFM and Bar; making him Australia's most-decorated NCO airman of 1939-45.

On the night of 15 February 1944, Flight Sergeant G. C. C. Smith, another Australian air gunner, was in the rear turret of a Lancaster bound for Berlin. Smith's aircraft was one of the Path Finder element spearheading a main force attack of almost 900 bombers on the 'Big City'. With a score of operations already under his belt, Smith was no novice, and when, during the final leg towards the objective, he spotted a Messerschmitt Bf 110 nightfighter on the beam, coolly displaying its white and green navigation lights, his immediate reaction was to search the sky for its companion. At this stage of the air war the Luftwaffe often employed its *nachtjäger* in pairs and threes; one acting as decoy to distract the rear gunner, while its companions slid in from a different angle for the kill. In the mid-upper turret Sergeant A. C. 'Nobby' Clarke, was equally anxious to find the 'other bastard', swinging his turret steadily. Smith meanwhile warned his skipper, Flight Sergeant K. P. C. Doyle, of the danger, then lined his sight on the Messerschmitt, waiting for its first move.

68 *Inside a Halifax rear turret. The four .303 Brownings are fitted on their sides; while the single control column is located in a central diamond-shaped cut-out panel. Just above the control stick is the reflector gun sight. Bottom right, adjacent to the seat pad, is the manual rotation crank handle.*

The German, however, finessed the normal tactic of playing decoy, and bore in swiftly at Smith. Yelling over the intercomm to Doyle, 'Corkscrew port, Go, Go, Go . . .', Smith poured 150 rounds straight into the oncoming Bf 110. There was a blinding flash and the Messerschmitt exploded. At the same moment flecked lines of green tracer laced past Smith's turret from below; a Focke Wulf Fw 190 – the 'other bastard' – had made his move, but was off target due to Doyle's immediate response to Smith's call for an evasion corkscrew manoeuvre. Diving fast, Doyle lost the Fw 190, but not before his Lancaster had absorbed considerable damage from both fighters' cannons. One stream of shells had sliced through the rear length of fuselage, shattering the mid-upper turret's hydraulic lines, igniting the escaping oil, and knocking Clarke sideways. Other shells smashed through Smith's turret mechanism and set his stowed parachute bag on fire; while one shell hit Smith in his right ankle, smashing the leg. Clarke, with a fractured left leg, lost his face oxygen mask and was almost unconscious from pain and lack of oxygen.

Doyle, once he felt sure the fighters were nowhere near, called up his crew to check casualties. On hearing nothing from Clarke, the

69 Halifax rear turret after an attack by a Messerschmitt Bf 110 over Berlin on 23 August 1943. Note Monica aerial 'arrow' just below turret.

wireless operator went back, found Clarke on the floor gasping for air, and slipped a spare oxygen lead into the gunner's mouth, then climbed into the turret to keep a lookout for any other fighters. Smith, on hearing his skipper say he would send someone to help him out of his turret, refused the offer, and continued to work his guns by hand; while the navigator dealt with Smith's burning 'chute pack. The Lancaster soon crossed a coastal flak belt and was hit again; two engines going out of commission and having to be feathered. By now the intense cold of the night's rarified air had frozen up Smith's oxygen supply line, and he had taken off his mask to gulp the icy air.

Once clear of the coast, over the sea, Doyle came lower to a warmer altitude, then sent the navigator back to free Smith, whose turret doors had also frozen solid. Chopping away the doors, they spent nearly an hour extricating the rear gunner, whose shattered leg was enmeshed in his ammunition feed belt and lower turret controls. The turret itself was a horrifying sight, 'drenched in blood', to quote a later report. Finally easing Smith out of the shambles they laid him on the fuselage floor and gave him shots of morphia. Doyle meanwhile prepared for an inevitable belly-landing; but the Lancaster's bomb doors refused to close, and the undercarriage was damaged. To protect Smith from the coming crashlanding, the bomb aimer and wireless operator lay on either side of him on the floor, but Doyle set the bomber down smoothly along Woodbridge's long runway for a good landing. The ground crew hacked out the side of the fuselage and removed the two wounded gunners gently. Next day Smith had to undergo amputation of his smashed leg, but was later awarded a CGM for his courage in remaining behind his guns. His reaction to the award was typical, 'If it hadn't been for the skipper, we'd never have got back at all.'

Occasionally there were cases of gunners who stayed at their posts to the bitter end quite unwittingly, and without any aggravation on the part of any enemy. On the night of 27 October 1939 five Whitley bombers of 51 Squadron, temporarily based at Villeneuve in France, were detailed for immediate take-off. Their 'targets' were five major German cities, including Stuttgart, Frankfurt and Munich; while their 'bomb loads' were simply bundles of propaganda leaflets. The met forecast was foul, promising rain, hail, sleet, 7 to 9/10ths cloud with 1,000 feet base, a freezing level at 1,500 feet, and heavy icing anticipated up to 12,000 feet. At that early stage of Bomber Command's war the aircraft had little in the way of adequate oxygen supply points, internal heating, or electrically-heated flying clothing for the crews. Yet all five crews set off cheerfully enough despite the weather prospects. At cruising height, however, the ultra-cold upper air quickly nullified one crew's attempt, and its skipper aborted the sortie and returned to Villeneuve.

The remaining quartet pressed on to their individual objectives – and troubles began to accumulate. One crew reached Stuttgart,

70 *Bumf Bombs. Loading propaganda leaflets in bundles into a Whitley on 12 January 1940. Note Corporal Wop/AG's 'Brass Bullet' arm badge, even on that date.*

released its paper 'bombs', then began its struggle to return to base. With control surfaces coated in inches of ice, frozen instruments, frosted windscreens obliterating vision in any direction, with an outside (and inside) air temperature of minus 38 degrees Centigrade this crew eventually arrived safely after flying virtually blind for more than six hours. A second Whitley also reached Villeneuve, with flak damage, iced controls and instruments, a semi-comatose crew and a sick pilot. The third victim of the weather conditions was a Whitley which reached Frankfurt, dropped its leaflet load, then struggled back with an oxygen-starved crew, iced wings, and a fire in the starboard engine. Finally crash-landing in a French wood, the crew were refused shelter for the night by a nearby farm owner, and spent a frozen night in their aircraft.

The fourth Whitley, bound for Munich, reached the target, lowered the under-belly 'dustbin' turret through which were dropped the bundles of leaflets, then tried to return. Already the fuselage floor internally had snow as a carpet, and now the under-turret froze and refused to retract. Next the starboard engine blew a cylinder head, erupted in flames, and caused the Whitley to descend through dense snow clouds. Soon the port engine faltered. Finally, at some 2,000 feet, with a chain of hills looming ahead, the captain ordered the crew to abandon the aircraft. The front gunner jumped and nearly strangled himself on his intercomm leads, before being released by the navigator. The navigator then jumped; followed by the wireless operator clutching an oxygen bottle which had frozen to his hand, who landed dead centre amongst a herd of indignant French bulls – and broke the world's record for the 100-yards' dash to the nearest fence, in full flying clothing. The pilot, having trimmed the Whitley for a gentle descent angle, then evacuated his aircraft.

Unconscious of the activity 'up front' – his intercomm had failed to convey the bale-out order – Sergeant A. Griffin in the rear turret remained in his seat. Peering somewhat anxiously through frosted perspex, he realized the bomber was descending fairly quickly, and presumed his skipper was trying a forced landing somewhere before that engine fire got worse. There came a severe bump and lurch, then several lesser bumps, and then silence. Hastily evacuating his turret, Griffin made his way up the long fuselage tunnel to check that the rest of the crew were okay – and only then realized that he was all alone! Cut, bruised, and partly suffering from minor burns, Griffin staggered away from the Whitley towards the lights of a nearby village – to be greeted by the rest of his crew who had joined up after landing and trekked to the same village.

Yet another victim of recalcitrant communications and to some extent freakish weather conditions was a very young Lancaster rear gunner, returning from his first operational sortie over Germany. The outward trip had gone well, with no opposition until the target approach leg. Then flak came up in a terrifying hail of shells and

71 *Tail defence. An FN20a four-Browning turret in the tail of Wellington III, X3763, KW-E of 425 ('Alouette') Squadron, RCAF.*

tracers, exploding all around the wallowing bomber. For nearly ten minutes the Lancaster was buffeted and bounced around the sky, but it released its bomb load over the target, then swung out of the flak zone in a fast climbing curve, heading for safer air.

In the rear turret the eighteen-year-old gunner was 'paralysed with fear, and feeling distinctly sick in the guts'. Nothing in his training had prepared him mentally for such an ordeal; while the sight of another Lancaster exploding in mid-air in a huge gout of flame merely added to his terror. Fighting against an almost over-whelming desire to faint, the gunner remembered his skipper's last words before take-off; 'It may become a bit rough over there, but for Christ's sake keep watching for fighters, Smith.[1] I'll take care of anything else'. The Lancaster seemed to have survived the holocaust of flak, and was drumming steadily homewards, so Smith began quartering the skies methodically, over-anxious, with the pedantic seriousness of purpose of the newcomer to ops. Nervously reacting to every change of shadow, Smith saw one shadow deliberately slide into his vision from the port quarter behind – then solidify into a straight-winged silhouette; fighter! Yelling a warning into his microphone, Smith let loose with all four Brownings as the silhouette grew larger, with strings of tracer leaping directly at the rear turret, then rushing past Smith on each side.

The ensuing few minutes were a kaleidoscope of lights, wheeling clouds and moon, cordite stink and rattling; with Smith valiantly trying to keep his seat and still bring his guns to bear. Unbeknown to the gunner, the fighter had done its work only too well. Cannon shells had ripped out most of the pilot's instrument panel, smashed the wireless set, wounded the navigator and knocked him un-conscious, and slashed chunks out of the forward length of fuselage. The port inner engine had been hit badly, putting it out of action, though mercifully without creating any fire – yet. The pilot eventually evaded any further fighter onslaught, then took stock. He had no way to obtain a position fix, his navigator was in no state to help, and the Lancaster was sloppy on the controls. The port inner engine began pluming smoke ominously – he could expect a fire any second. A rough check on the time told him he should be somewhere near the coast, but where? The intercomm was obviously 'out', and to add to his problems he was heading into a sky of dense black cloud which eliminated any hope of guidance from the stars.

Determined to try for home, the pilot set a guessed course north-westwards and struggled with reluctant controls for as long as he could. Then, on the point of physical exhaustion, he realized that the fuel state was almost zero – the fighter must have hit the tanks or the supply lines. The port outer engine grunted to a stop, starved of fuel; then the starboard inner began to slow. He had little choice now. Yelling to the bomb aimer to tell the others, he gave the

[1] 'Smith' is a pseudonym here, at the request of the gunner concerned.

72 *Lancaster B.III, LM418, PG-S of 619 Squadron, RAF, which was destroyed in a crashlanding at Woodbridge on return from the notorious Nuremburg raid of 30/31 March 1944. This view demonstrates clearly the fields of fire afforded to all three gunners in most heavy bombers.*

order to bale out. This was done, and each man made his way to the escape hatch; the navigator, now conscious though still dazed, was helped into his chute and through the hatch by the wireless operator. The mid-upper gunner, on getting the order, climbed down from his turret, made his way back to Smith's rear turret and banged on the doors. Smith later said he had no recollection of this, though the mid-upper gunner was certain his knocking had been acknowledged, after which he had gone forward and baled out.

Smith stayed in his seat, still searching fearfully for fighters, conscientiously remaining on the *qui vive*. Only later – the time lapse is unknown – did Smith begin to 'unwind' and relax, as it seemed clear that they were well out of Luftwaffe range. On receiving nothing over his intercomm, Smith flipped open his rear doors and looked down the fuselage – to his horror he realized he was on his own. Panic set in. Closing the door, he rotated the turret to the beam, having grabbed his parachute pack from its stowed position; then, in the approved trained procedure, back-flipped out of the turret.

Coming to earth at the edge of a small copse, Smith continued to heed his training and made for cover in the copse, where he got rid of his 'chute and harness and buried them as best he could. Then, in inky darkness, he set off to put as much distance as

73 *Lancaster ED413, 'M', after a raid on Oberhausen on 14 June 1943. The rear gunner, Sgt P. F. Hayes, was killed fighting off at least three nightfighters during the bomber's approach run to target.*

possible between him and the copse. For the next 18 hours Smith lay low, avoiding all paths and roads, and snatching sleep in a thick patch of gorse. As darkness approached again he set out in a vaguely northern direction. Near-exhausted, hungry, and dying for a drink of cool, clear water, he came out of a small clump of trees – and nearly tripped over an RAF corporal engaged in the art of gentle wooing with a very blonde WAAF! The astonishment was mutual . . . Smith then learned that for some 18 hours he had successfully 'evaded capture' within two miles of a tiny RAF signals unit near the coastline of Kent.

9. Bale-out

The rear gun turret of a bomber on a night sortie could be the loneliest place in the sky. Encased in a metal and perspex cupola at the extreme end of the fuselage, the rear gunner was almost literally on his own, with only occasional crackling or muted voices bouncing into his earphones to reassure him that the rest of his crew were nearby. Most of his airborne hours were suffered in silence except for the soft hiss of his own oxygen tube when flying high, and the spasmodic creak and groan from his metal surroundings and immediate impedimenta of his trade. At times it took a conscious mental effort to remember that he was not the sole occupant of the aircraft. Every second inside the turret was spent in constant vigilance, searching the surrounding inky blackness methodically, quarter by quarter, for the tell-tale grey shadows which might at any moment solidify into an oncoming German nightfighter. At night the majority of Luftwaffe interceptors favoured initial attacks from the rear or from under the belly of an Allied bomber, thereby placing every rear gunner first in line for elimination.

Flight Sergeant Eric Sanderson, cloistered in the rear turret of his 578 Squadron Halifax on a night in March 1944, was well aware of all these hazards and discomforts. It was the last sortie of his first tour of operations, and he might have been excused for any momentary relaxation in vigilance thinking of the inevitable celebration back at base on his return, to be followed by the customary 'rest' posting to some form of instructional job. If such thoughts crossed Sanderson's mind, he was too experienced to let them interfere with his job. If anything, this being his last 'op', Sanderson was even more than usually alert – he wanted to get back from this one particularly. Then, halfway to the target, Frankfurt, things began to go wrong.

It was Sanderson who first spotted the grey outline of a Junkers Ju88 lining itself up beneath the Halifax. 'Fighter', he yelled over the inter-comm. Immediately his pilot jerked the bomber into a weaving standard corkscrew evasive manoeuvre, but the Ju88 pilot was evidently no novice and knew about corkscrew evasions. Following the twisting bomber, move for move, the nightfighter clung to its intended victim. The Halifax went into a diving turn and half-roll in order to offer possible firing opportunities to either Sanderson or the mid-upper gunner, but the half-roll at full throttle developed into a full roll, leaving the ponderous bomber wallowing helplessly on its back. Snatching this chance the German pilot raked the

74 *A Wellington victim of flak which crashed during a leaflet raid, near Eifel on 23 March 1940.*

Halifax from stem to stern with a stream of cannon shells, and before the pilot had brought the bomber back onto an even keel its wing root was ablaze. The Ju88 then bore in for the kill, but Sanderson's warning gave his skipper time to weave out of the German's path in time. The fire was now spreading rapidly along the wing, and over the inter-comm came the order, 'Jump, jump'.

Sanderson, still searching for the elusive Ju88, heard the rest of his crew acknowledge their skipper's order, 'Mid-upper gone! Navigator gone!... until the pilot, undoubtedly believing he was alone in an empty aircraft, added his personal cryptic farewell. Normally Sanderson should have been one of the first to obey the order. His immediate drill should have been to flip open his turret doors, reach into the fuselage for his stowed parachute pack, clip it on, rotate his turret to the beam, jettison his back doors and – as best he could – do a back-flip out into the darkness. He had other ideas.

Somewhere out there, he was sure, that bloody Junkers was still lurking about, and Sanderson was still determined to fight it if it came in again, and thereby give his friends a further chance of survival. The sky outside his turret was brilliant red at one side where the wing fire was raging, and acrid smoke was now drifting into his turret. It then came to Sanderson that he was literally alone, and very calmly and dispassionately, he decided it was time to go. As he methodically disconnected his inter-comm lead and oxygen pipe, his main thought was one of bitter regret. Throughout a tour studded with dangers his crew had nevertheless always come back. Now – the last op – they had got the chop. It was almost ironic.

Sanderson forced open the turret doors and, raising his knees, swung his body backwards . . . then hung helpless, trapped by some hidden obstacle gripping his legs. The howling slipstream buffeted the breath out of him as he frantically heaved and twisted, half in and half out of the Halifax which was already nosing over into its final blazing dive. Desperately he attempted to heave himself back into the turret in order to find whatever was holding his legs, but he seemed drained of strength. He tried to pull his feet out of his heavy flying boots, held in a vice-like grip inside the cupola, but with half his body hanging loose he could get no purchase or leverage. Suddenly his mood changed from its former passing regret to a black hopelessness of desperation. The doomed Halifax was diving steeply now, and Sanderson knew he was going with it and would die in the instant it exploded into the earth. The rest of the crew had abandoned the bomber at some 15,000 feet, but Sanderson was now trapped at the rear end of a fiercely burning torch of an aircraft fast approaching a mere one thousand feet altitude.

Then blinding inspiration came. It was a slim chance, but he would be dead in a few more seconds anyway, so why not take it? He wrenched the rip-cord of his parachute. The silk shrouds streamed out smoothly, there was a loud crack and a moment of blinding pain throughout his body, then he was free. He had only time to see the canopy of his 'chute billow, and then he was smashing his way through a host of tree branches. It was then that he blacked-out. As consciousness gradually returned, Sanderson realized he was lying on his back in a wood, surrounded by complete blackness and utter silence. His first reaction was 'I'm dead', but as his hearing slowly returned, he heard water trickling somewhere nearby. Then his vision cleared and he could see a winking star high above. He was alive! Checking himself all over for expected fearful injuries, his shoulder hurt (his collar bone was broken), his head was painful, and as he pressed a handful of snow to his face to relieve the pain, he realized that the hand holding the snow was a bloody shrivelled mess of burned flesh. But he was alive. Eventually crawling to a nearby clearing, he saw four German soldiers watching the burning wreckage of his Halifax, R-Robert. Sanderson knew that his extensive burns and injuries ruled out any possibility of

75 *Name, rank and number. An air gunner begins the long wearisome prospect of becoming a 'Kriegie' (prisoner of war).*

evasion, so he hailed the Germans, who, on seeing his parlous state, carried him carefully to the nearest village. Later, in a prison hospital, Eric Sanderson met all his former crew members who had baled out safely and survived intact.

For Flight Sergeant Francis Smith, rear gunner in a Halifax of 58 Squadron, the ultimate use of his silk parachute shroud, even in the last-minute perilous state which succoured Eric Sanderson, was to be denied; yet he survived in circumstances which came as near to the proverbial 'miracle' as most men are ever likely to get. Based in early 1945 at the remote Stornoway base, 58 Squadron was temporarily attached to RAF Coastal Command, employed in anti-shipping sorties and attacks against enemy-occupied coastal installations in Northern waters. Smith's Halifax had just completed one such attack on a German coastal base, and was circling the objective, when Smith asked the mid-upper gunner to swap places for a spell, in order to 'stretch his legs'. As he came forward along the fuselage and squeezed past his fellow gunner, the bomber's captain gave an order to release the photo-flash canister in order to check bomb damage on the target. Smith stopped to give another crew member a hand in manoeuvring the photo-finish into its release 'chute, then began to make his way back to the midships' rest bunk, when the fuselage was lit up by a blinding white explosion of light.

For a few moments there was confusion, with nobody able to understand what had happened. In fact, the photo-flash had detonated prematurely only seconds after its release, and the explosion had torn a wide jagged hole some four feet in width in the floor of the Halifax's rear fuselage. Smith, plugged in to the aircraft intercomm, heard his skipper yell, 'Emergency. Stand by to bale out. Wait till I give the order.' Smith's parachute pack was still in its normal stowage at the rear, and he immediately unplugged from the intercomm and hastened down the dark fuselage to retrieve his 'chute. He had only taken a few steps when he felt himself pitched forward and downwards, helpless to stop himself. Then, just as suddenly, he stopped falling, abruptly, and found himself breathless and being battered by an icy slipstream *outside* the fuselage. As the rushing air slammed him violently against the underside of the bomber, Smith took lightning mental stock of what had happened to him.

Cautiously exploring with his hand, his gloved fingers met jagged metal, and he realized that the hooks on his parachute harness had somehow caught and wedged into the thin duralumin

76 *Ammo tracks. The internal ammunition tracks supplying a Halifax's rear turret.*

fuselage, arresting his headlong plunge through the hole torn out by the explosion. Thousands of feet below him was the open sea, and Smith began to wonder how long it might be before the harness hooks worked loose and dropped him into the black void below. His life was literally hanging on two metal hooks and a short length of webbing strap. With the howling slipstream searing his face into icy numbness, Smith very carefully turned his face around, out of the draught, then slowly raised his hands and got a good grip on the webbing to support himself better, while he thought about his precarious state. At any second the hooks might give. On the other hand, supposing the skipper had ordered the rest of the crew to bale out? He would be alone, tethered to a empty aircraft destined to oblivion, and helpless to avoid certain death.

Up in the Halifax cockpit, however, the pilot had finally sorted things out. All engines were still going strongly, and all controls responded. By then the wireless operator had discovered the hole in the fuselage floor and reported it to the pilot; then said, 'By the way, is Smithy up there with you?' 'Negative. Must be down the back. Hello Smithy, check in.' Receiving no answer, the navigator suggested Smith might have misheard the skipper's standby order and actually baled out. 'Negative again,' reported the other gunner. 'His 'chute's still here, and I didn't give him mine.' The final consensus was that Smith must have been blown out of the bomber by the explosion – a hell of a way to get the chop. Getting a course for England, the pilot turned onto this heading and settled down for the home run.

As the Halifax droned its way across the North Sea, the dangling Smith became numb from the intense cold and unceasing buffeting of the roaring slipstream. After a while his mind dimly registered the fact that the aircraft was still flying steadily, not diving to destruction, and a faint hope began to filter through his numbed senses. *If* the hooks still held, and *if* the 'Hallie' reached base OK, and *if* his skipper brought off his normal smooth landing, there *might* be a chance. Then his brain registered the next, obvious thought. Landing! 'My God,' he thought, 'I'll be wiped off on the runway when she lands!' For a moment blind panic hit him and he shouted at the top of his lungs, 'Skipper, I'm here! Smithy! I'm caught underneath! Give me a hand somebody'. It was a cry of sheer, hopeless despair. His mind slid away from the horrifying thought into a semi-delirium.

How long he hung there he had no idea. Then came a change in the note of the droning engines above him, and dimly he realized that the cruel, buffeting wind had lessened. He was vaguely conscious of movement beneath the wings – the wing flaps and under-carriage were being lowered. He braced himself for death, then mercifully lapsed into near-unconsciousness. Suddenly it was silent, he heard voices, then shouts, felt strong hands gripping him and relieving him of the intolerable strain on his arms and body, then

an exquisite softness beneath him as he was lowered to the grass verge alongside the runway. Only days later after solicitous hospital care had coaxed warmth and life back into his frozen body did Smith learn what had happened. Dangling at full height beneath the fuselage, his toes had cleared the ground by mere inches as his captain had brought the Halifax in for a perfect arrival.

They told him later that he had hung beneath the bomber for two and a half hours, from the Norwegian coast, across the North Sea, until landing at the first available emergency airfield on the home coast. They also told him that, although he had no recollection of it, just as his anxious fellow crew members eased his body onto a stretcher, he had mumbled through cracked, frost-bitten lips, 'Good show, Skip', before lapsing into a blissful coma.

If Flight Sergeant John Vivash, a mid-upper gunner in a Halifax of 466 Squadron, RAAF, had any thoughts about his parachute, they were probably similar to most aircrews' thoughts on that subject; a deeply felt hope that he would never need to use it, but if he did, a fervent wish that the thing would hold his weight for the 'big drop'. The chunky Australian's wish was amply fulfilled on the night of 4 November 1944. Piloted by a fellow Australian, Flight Lieutenant Joe Herman, Vivash's aircraft left base at Driffield that evening, bound for Bochum in the Ruhr. Twice on the approach to their

77 External view of a Halifax rear turret, showing the Browning guns, on their sides with breech covers raised preparatory to linking up ammunition belts.

target the crew had suffered searchlight coning yet managed to evade punishment from the German flak due to Joe Herman's skilful manoeuvring. Running into a fierce barrage of flak soon after, Herman experienced a strong premonition of imminent trouble, and called up each crew member, suggesting that they should clip on their parachute packs; though the tall Queenslander was too occupied 'up front' to follow his own advice for the moment.

The bombing run itself went smoothly, all bombs were released over the objective, and Herman thankfully turned westwards to start the return leg, out of the menacing flak and searchlight defence belts. Once on course for home he gently let down from 18,000 feet to 10,000 feet in accordance with his pre-briefing instructions, but had hardly begun his gentle descent when the Halifax shuddered violently – hit by flak in the fuselage just behind the wing's rear spar. Instinctively, based on long experience, Herman immediately swung his aircraft to port, but was hit twice more, in the wings. Both wing fuel tanks were ruptured and within seconds the Halifax was afire along its whole wingspan. Realizing that it could only be minutes at most before the aircraft fell apart, the pilot yelled 'Bale out, bale out' over the intercomm; meanwhile holding the stricken bomber as steady as possible to let his crew get away safely. In the mid-upper turret 'Irish' Vivash (his unlikely nickname in the crew) had suffered a shard of flak deep in one leg, and painfully wormed his way out of his turret. Finally inside the fuselage Vivash started crawling forward towards the escape hatch, noticing his pilot leaving his seat to find his own 'chute, stowed in the flight engineer's crew station. At that moment the Halifax's starboard wing folded back with a blinding flash of burning petrol and the bomber flicked onto its back and then began to spin down.

The explosion of the wing root was the last Vivash remembered; his next conscious memory was feeling a draught of cold air on his face and a not unpleasant sensation of falling. He had no recollection of operating his ripcord, yet above his head the silken canopy was fully deployed, swinging him in long gentle arcs through the black air. Suddenly the see-saw swinging motion abruptly stopped and he realized he was falling straight down, still supported by his parachute, but with a puzzling heavy feeling in his legs. Reaching down with one hand Vivash had a shock – he was not alone! Remarkably calm in such circumstances, Vivash later recalled his exact reactions. Firstly he called, 'Is there anyone else around here?' A voice he recognized replied, 'Yes. Me. I'm here, hanging on to you.' 'Is that you, Joe?' queried Vivash. 'Yes, but I haven't got a 'chute, Irish. I seem to have bumped into you on my way down.'

The explosion in the Halifax had blown Herman and Vivash clear, but while the gunner had his parachute deploy and begin to carry him safely down, Herman had no 'chute. Falling from some 17,000 feet, the pilot was conscious but resigned to death, when by an astounding fluke of coincidence he had bumped into

Vivash as the latter reached the top of one swinging arc of his original descent. Sheer unconscious reflex action made Herman wrap his arms around the 'object' he'd collided with – Vivash's legs. Both men were descending on one parachute. Minutes later Herman saw some tree-tops rushing up towards him and had just time to yell a warning. Then he thudded onto the ground, and Vivash landed heavily on top of his pilot.

Once both men had recovered their breath and senses, Herman realized that his gunner's weight had broken two of his ribs, but apart from a tattered uniform and many cuts, slashes and bruises, he was otherwise intact – and amazingly, alive. Turning to his inadvertent 'saviour' Vivash, Herman ripped up strips of parachute silk and bound the gunner's leg wounds; then both men began planning how best to evade capture. Four days later, when well en route to Holland, they were made prisoners. Both men survived the war and returned to their native Australia, but tragically, John 'Irish' Vivash was killed in a road accident a few years later.

10. Tales from the Bombers

If a preponderance of publicity has usually been accorded to the air gunners in heavy bombers, it is merely in relative proportion to the overall total of gunners employed in such aircraft when compared with all other forms of multi-crew operational aircraft. Patently, in such 'heavies' as the Lancaster, Halifax, Stirling, B-17 Fortress or B-24 Liberator, more air gunners were carried per crew than any other crew category. By day the gunners were often a bomber formation's only effective defence against enemy air opposition; by night, when the bomber was (usually) alone, without the comforting back-up of other formation gunnery, the air gunner was a crew's sole shield. Over Europe, by 1943, nose gun turrets in RAF bombers were seldom occupied, or were deleted. Head-on attacks by night were relatively few, and defence relied heavily upon mutual co-ordination between the mid-upper and rear gunners who between them commanded a wide field of fire. The weak spot remained under the belly, and – in the RAF particularly – few bombers were fitted with any form of ventral turret. The 'kick in the gut' was a favoured mode of Luftwaffe attack by 1944-5; often by fighters with *Schrägemusik* armament – upward-slanting cannon batteries in Messerschmitt Bf 110s and other *nachtjäger*.

The 'adventures' – to use a contemporary expression beloved by journalists – of bomber gunners were myriad. Incredible escapes from death, near-miraculous survivals in the face of overwhelming odds, unbelievable quirks of fate or circumstance which leave a 'spectator's' credibility stunned. Nor were such experiences entirely exceptional. For every individual's story related here, probably another hundred similar stories could be told. Sift through any bomber squadron's operational record and the perilous position of the air gunner is clearly evident; with crew after crew returning with a shattered rear turret and – so often – a dead gunner inside. The bulk of Luftwaffe attacks came from behind or below, with the gun turrets as the German fighter pilot's first target. Once the turrets were knocked out a bomber was at the fighter's mercy. It was this stark fact that kept most gunners in their turrets, even when wounded, with only half a turret left around them. As long as they had at least one gun still operative, they continued the fight. Even without guns, many gunners continued to act as a warning 'outpost', advising the pilot on evasion manoeuvres as each fighter attack bore in; sitting, defenceless, directly in front of the fighters' cannons and machine guns.

The accounts which follow are simply individual examples of gunners' experiences; each illustrating some aspect of the deadly war fought by the air gunner. Though each story applies to one individual, the overall pattern was all too common in other gunners' experiences. Raw courage is not the prerogative of any particular species of the human race, and in mortal combat race, creed or origin is irrelevant.

On the night of 31 August 1943, Berlin was the target for the Short Stirlings of 75 Squadron, seven of which failed to return. Among the crews of those seven Stirlings were nineteen New Zealanders, one of whom, Sergeant (later, Warrant Officer) J. S. Grant, survived by the merest chance. An ex-farmer who had initially enlisted in the RNZAF in February 1942, Grant gave this account of that night's experiences:

On reaching the target area we found plenty of enemy action. The whole sky was alive with searchlights and anti-aircraft fire and fighters. Cruising in on our bombing run at 15,000 feet, we had to pass through a heavy barrage of flak and a screen of night fighters. With the bomb doors open and on a straight and level course, we were slowed by a shell which hit the port inner engine, and we made a sitting target for the fighters. Just as we were about to drop our bombs a Ju88 began to tail us and, when the bombs had gone, closed in with guns blazing.

I returned the fire but was unable to give instructions for evasion as I was having trouble with the intercomm. Meanwhile the mid-upper gunner was firing at another enemy aircraft to starboard and managed to drive it off. Then another attacked from the port beam and succeeded in putting his turret out of action. The Junkers at our rear scored many hits on the fin and tailplane and knocked out my two right-hand guns, wounding me in the right arm and shoulder, while my face was peppered with shrapnel. Before I could get my remaining guns to bear this fighter closed in on our slow-moving aircraft for the kill.

I again opened fire and the enemy machine belched forth a cloud of smoke and flame and disappeared. We were further attacked and one fighter came up from below and raked us with fire from stem to stern, completely crippling our aircraft and putting my turret out of action. I had again been wounded and was cut off from the rest of the crew. My intercomm was by this time completely useless but I managed to repair it enough to hear what was going on. The crew thought I had been killed during the attacks, but after I had signalled by flashing my lights the wireless operator freed me from my turret.

We had been flying for about an hour when we ran short of fuel and were ordered to abandon aircraft. On taking my parachute out of its stowage I found it had been shot to pieces, so I was forced to watch the rest of the crew bale out and sit waiting for the crash, which came on the top of some high hills. I managed to scramble out of the burning machine and crawled away and went to sleep, only to be awakened some six hours later by a German search party.

78 *Stark evidence of the effect of cannon fire on the rear turret of Stirling 'O-Orange' of 75 (NZ) Squadron, after a raid on Duisburg, 26 April 1943.*

For Flight Sergeant Nick Alkemade, a 115 Squadron Lancaster rear gunner, the night of 23 March 1944 was just another op. His fifteenth, and the half-way mark of his operational tour. The target was the 'Big City' – Berlin – so he knew he could expect heavy flak and night fighter opposition. The Lancaster left Witchford on time and settled on track across the coast, with Alkemade and his fellow mid-upper gunner steadily scanning the sky around them. Reaching the last leg of the outward trip, the Lancaster began

79 *Lancaster B.II (Hercules engines) DS771, which served with 426 Squadron and was eventually lost over Stuttgart on 15/16 March 1944.*

encountering flak, and the gunners increased their vigilance. Then came the bombing run, threading a path through fierce shell-bursts which seemed to surround them, and a lattice-work of probing searchlights; while below could be seen the 'brew-up' of burning incendiaries punctuated by bomb blasts. Finally, thankfully, the bombs were released, aiming point photo taken, and the skipper could at last turn away from the immediate danger zone and seek safety in quieter air.

It was now nearly midnight, with the Lancaster about to settle on its return trip – when Alkemade's world seemed to fall apart. Without warning the whole aircraft shuddered violently and reared as a Junkers 88 gave it a broadside of cannon and machine gun fire; slashing along the whole length of fuselage and ripping open the starboard wing. An instant explosion of burning fuel lit up the sky around Alkemade's turret, and hungry flames began eating their way rearwards threatening to engulf him externally. Within seconds his pilot's voice came through his ear phones. 'Sorry boys, can't hold her. Bale out, bale out!' Knowing that seconds counted if his skipper was to have any chance, as the last man to leave in any crew evacuation, Alkemade acknowledged the order, 'Rear gunner gone'; then he rotated his turret facing aft, opened his back doors, and twisted round to grab his stowed parachute pack.

The sight which greeted him made him recoil. The whole internal fuselage was a tunnel of roaring flames, wind-driven with a blowtorch intensity, fed by the slip-stream howling through the shattered metal skin. Nick's face and wrists were instantly scorched and the rubber face mask of his helmet began to melt. He could see his parachute pack was already burning. Instinctively he retreated back into his turret and pulled the doors closed. With his brain racing, and feeling heat on the doors pressed against his back, Alkemade made his decision – a clean death rather than being shrivelled in burning petrol and oil. Hand-rotating his turret to a beam, he pushed himself backwards through the doors and plummetted down in the night sky. He had 'jumped' at some 18,000 feet height – more than three miles high – with only his parachute harness.

He dropped head-first, almost in the drill position of 'attention', but felt no falling sensation; just coolness and peacefulness after the vivid horror of the burning Lancaster. No condensed past life 'paraded' before him; only a calm thought, 'If this is dying, it's not at all strange'. His only concession to reality was the decision not to look down at the earth – let death come unexpectedly.

Just over three hours later Alkemade regained consciousness. He was lying on his back, in snow, in a wood of pine trees. Far above him he could see a star. His mind refused to believe. He wriggled his toes, flexed his fingers – they worked! 'Jesus Christ, I'm alive!' was his first reaction. He explored his body further – some cuts, bruises, burns, but he was in one piece. Rummaging in the pocket of his Irvin

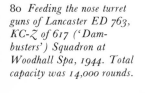

80 *Feeding the nose turret guns of Lancaster ED 763, KC-Z of 617 ('Dambusters') Squadron at Woodhall Spa, 1944. Total capacity was 14,000 rounds.*

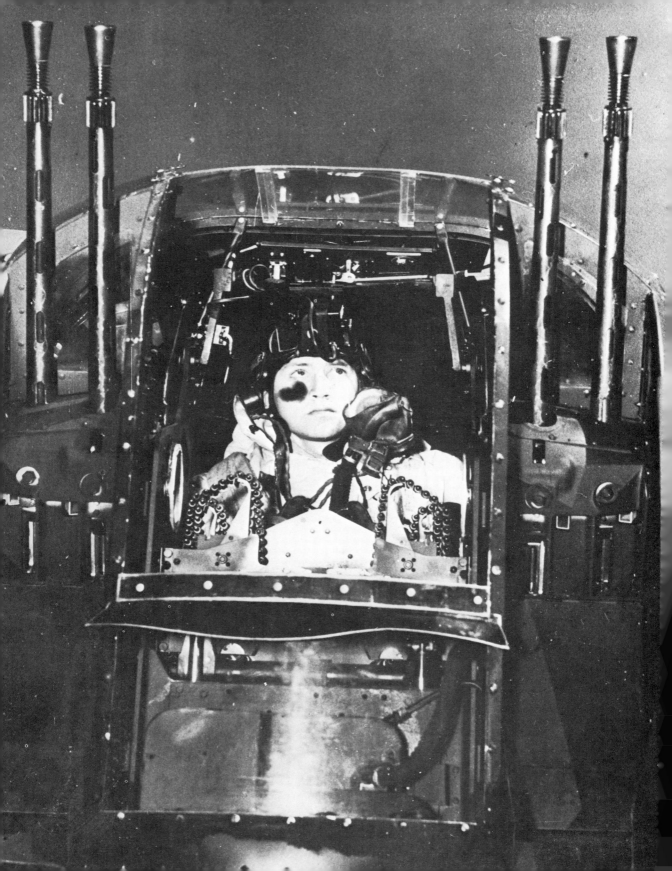

81 *Lancaster rear gunner.*
The centre perspex panel has
been removed for better
vision. Note ammunition
belts feeding guns from
centre.

suit, he took out his watch – still working and showing the time to be 3.10 am. He found his cigarettes and lit one, pondering how all this could be real. Minutes later he stood up, and immediately crumpled to the ground again; one leg was unable to take his weight, probably twisted. His flying boots were gone, the legs of his flying suit charred, but his parachute harness was still in place. He took the harness off and dropped it in the snow – then realized that the snow was at most eighteen inches deep, and only here among the trees. Outside the copse the ground was dry.

Reconstruction of his fall later – he had no recollection of the final moments – showed that Alkemade had plunged into the tops of some highly-sprung pine tree branches, which had let him down relatively gently into the shallow snow drift. His twisted leg and general state precluded any attempt at evasion of capture, so Nick blew the whistle attached to his jacket lapel to attract attention to him. Soon a torch shone in his face. His captors, German equivalents to the British Home Guard, first robbed him of his cigarettes, then dragged him like a sack to a nearby cottage. Later some Gestapo men arrived and took him by car to Maschede, where he received medical attention.

His interrogation next morning sought mainly to establish the location of his (presumed) parachute, but all Alkemade could do was to repeat that he hadn't used it. Understandably disbelieving, his captors only became convinced of the truth of Alkemade's incredible escape from death when his parachute harness was retrieved and examined. Had he used his 'chute, the lift webs which extend when the parachute opens would have torn away their restraining stitches; Alkemade's were still intact. As proof of his unaided fall from three miles up, the German authorities later presented Alkemade with a signed, witnessed testimony at a parade of RAF prisoners of war at Stalagluft III, Sagan. Final proof had been the discovery of his burned-out 'chute, in its correct stowage, in the wreckage of his Lancaster.

Sergeant J. L. Loudon was rear gunner of a Halifax crew of 158 Squadron in early 1943, and his crew were one of 24 from the squadron detailed to attack Essen on the night of 25 July. The main force, benefiting from the use of 'Window' anti-radar foil, was largely unscathed by the German defences; but Loudon's crew were late in getting away from the unit base at Lissett, leaving them in the unenviable naked position of a 'straggler' and easy prey for the enemy night fighters. In Loudon's own words;

> We had made a successful attack on Hamburg the night before but on the return flight our aircraft developed engine trouble, and an emergency landing was made at Catfoss. After de-briefing at Lissett the skipper (Sgt K. R. Larkin) and myself returned to Catfoss to attend to the aircraft. We had not expected to be back on operations that evening, but a

82 *Halifax HR868 of 51 Squadron, Snaith after a sortie to Frankfurt, 20 December 1944; merely part of further extensive damage caused by nightfighters.*

message came through from the squadron informing us to return as soon as our aircraft was ready. This we did and, on landing, were told that Essen was the target. We had little time to spare and it was not long before we were bombed up and airborne again.

We seemed to be way behind the rest of the squadron, and I suppose we were about half-way across the North Sea when the troubles started. The mid-upper gunner was complaining about feeling unwell, and the navigator was having difficulty with readings from his instruments, and to cap it all *Gee* and *Monica* failed.

We had just crossed the northern tip of Holland, over Dan Helder, when the skipper said he could see what could be the target as there was a substantial fire in the direction of Essen. I completed a search of the sky above and leaned forward in order to look below. There, pointing up at around forty-five degrees, was a night fighter, probably a Ju88. I went to switch on my intercomm to give warning, and at the same time went to fire my guns. In that time the fighter struck, and I saw and felt a hail of cannon shells strike the belly of our aircraft.

We immediately pitched forward, as if the skipper had been hit and had slumped forward over the controls. We had a full bomb load, and flames were pouring past me from the engines and forward compartments. There was no word from anyone from the moment we were hit. I was completely uninjured and decided to bale out. I carried my parachute in the turret, although the normal stowage was in the rear fuselage. This probably saved my life, as opening the turret doors into the fuselage would have let in the flames. I swung my turret to beam and was whipped out of the aircraft by the slipstream, damaging my left leg which was caught underneath the turret seating. It finally came free, minus a boot. The parachute harness had also broken loose and the pack was following me down. Somehow I managed to refix the clips properly – luck was still with me – and a few minutes later I landed in the soft dug earth of a garden, just missing a house.

The owner, a Dutchman, took me in and disposed of my parachute but indicated that he could not give me further shelter. I trudged down a road, hiding in ditches whenever German patrols came by, but three or four hours later I walked smack into two German soldiers. In a way I was not too sorry as my left leg was paining me and I was suffering from shock. After medical treatment I was transported to Amsterdam gaol, where I was told my crew had died and would be accorded a proper military funeral.

The value of silk-smooth co-ordination and understanding between a bomber captain and his gunners was borne out in every engagement with Luftwaffe night fighters. Given an evasion manoeuvre instruction from the rear or mid-upper gunner, a pilot immediately reacted accordingly, and – usually – saved his crew and aircraft from certain destruction. Two raid reports illustrate the effectiveness of such crew teamwork. The first was written by Warrant Officer J. A. R. Coulombe, the skipper of a Lancaster B.II of 426 Squadron RCAF ('Thunderbirds'), based at Linton-on-Ouse and referring to his part in a raid on Berlin on 2 December 1943.

83 *A Lancaster rear gunner about to get grey hairs, as a 500 lb HE bomb from another Lancaster plunges down. In the event it missed – by inches.*

While over the target this aircraft was coned by 50-70 searchlights from 2024 to 2029 hours, during which time we were attacked five times by e/a (enemy aircraft) and damaged by flak. The MU/AG first sighted a Ju88 on the port quarter down at 400 yards range and gave combat manoeuvre corkscrew port. The fighter immediately broke off his attack. No exchange of fire by either aircraft. The second attack developed from starboard quarter down and MU/AG saw e/a at 400 yards, so gave combat manoeuvre corkscrew starboard. Again fighter immediately discontinued his attack and broke off at port beam down. No exchange of fire. The third attack came from the port quarter down at 400 yards range. Again MU/AG gave combat manoeuvre corkscrew port and e/a broke off his attack to starboard beam down. Fourth attack developed from starboard quarter down at 400 yards range and MU/AG once again gave combat manoeuvre corkscrew starboard and again the fighter discontinued his attack and broke away port beam down.

The fifth and last attack developed from port quarter down at 200 yards and MU/AG gave combat manoeuvre again corkscrew port and at the same time opened fire. E/a came in to 60 yards range and broke away to port beam above, giving MU/AG a sitting target. Tracer appeared to enter belly of e/a; sparks and tracer were seen to ricochet off fighter which dived steeply and was lost to view. During this attack our aircraft sustained damage to port inner engine and the R/T was rendered u/s (unserviceable). The rear gunner was completely blinded by the blue master and other searchlights throughout these five attacks. During all these attacks an Me109 was sitting off at 1,000 yards dropping white fighter flares. Just as the Ju88 opened fire on his last attack an Fw190 was seen by the pilot and flight engineer off on the port bow up at 400 yards coming in for an attack. The cannon fire from the Ju88 caused the FW to break off his attack to the port beam and down at 100 yards range. He was not seen again. The MU/AG claims this Ju88 as a probable. The port tyre, port outer tank and hydraulic system were damaged.

The second example of gunner-pilot co-ordination came from another Linton-based Canadian squadron, 408 ('Goose') Squadron. The unit diary gives the following rather prosaic description of attacks on Lancaster B.II, 'S-Sugar', piloted by Warrant Officer 2 J. D. Harvey during a raid on Berlin on the night of 27 January 1944:

The e/a (identified by rear gunner, Flight Sergeant S. E. Campbell as an Me110) was first sighted below and slightly to port, range 600 yards, commencing to attack; Campbell instructed the pilot to turn port towards dark side of sky. The fighter appeared to be trying to position himself to fire rockets. The rear gunner opened fire at 300 yds with long bursts of approximately 300 rounds. He observed his tracer entering the e/a's starboard wing, hitting the engine and knocking off one of the rockets. The fighter broke off down to port, and the rear gunner instructed the pilot to climb starboard, do a banking search, then resume course. The rear gunner again sighted the e/a right below at a range of 300 yds and opened fire with another long burst of 300 rounds, his tracer entering rear of fighter's cockpit. A large blue flash appeared in the cockpit and every light came on. The Me started to weave, going over to port quarter down and back again underneath bomber and commencing to attack with all his lights on. The rear gunner again opened fire with a long burst of 300 rounds, his tracer entering fighter's cockpit; the Me caught fire, rolled over and went down out of control, disappearing beneath the clouds with flames completely enveloping fuselage. This was seen by the rear gunner, MU/AG and WAG. Then a glow appeared beneath the clouds, which was assumed to be the fighter hitting the ground.

Successes in the nightly gunners-*v*-Luftwaffe mortal battle depended to a very large extent on the element of surprise in attack, and constant vigilance in defence. It has been estimated that almost 90 per cent of Allied bombers over Germany throughout the intensive 1943-5 assaults went virtually unmolested by German fighters; yet of the other 10 per cent almost half were brought down by *nachtjäger*. Be that as it may, the vital need for every air gunner to be ever-alert, from take-off to landing, was crucial. Take the case of Halifax 'K-King' of 429 ('Bison') Squadron RCAF, based at Leeming, and attacking the Krupps works at Essen on the night of 26 March 1944. Its pilot, Flight Sergeant S. Puskas reported afterwards;

Attacked by three unidentified aircraft believed to be single-engined at 2249 hours. The first indication of attack came when the rear gunner, Sergeant W. Faulkner, saw yellow tracer coming from both quarters and dead astern. He immediately ordered the captain to corkscrew starboard and at the same time opened fire. From then on the Halifax was attacked more or less continuously until 2320 hours when the captain was able to resume course.

No searchlights were in evidence at the time of combat but two fighter flares were dropped dead astern of the bomber just before. There were no other signs of imminent attack. Following one long burst from the rear gunner a bright explosion appeared in the sky, and the captain, engineer, mid-under look-out and rear gunner saw an aircraft fall earth-wards and end in a flash on the ground. The mid-upper gunner was in the under-blister[1] at the time and the wireless operator/air gunner, Sergeant W. R. Wilson, went over to the mid-upper turret. A few seconds after getting in he saw tracer coming from the starboard beam and, ordering the captain to corkscrew starboard, opened fire in the direction of the tracer. The enemy aircraft moved round to the star-board quarter, still firing, when the rear gunner joined the mid-upper in firing a long burst. Suddenly a burst of yellow flame appeared, followed by a red glow and the outline of a single-engined aircraft as it dived, and a few seconds later was seen burning on the ground. Both enemy aircraft are claimed as destroyed.

[1]At this time some Halifax bombers were fitted with a two-gun under-blister 'turret'; most were removed when H2S radar became available and replaced the item.

In stark contrast were the increasingly successful 'mass' victories being claimed by German night fighters from early 1944, particularly those aircraft fitted with 'Slanting Music' *(Schrägemusik)* upward-firing twin 20 mm cannons, using no tracer ammunition. Piloted by a veteran, this new breed of *nachtjäger* exacted a heavy toll of the unprotected (from below) RAF bombers. One such *'experte'* was Major Prinz Heinrich zu Sayn-Wittgenstein, commander of *Nachtjagdgeschwader* Nr 2. On the night of 21 January 1944, the RAF despatched a total of 648 bombers – virtually 70 per cent of its average available first-line strength in bombers – to attack Magdeburg, south-west of Berlin. Fifty-six of these failed to return, and German night fighters claimed more than 40 of this casualty figure.

Wittgenstein, at that date the Luftwaffe's highest-scoring night fighter pilot, with 79 *luftsiegen* credited, took off in his Junkers Ju88, with his radar operator Feldwebel Ostheimer. It was to be his last

84 *Another victim of 'friendly' bombs – Liberator B.VI, KK320, 'V-Victor' of 37 Squadron (Sqn Ldr L. C. Saxby) after a raid against Monfalcone, Northern Italy on 16 March 1945. Hit by two bombs by a higher Liberator, one of which demolished the upper turret – fortunately unoccupied at that moment – the Lib was flown safely back to base, 300 miles away.*

sortie. Ostheimer's combat report for this fateful patrol illustrates only too well the comparative ease with which an experienced fighter crew could cut a swathe through any bomber stream:

At about 2200 hours I picked up the first contact on my search equipment. I passed the pilot directions and a little later the target was sighted – a Lancaster. We moved into position (below) and opened fire, and the aircraft immediately caught fire in the left wing.[1] It went down at a steep angle and started to spin. Between 2200 and 2205 hours the bomber crashed and went off with a violent explosion: I watched the crash. Again we searched. At times I could see as many as six aircraft on my radar. After some further directions the next target was sighted: again a Lancaster. Following the first burst from us there was a small fire, and the machine dropped back its left wing and went down in a vertical dive. Shortly afterwards I saw it crash; it was some time between 2210

[1] Most German pilots deliberately avoided firing into a bomber's belly, because of the danger of the bomb load exploding; preferring to strike in the wing-roots and wing fuel tanks.

85 *Halifax HR837, NP-F of 158 Squadron after a raid on Cologne on 29 June 1943. The mid-upper gunner (seen here in his seat) escaped death by inches when a 'friendly' 1,000 lb bomb hit his aircraft.*

and 2215 hours. When it crashed there were heavy detonations, most probably its bomb load.

After a short interval we again sighted a Lancaster. There was a long burst of fire and the bomber ignited and went down. I saw it crash some time between 2225 and 2230 hours; exact time is not known. Immediately afterwards we saw yet another four-motored bomber; we were in the middle of the so-called 'bomber stream'. After one firing pass this bomber went down in flames; at about 2240 hours I saw the crash.

Yet again I had a target on my search equipment. After a few directions we again sighted a Lancaster, and after one attack it caught fire in the fuselage. The fire then died down, so we moved into position for a fresh attack. We were again in position and Major Wittgenstein was ready to fire when, in our own machine, there were terrible explosions and sparks. It immediately caught fire in the left wing and began to go down. As I heard this the canopy above my head flew away, and I heard on the intercomm a shout, *Raus!* I tore off my oxygen mask and helmet and was then hurled out of the machine. After a short time I opened my parachute and landed east of the Hohengöhrener Dam, near Schönhausen.

Wittgenstein's body was discovered in the wreck of his Ju88 next day – victim of a belly-shot from one of two air gunners who claimed Ju88s in that area at that time, or possibly a Mosquito night escort fighter.

In the closing months of the bomber assault on Germany, Allied crews began meeting some of the desperate measures employed by the Luftwaffe in its last-ditch efforts to protect the Fatherland. Among these weapons were several designs of jet-powered fighters;

86 *Devastating effect of combined cannon fire from two Focke Wulf Fw190s on this Lancaster over Cologne on 28 June 1943. The whole turret (and gunner) was chopped off.*

sleek, deadly fighters capable of speeds far in excess of anything encountered by Allied air gunners throughout the war. The initial impact of a Luftwaffe jet interceptor on any air gunner was to shock him – the sheer speed of a jet baffled his senses and crumbled the lessons hard-won by dint of long experience in bomber-fighter combat. Nevertheless, such an adversary was not immortal. They could be caught, and destroyed. It needed hyperfast reactions and instinctive gunnery, but it could be done. Proof lay in the various successes achieved by some gunners on meeting their first jet fighter.

In April 1945 Ted Beswick was the mid-upper gunner of Lancaster QR-Y of B Flight, 61 Squadron, stationed at Skellingthorpe. On the afternoon of 9 April, at 1741 hrs, his Lancaster, in the leading Vic of a formation of 55 bombers, had just released its bomb load over the U-Boat yards at Hamburg when the Luftwaffe struck:

We had just left the target when suddenly the flak ceased and I saw several black specks in the sky behind us, growing larger every second and coming down on us at incredible speed. As I watched the Lancaster behind us, piloted by Flying Officer Greenfield, suddenly reared its nose up, burst into flames, then exploded. Out of this cloud of smoke and debris appeared a Messerschmitt 262 jet fighter, which continued its attack on us. Jimmy Huck, our rear gunner, immediately opened fire. I could not depress my guns low enough to add to his stream of bullets, but I yelled to the pilot over the intercomm to corkscrew like hell to port! This brought the Me262 up over the port fin and rudder and I could clearly see its pilot. I got him fair and square in my sight and kept the triggers down, following him as he overhauled us. Then, as he was abeam, I and the rest of the crew saw black smoke begin to belch back from the cockpit area and the Me's nose pitched over in a vertical dive down out of sight.

Incidentally, this was not the end of our troubles, for we then discovered that we had a 1000 lb bomb hung-up in the bomb bay. Over the sea we tried to get rid of it but could not dislodge it until we landed when the shock of landing did the trick. Unfortunately by this time we were on the ground and could clearly hear it rattling around, live, inside the bomb bay. We turned off the runway and held there while the armourers came running to us. They rigged a winch inside the aircraft and dropped cables through apertures in the fuselage floor. The bomb doors were then wedged open just enough for an armourer to get an arm through, make the bomb 'safe', and attach winch cables. Then they lowered it down. We may have had a 'shaky-do' that day but afterwards our hats went off to those armourers!

German jet interceptor opposition to the Allied bomber tidal waves reached its peak in March-April, 1945; the last desperate attempts to prevent an inevitable collapse of Hitler's vaunted Thousand Year Reich. By then almost all Allied bombing raids were flown by day, such was the aerial superiority enjoyed by Allied airmen. On the morning of 31 March 1945 a force of 428 bombers were despatched by the RAF to destroy the Blohm & Voss ship-building yards at Hamburg; an important centre of U-boat construction. Of these nearly half came from the all-Canadian No. 6 Group, RCAF, including Lancasters and Halifaxes representing every one of the Group's 14 squadrons. The spearhead Pathfinder and other Lancaster formations became heavily engaged by at least 30 Messerschmitt Me262 jets over the target area, but had plentiful fighter escort protection and lost few bombers to the flashing Me262 assaults. At the rear of the stream, however, a gaggle of Canadian Lancasters, ten minutes late over target and thus without escort, suffered heavily. For some five minutes of non-stop assaults the Canucks lost five Lancasters (three other 6 Group aircraft had already fallen victims to fighter attacks); totting up a total of 78 individual attacks, with 28 crews later reporting actual engagements. Canadian gunners

87 *Literally 'getting the chop' – a Lancaster which returned without gunner or turret from Germany after being hit by another Lancaster's bombs. Note severed ammunition belts and hydraulic pipelines.*

88 *Flak tore away this Mitchell bomber's tail turret.*

redressed the balance to some extent by claiming four Me262s destroyed, three probables, and four others damaged.

Of the eight RCAF Lancaster squadrons, No. 433 ('Porcupine') was probably the most heavily engaged; with seven of its ten crews being attacked, and fighting 16 actual engagements. A pair of Me262s bore in towards Squadron Leader P. D. Holmes' aircraft simultaneously from the rear and port quarters. Warrant Officer E. J. Ash, in the rear turret, opened up at the first jet, then was joined by his mid-upper (WO V. M. Ruthig) in converging fire at the second. Their combined tracer splashed the Me262 in the wing, engines and nose, and it broke away, scattering metal debris and pluming smoke as it plumetted downwards. Ruthig then coolly directed his skipper in necessary evasive action during five further attacks, and was later awarded a DFC. Another 'Porcupine' crew, captained by Flying Officer D. Pleiter, whose gunners were Flight Sergeants C. H. Stokes and M. A. Graham, claimed one jet as probably destroyed.

89 *Bristol Blenheim IV, with the later, improved Bristol mid-upper gun turret – having lower profile and twin .303 Brownings – after a daylight 'Rhubarb' sweep over occupied France, early 1941.*

An aircraft of 431 ('Iroquois') Squadron, piloted by Flying Officer E. G. Heaven, was the focal point for the combined onslaught of three Messerschmitts. In the rear turret Flight Sergeant Bill Kuchma lined his sights on the first at 700 yards and waited until it was a mere 50 yards away before ceasing his fire; at which point the jet veered crazily to starboard, trailing smoke and debris, and fell away. A second later its complete tail assembly tore away and the forward section tumbled head over heels down into the clouds. Of the other two one was sent packing with a thin banner of smoke pouring behind it.

Another Me262 was sent down in flames by the combined firepower of a 428 ('Ghost') Squadron bomber's gunners (Flight Sergeants R. C. Casey and A. E. Vardy); while Flight Sergeants C. K. Howes and S. J. Robinson, in a 424 ('Tiger') Squadron aircraft successfully countered two simultaneous attacks. Howes engaged one jet on the starboard quarter but had all four of his guns jam; while at the same time Robinson hammered a burst into the second German at dead astern. Its engines erupted in smoke, then the plane fell away in a spiral dive obviously out of control, and disappeared with blue flames rippling along the belly of its squat fuselage.

Seven 'Bluenose' (434 Squadron) crews reported 10 combats, resulting in one Me262 being probably destroyed, and two others at least damaged. For 429 ('Bison') Squadron this was its first operation since converting from Halifaxes to Lancasters; with ten crews participating. Five were attacked, engaging in nine separate combats. Flight Sergeants D. H. Lockhart and R. Jones, rear and mid-upper gunners respectively in the aircraft skippered by Flying Officer A. M. Humphries, both opened up at one Me262, though all four of Lockhart's guns ceased firing after about 20 rounds. As the jet broke away, however, Jones sank in a fierce burst and the German fell into the clouds apparently out of control and shedding metal from its starboard wing. In a companion 'Bison' bomber the mid-upper gunner, Flight Sergeant J. O. Leprich, was attacked directly over Hamburg. With his electrical firing circuit already out of commission, Leprich worked his guns with one hand, while hand-rotating the turret. He continued firing one gun after the other until the jet was finally driven away by three escort Mustangs which had returned to cover the Canadian 'straggler' formation. When last seen the Messerschmitt was spuming black smoke. Leprich was awarded a DFM for his cool courage and determination.

In a 427 ('Lion') Squadron aircraft Warrant Officer J. G. Jarvis was in the rear turret, and watched his tracers stitch along the belly of another jet as it rolled over and dived into cloud with dense black smoke trailing from its engines; though not before the Messerschmitt's twin 30 mm cannons had gouged chunks out of Jarvis's aircraft fuselage, engines, elevators and rudders. Evidence of the determination of the German fighter pilots' onslaught was starkly illustrated by the widespread damage caused to many of the bombers when they eventually reached their respective bases. Flight Lieuten-

ant J. L. Storms of 427 Squadron piloted his aircraft back from Hamburg with one shattered aileron, and a five feet chunk of one wing missing, but finally achieved a safe return, thereby earning himself a DFC. The Canadians' 'Day of the Jets' had been the Group's greatest daylight battle of the war.

11. A Gunner's Diary

Flying Officer Cliff O'Riordan, RAAF, was a man of rare quality of character, who possessed (to quote a fellow squadron member) '. . . all the fine qualities which go to make up a gentleman, and was universally popular with all who had the pleasure and privilege of meeting him'. In civilian life O'Riordan was a leading member of the Sydney Bar, a King's Counsel, and could thus, justifiably, have entered the Services in a non-combatant capacity. Apart from his legal skills, he was distinctly over-age for aircrew duties – officialdom recorded his birthdate as 12 May 1909, but virtually everyone who knew him placed his seniority at least ten years older. Neither age nor qualifications prevented Riordan from volunteering for training as a pilot, and when he was rejected for such he undertook air gunner training, qualified, and found his way to England in early 1942. After brief service with 103 Squadron, RAF, Riordan joined 460 Squadron RAAF in late 1942 as an 'odd bod' – a 'spare' gunner affiliated to no particular aircrew.

With 460 Squadron Riordan proceeded to tag on to any operational crew temporarily short of a gunner, and flew many sorties over Germany. His legal background soon led to him undertaking the role of defence counsel in many apparently hopeless courts martial cases, determined always to see justice properly done. He seldom 'lost' a case, and became a friend to many men needing such counsel, irrespective of their rank or position. Innately modest, and immensely popular with all members of his squadron, Riordan kept a daily diary of his life on an operational bomber squadron. The following extracts reflect not only his personal views, thoughts, opinions and experiences, but exemplify to a degree the contemporary 'scene' – the hopes, fears, frustrations and highlights of life on a bomber unit in the summer of 1943.

APRIL

Tuesday 13th.   Big do on and we're operating. 2,250 gals petrol and ammunition cut down to a minimum. Much speculation as to the target. Austria? Czechoslovakia? New navigator in crew and did x-country in afternoon to try him out. Dropped in at Elsham and saw Blue Freeman whom I'm defending at Ct Martial, since Tom McNiel has gone. Seems to have an outside chance.
Briefing at six. Target Spezia, Italy. They think there are battleships there.

Uneventful trip out. The Alps looked like a travel poster. We were bang on course and the first aircraft at the target. The town lights were on and we could see cars and buses going up and down in the streets. Stooged across and had a look. Height 7000. No ships. Made a second run. Some of the town blacked out. Made a third run and dropped in on the docks. Caught in searchlights and lots of light flak. Climbed into cloud. Extraordinary effect of reflections in cloud, with coloured flak and own aircraft silhouetted a dozen times. Soon out of trouble and heading for home. After an hour or so Camp asked if we had crossed the Alps. No one had seen them. Later we passed over lighted towns which hastily blacked out. Hopelessly lost and the navigator couldn't take an astro shot. Later we came over the sea and kept stooging along. Airborne for eight hours and lost. Mitch, the WOP, finally got a QDM and we set course due south of Southampton. After a while land appeared and we lost height to find where we were. Flak came up to welcome us and we were over Lorient. For good measure our navigator took us over Brest and a convoy. They all had a poop at us. Diverted to Harwell. Bright sunlight and down to 1000 ft, feeling secure, when we went straight through the Yeovil balloons. Finally made it, but well overdue, 11 hours 5 minutes in the air. Found we had set course wrongly from target and went bang across Spain and up the Bay of Biscay. Shaky do. Got to Breighton at 4 pm and left for London at 5. Caught midnight train.

Thursday, 15 Stayed at Golfers' Club. Met crew and the Wingco at the Codgers, did a pub crawl. Finished up at the New Yorker. Quite a day.

Friday 16 Went for a steak dinner with the boys and ———. I've got him blackmailed for life for having a pee into a flower vase.

Saturday, 17 Was going to Taunton-on-Sea to visit Brian and Babs Smith, but fate decreed otherwise. Tamagno and McLaughlan rolled in and then Jimmy Crabb who didn't know he'd been given a gong that morning. Party – finished up at the old pub in Watling Street. Stan Ricketts in fine form climbing lamp posts.

Sunday, 18 Got to Mass. At 1230 I arrived in Strand to quench a great thirst. There wasn't a taxi, pedestrian or even stray cat in Fleet Street, but when I turned the corner there must have been 50 Australian airmen waiting outside Codgers for it to open.

Monday, 19 George Peterson and I met two nice show girls from George Black's Revue. Went to Star-Spangled Rhythm.

Tuesday, 20 Just about to leave London when I ran into Pat Crennan. He's a Sq. Ldr and came over with a draft of airmen. Caught train to Scunthorpe and met by Blue Freeman who drove me to camp.

Wednesday, 21 Court Martial. G/C Edwards, VC, DSO, DFC, the President. They laid it on thick for Blue, but the county police were just a piece of cake in cross-examination and to my surprise and delight we got away on every charge. Celebration later at Scunthorpe with Blue and Jake Kennard, my old skipper. Stayed at the Oswald as guest of the Harrisons.

Friday, 23   Good Friday, but no stations at our church. Incidentally, we used the little Methodist chapel for Mass on Sundays!

Monday, 26   Duff weather. Ops scrubbed.

Wednesday, 28   Still the same. Brassed off.

MAY

Saturday, 1   Detailed to make a speech at a Wings for Victory rally at Allerton. Got there and no crowd. Only 24 hours late.

Sunday, 2   Ops scrubbed when the aircraft were running up. Went to Seven Sisters with Wingco and Speare.

Monday, 3   Another scrub. Party in Mess.

Tuesday, 4   Ops. Dortmund. Good show. 19 kites in from Breighton. Jaekel's crew missing and five kites from Holme Jaekel's observer, Russ, used to be a bullock driver and timber fettler in Queensland. Quite a character.

Wednesday, 6   Ops on again but scrubbed at 5.30.

Friday, 7   Another scrub. F/O Anderson and F/S Furhmann have been given immediate gongs for their last show. They are still in hospital.

Saturday, 8   The stationary front is still about and another scrub.

Sunday, 9   I'm OC advance party to Binbrook. Leaving tomorrow. Another scrub and had a farewell party at the Terry.

Monday, 10   Travelled to Binbrook with five Fl/Sgts and 20 erks. Getting things in order for the squadron. Lot of GHQ deadbeats here!

Tuesday, 11   Run off my feet. Have signed for three hangars and four living blocks. Every detail needs my signature. Why?

Wednesday, 12   My birthday, but no chance to celebrate. The boys went to Duisburg tonight and it was Laurie Simpson's last trip. Got through on three engines. Had a beer in the village before turning in.

Thursday, 13   Still cracking on amidst glorious confusion. The boys bashed Bochum. That sounds like 'Truth'.

Friday, 14   The squadron started arriving by glider at 8.30. By midday most of ground crew and equipment were here. In the afternoon the Lancaster party arrived with the ground crew of each kite. Hell of a flap getting them all settled in. Went back to Farewell at Breighton by glider. Party started with shoot-up of Mess by Grant in a Lanc, and then a pyrotechnic display by Camp which grounded aircraft for miles around. Two motor bikes in the Mess and Group Captain Crummy got a black eye when thrown through a screen. I slept in the Mess from 5 am after playing accompaniment to Mochetty on the violin.

Saturday, 15   Party resumed at 10 am. Dale with Very pistol made everyone drink a '460 Special'. Quite a bright party. Tried to ride a horse in the field and fell off. Was going back in Bruce Bennett's car (4d a pound peas!) till I found he had no clutch or brakes. Bought Phil Ward's car on the spot and drove myself to Binbrook. Arrived at 1 am.

Sunday, 16   Arm a bit sore. Saw the Doc and he put it in splints. Says it's fractured.

Monday, 17   Into Grimsby for X-ray. Doc was right. Comminated fracture of the lower radius. Felt a fraud when an old lady offered me a seat in the bus coming back. Look like a Red Cross poster.

Tuesday, 18   Five fresher crews on a mining stooge to the Gironde. All back safely.

Thursday, 20   No ops. Cross country practice for crews.

Friday 21   No ops. Drove to Tielby with Frank Arthur, Cappi and Eddie Hudson. Lovely spot with Tennyson's 'Brook' running past the pub.

Saturday, 22   Still no ops. Liberty bus to Grimsby. Went to the Officers' Club and danced a while.

Sunday, 23   Ops. Dortmund. Biggest effort yet by Bomber Command.

Monday, 24   Furhmann's kite 'B-Beer' an awful mess. 150 holes by fighters and no one hurt. Gongs have been given to Ted McKinnon,

91 *'Arse-end Charlie' – rear gunner of a Lancaster seated at the controls of his 'Mighty Wurlitzer'.*

Geoff Heath, Moore and Sgt Smith. Hadley won the 'picture pool' for last night on Dortmund. Stiffy Horne is very proud.

Tuesday, 25   Ops. Dusseldorf. 26 on.

Thursday, 27   Five aircrew told to parade outside the Mess at 1100. Didn't know what it was all about but Camp told me to be there. At 11 their Majesties arrived. I tried to hide behind Panos, but the King asked me what happened to my arm. The AOC was there, but I told him the truth. He laughed like Hell and said, 'Did you borrow the horse or scrounge it?' Told him I scrounged it. The Queen was grand. Ops were on to Essen. Nothing for me to do so drove to Market Rasen with Frank Arthur.

Friday, 28   Stand down. Mac and I went to a 'Musical Evening' in Grimsby and came back in time for the Sergeants' Dance.

Saturday, 29   Ops again. Two crews missing.

Monday 31   Stand down. Into Grimsby for another X-ray. Chap in the guardroom tried to commit suicide by cutting his throat. Ivan Galbraith and Tom Osborn have got their commissions.

JUNE

Tuesday, 1   On leave. Got to London at 6 pm. No trouble with seats or porters with arm in a sling. Booked in at Waldorf and went to Codgers.

Wednesday, 2   The whole crew arrived and I took a room with Camp at the Strand Palace.

Wednesday, 9   Back at 8.30. Two new crews as raw as carrots. Ops scrubbed at 10 pm.

Thursday, 10   Stand down. Formation flying in afternoon. Went by bus to Grimsby and struck 'Count' Doleman, now a P/O, and doing an AGI course at Manby. He has a guard's moustache and takes snuff, but all in fun.

Friday, 11   Ops again, 27 on and one waiting.

Saturday, 12   Ops on. Two crews missing, Hadley and Stiffy Horne and Bennett from the Mess. No more '4d a pound peas' Cope's crew got an incendiary from one of our own kites and Hugh Gordon put the fire out.

Monday, 14   Went in for another X-ray. Grimsby was raided last night very lightly. The people look very tired. Wonder how they feel in the Ruhr. Ops again. 23 on and three crews missing. Not so good.

Tuesday, 15   Bullseye exercise. A bus ran to Cleethorpes. Max Keddie and Ron Friend have been given DFCs.

Thursday, 17   It was announced today that nine gongs had been given to 460 this week. Good show. The boys earn them.

Sunday, 20   Ops, mining in the Gironde. Giles finishes his tour. McLaughlan has been posted to Lindholme and MacWilliams is taking his place.

92 *Birthday toast. Sergeant Cliff Fudge, DFM, gunner in Lancaster R5868, PO-S of 467 Squadron RAAF, is toasted in cocoa on return from Berlin on 16 February 1944. Fudge had become 21 years of age over the target at midnight. His captain, Plt. Off. J. McManus, RAAF, is second from right. Lancaster R5868 is now on permanent display in the RAF Museum, Hendon.*

Monday, 21 Ops. Krefeld. 1 crew missing. To date we have dropped (on this squadron) 3,000 tons of bombs, made 1,477 sorties and lost 61 aircraft.[1]

Tuesday, 22 Camp has been posted to Lindholme. Have to get another skipper. Had another Ct Martial today for AC2 L——. I defended him on a similar charge at Breighton and since he only got 26 days detention that time thought he would go AWL again. Think they'll throw the book at him this time.

Thursday, 24 Fighter affiliation this morning. Baron Keys came over in the afternoon and seemed quite happy at Lichfield. Ops were on and Wuppertal the target. Stooke's crew did not return.

[1]This casualty total resulted from some 15 months of bombing operations, since 460 Squadron's first-ever operation on 12/13 March 1942; representing approximately 500 crew members 'missing' . . . Author.

Friday, 25   Ops again. P/O Naylor shot the following line. When asking what was doing was told that he was on another Ruhr bash. He said, 'I'm sick of that bloody place.' He made his first trip there last night. (Delightful).

Saturday, 26   Stand down. Bullseye exercise on. Sergeants' Mess party. Cappi got tangled with Spanner and was in good voice.

Sunday, 27   Three crews on Gardening, all returned safely.

Monday, 28   Ops again. 17 crews on. All came back.

On 29 July 1943 another squadron member wrote in Riordan's diary:

29 July   24 aircraft from squadron attacked Hamburg, and from reports raid was very concentrated. More searchlights were reported than before and these appeared to line the route in leaving the actual path itself in darkness, flak was being pumped up in the searchlight zones. Pilots stated they saw many fighters milling in the dark areas. Unfortunately the squadron lost two aircraft on this do, F/Sgt Furhmann, DFM and F/O Johnson being the captains. F/Sgt Furhmann and his crew had been through many shaky do's together as they almost invariably seemed to be shot up, and he and his navigator F/O Anderson, had both received decorations for bringing their aircraft back under difficulties on a previous occasion.
F/O Johnson's crew contained a number of old identities of the squadron including Cliff O'Riordan. Cliff had been on the squadron since August 1942 and had been regarded as one of the squadron's fixtures. As one of the oldest members of the squadron he had been compiling the squadron history. He will be sadly missed by everyone in the Group and it is hoped that he will be found to be a prisoner war.

The unknown writer's hope was not fulfilled – Flying Officer C. T. O'Riordan, RAAF, was killed over Hamburg that night along with his crew.

12. Over 'Over There'

Just before 4 pm on the afternoon of 17 August 1942, twelve Boeing B-17 'Fortresses' of the 97th Group, USAAF, took off from Grafton Underwood, bound for the French coast and their objective the marshalling yards at Rouen-Sotteville. In the lead ship, *Butcher Shop*, Colonel Frank Armstrong was pilot, while his co-pilot was a certain Major Paul W. Tibbets (who in August 1945, was to skipper a B-29 Superfortress over Japan and release the first-ever atomic bomb on a town titled Hiroshima). The target was reached, duly bombed, and apart from minor flak damage, every Fortress returned to base safely. It was an historic raid in one sense, because it was the first bombing mission undertaken by bombers of the Eighth Air Force, USAAF – the initial mission of US bombing power which was to play a massive part in final destruction of Hitler's Germany within less than three years.

If the veteran bomber crew of the RAF in 1942 tended to look askance at the unbridled eagerness of the 'sprog' Yankee crews, and particularly at the brash publicity accorded to the words and

93 *Boeing Y1B-17, progenitor of the highly successful 'Flying Fortresses' of the USAAF. No turrets were fitted, but it carried five single .50 machine guns in various 'blister' locations.*

deeds of these newcomers to the aerial war, they might be forgiven for being patronising. Apart from the divergence in national characteristics in such matters, the RAF had finally learned the brutal lesson of not attempting major bombing raids over Europe by day without long-range fighter escorts. Instead RAF Bomber Command was concentrating on night bombing on an escalating scale. USAAF bombing policy, on the other hand, was determined to prove the efficacy of high altitude, daylight precision bombing – despite the tragic experiences of the RAF's early war years.

Within the 8th AAF (and USAAF generally) air gunners were almost invariably 'enlisted men', i.e. non-commissioned ranks, while each usually held a dual role in any crew, as bombardier/gunner or wireless operator/gunner, and often switching roles on different missions. The state of aerial gunnery among the USAAF's early combat crews was frankly poor. Many of the first gunners to see combat over Europe were sparsely trained, and some had never fired from an airborne gun turret before their first bombing mission. RAF help with training facilities and technique was quickly sought and obtained. In the main the early Fortress and Liberator gunners were handling single .50 machine guns in the various nose and waist locations – no easy task when attempting to swing a vibrating, jerking gun weighing 64 lbs into a 180 mph-plus roaring slipstream against the fury of a Luftwaffe's cannon-armed fighter.

One long-standing criticism of USAAF gunners in the Fortresses by outsiders was the question of gunners' claims for enemy aircraft shot down; especially during the first eighteen months of operations over Europe. Postwar investigations of USAAF claims and Luftwaffe records, incomplete as the latter were, showed clearly highly exaggerated victory totals. Indeed, for the first year's operations it has been calculated as approximately ten times the true figure! Undoubtedly such inflated claims resulted from a combination of several, natural factors; inexperience, over-eagerness, heightened nervous reaction and tension, and – inevitably in the huge, tight box formations flown by all Fortress formations – multiple claims for a single enemy aircraft sent down, where perhaps a dozen or more gunners had concentrated on the individual opponent. Luftwaffe pilots encountering the early American bombing formations soon learned to respect the deadly barrage of .50 bullets awaiting any attempt to attack from the rear, and changed to the more fruitful head-on plunge through the Fortress boxes. As the American bombing programme increased steadily, both in strength and in depth of penetration over Germany itself, Luftwaffe opposition mounted in huge proportion. Fresh tactical schemes and weaponry were employed to combat the sprawling formations of Fortresses and Liberators, including the use of air bombing and, later, rockets.

In many ways typical of the depth and fury of the opposition awaiting any daylight bombing mission was the raid mounted by the Eighth AAF against Regensburg and Schweinfurt on 17 August

1943. A total of 147 B-17s were despatched to Regensburg to destroy the Messerschmitt factory there, then continue their flight to bases in North Africa. At almost the same time a second raid, comprising 230 B-17s were sent to Schweinfurt. The Regensburg force first met Luftwaffe attacks when only 15 minutes past the Belgian coast, and these continued in successive waves, without pause, for the next one and a half hours. One observer-participant in a Fortress summed up the battle scene as, 'Fantastic, it surpassed fiction . . .' The Schweinfurt mission suffered most; and at the end of the day the grim casualty figures read 60 bombers lost, representing some 600-plus men. The gunners that day totted up initial claims for a staggering 288 enemy aircraft destroyed! Only after the war was it discovered that the true figure for German losses that day amounted to no more than 25 fighters.

If the RAF had tended to patronise the early crews of the 8th AAF, such pompousness quickly changed to sheer admiration for the dogged persistence and superlative courage with which the American bomber crews continued their dogmatic attempts to prove that daylight strategic bombing was possible. Returning Fortresses and Liberators displayed frightening damage on mission after mission; pilots brought home half an aeroplane and, too often, less than half a crew still alive; yet they returned to the battle, again and again. In a saga of outstanding courage and determination, many of the 8th AAF's aerial gunners were prominent. Two of the 17 Medal of Honor awards made to 8th AAF bomber crews went to gunners.

First to gain his country's highest honour was Sergeant Maynard H. Smith, usually nicknamed 'Snuffy'. On 1 May 1943 Smith was ball turret gunner in Fortress 42-29649 of the 423rd Squadron (306th BG) detailed for a mission against St Nazaire. It was Smith's first operational trip. The target was reached and bombed, despite intense opposition and thick cloud conditions, and the formation began its return journey. A navigational error brought the group over the Brest Peninsula where it was met with predicted flak. Smith's Fortress, piloted by Lieutenant Lewis Johnson, bore the brunt of several direct hits and near-misses, resulting in the intercomm and oxygen systems being wrecked, an engine damaged, top turret, nose, flaps and a fuel tank damaged, and fires starting up in the tail wheel housing and radio position. Escaping oxygen fed the flames, creating a furnace heat which began to melt parts of the rear fuselage structure and fittings.

Smith, on realizing that his turret had no power for operation, climbed out into the fuselage, to witness the two waist gunners and the radio operator bale out. Surrounded by fierce heat, flames and billowing smoke, Smith might easily have followed suit and abandoned the aircraft. Instead he grabbed a hand extinguisher and began fighting the fire. He next found the tail gunner, wounded and lying on the floor, and administered first aid, before returning to the main fire. By then the Fortress had come under attack by

95 *S/Sergeant Lusic of the 423rd BS, 306th BG, based at Thurleigh in early 1943, displaying the full flying gear worn at that period by USAAF gunners. Behind him is* Meat Hound, *a B-17F Fortress of his squadron.*

several Focke Wulf 190s, and between attempting to douse the flames, Smith operated the waist guns. As the heat began detonating spare ammunition boxes nearby, Smith threw these overboard or away from the flames. In all Smith fought the fire for some 90 minutes, using every extinguisher he could find, then his flying jacket, and finally – in a gesture of sheer defiance – urinated on the fire.

As Lewis Johnson in the front cockpit continued struggling to ride his weakened aircraft home, the English coast came into view. Smith also noticed this through the gaping hole burned out of the fuselage wall, and he started throwing out everything loose he could lay his hands on in order to lighten ship; the fuselage was so weak from damage it might break up at any moment. Spotting Predannack, Cornwall, Johnson brought his bomber in for a smooth landing without further damage. For his part in the action 'Snuffy' Smith, son of a circuit judge, was awarded the Medal of Honor a few weeks later, but only flew four more missions before being returned to the USA.

The second gunner to receive America's highest gallantry award was Archie Mathies, son of Scottish emigrant parents, who originally enlisted in the USAF as a ground mechanic. Sent to England as a replacement gunner in December 1943, Mathies was assigned to the 351st BG in January 1944; and on 20 February, on only his second mission over Europe, was the engineer/ball turret gunner in B-17G, 42-31763, TU-A of the leading formation bombing Leipzig. As they bore through the flak the Fortresses met a succession of head-on fighter assaults, and one put a brief burst of cannon shells through the pilot's windscreen of Mathies's aircraft. Exploding inside the cockpit, the shells killed the co-pilot and seriously wounded the skipper. The bomber staggered and fell into a wallowing dive, causing its bombardier to yell to the other crew members to bale out, then do so himself.

Mathies climbed out of his ball turret and went forward to see what was wrong 'up front' and, on finding a bloody shambles in the cockpit, leaned over the pilots' bodies and grabbed the controls and pulled the aircraft back onto an even keel. He was then joined by the navigator, Walt Truemper, and other crew men. A hasty 'conference' decided to try to get home rather than abandon their pilots. While other crew members extracted the still bodies of the pilots from their seats, Mathies and Truemper operated the aileron and elevator controls from between the seats; then, once clear, Mathies took the co-pilot's position. Through the shattered windscreen a freezing blast of air played directly onto Mathies, numbing him so badly that from time to time he had to be relieved at his post, but by letting down to lower altitude he continued to fly the bomber homewards.

Arriving over Polebrook airfield, Mathies and Truemper told the remaining crew to bale out; they were going to attempt a landing,

hoping still to save their wounded skipper. As the Fortress circled the field, traffic control made radio contact; while another Fortress took off, hoping to 'pair' alongside and talk the two men down in stages. Unable to get radio contact between the two aircraft, the control then ordered Mathies and Truemper to head out to sea, then bale out. Both men refused to do this – they still wanted to try to bring their injured pilot in. Given permission to try a landing, Mathies and Truemper let down for their first attempt, but were too high on approach and went round again. The second attempt was still too high for safety, so once more the Fortress circled the field. On the third approach the bomber slowly dropped towards the threshold – then stalled abruptly and crashed. Both Mathies and Truemper were killed in the crash, while the injured pilot, though pulled from the wreckage alive, succumbed to his grievous injuries shortly after. Both Archie Mathies and Walt Truemper were awarded a Medal of Honor posthumously.

A glimpse of the turmoil and tragedies of a heavy bomber daylight assault over Germany is provided by the personal account of Sergeant John Bode, a waist gunner of Liberator *Doodle Bug* of the 8th AAF's 392nd BG. On 18 March 1944, Bode's particular group, deep into German skies, suffered heavily;

Thing's didn't go right from the start. Just after the French coast a B-24 got into prop-wash and collided with another. I watched both planes all the way down with my binoculars but saw no 'chutes open. Heard later one man did get out. It was his first mission. As we neared the target I could see the Alps in the distance, but my attention was

96 *The notorious Sperry ball turret. Statistics after the war showed – surprisingly – that ball turret gunners suffered relatively less casualties than any other gun turret location.*

soon drawn to the biggest mass of flak I was ever to see. To jam the gun-laying radar I had to throw 'chaff' out. The Germans had us bracketed and we were hit in several places. Our bombardier was hit in the face and blinded; he screamed over the inter-phone. Looking out I was appalled to see five B-24s falling at once over the target – just like fingers on your hand. As the wounded bombardier was being removed from the nose turret I saw a gaggle of about 40 fighters flying parallel on our right at 3 o'clock. Looking through my binoculars I recognized them as a mixture of 109s and 190s, although our pilot (Lt William E. Meighan) at first suggested they might be our escort arriving. A moment later the air around us was full of white puff-balls. I wondered if they were a new type of flak but the pilot yelled, 'Here they come!', and sure enough outside my waist window an Fw190 flashed by from the front, doing a roll between us and the nearest B-24.

By now I felt it was only a matter of time before they got us as we were already crippled. I tried to swing my point-fifty after other Jerries as they streaked by. Our top turret was doing most of the firing, and the ball turret gunner was trying to get into the damaged nose turret. A fighter started pumping 20 mm shells at us from behind and though the tail gunner replied, the recently installed link chutes in his turret caused the guns to jam intermittently. Next thing I saw was a B-24 upside down, and then to my amazement an Me109 about 100 yards or so below us on my side going in our direction and not much faster.

97 Waist gunner in a B-17 Fortress – in this case a 'Fort' used by the RAF.

98 (Left) *The sting in the tail – a B-17 Fortress tail gunner with twin .50 Brownings and ring sight at the ready. Note two swastika claims for enemy aircraft destroyed to date.*

He was probably shooting at a B-24 ahead of us, and may have assumed our plane abandoned; at any rate he acted as if we didn't exist. I aimed my gun almost straight down, sighted point blank, and fired 30 to 40 rounds into his wings, engine and cockpit. His glycol sprayed but I'm sure I must have killed the pilot as the plane rolled over and went straight into the ground 20,000 feet below.

Our fighters finally came to the rescue of what was left of our formation. We now had two engines out but though we were losing altitude fast we managed to make a Spitfire field on the English coast. We had one flap shot away, a bad wheel and, as the hydraulic lines were cut, no brakes. We went off the end of the runway but out pilot brought the plane to a standstill without further hurt to us.

Surprisingly, relatively few USAAF gunners were thoroughly trained in the 'art' of gunnery, and the basic necessity of mastering deflection shooting was seldom put into practice. A majority of gunners tended to 'hose the air' around any attacking fighter, filling the intervening air space with 'hot lead' in a mini-barrage

99 (Below) *Combat crew (including ground crew chief, rt) of B-17G Fortress Dame Satan II of the 91st BG, 8th AAF – known as 'The Ragged Irregulars' – based at Bassingbourn. Note spare .50 barrels on ground, and chin turret.*

through which the fighter would need to fly in order to get in close. Known to American gunners as the 'zone system', this method of saturating the closing range with .50 shells was effective as a deterrent, if not exactly up to top standards of marksmanship. Equally it was grossly expensive in ammunition, in comparison with most RAF bomber gunners who preferred brief, crisp bursts aimed specifically at any target. The greater range of the .50 calibre shell lent credence to the American idea of keeping the opponent at 'arm's length'; RAF gunners, with their shorter range. 303-inch calibre Brownings had little option but to let a German fighter come in closer before they could register any strikes.

Despite the 'zone system', several 8th AAF gunners were credited with respectable victory totals. Highest scoring within the 8th AAF was Sergeant Crossley, tail gunner of the 94th Group's Fortress, *Brass Rail Boys,* who was finally credited with 12 enemy aircraft destroyed. Another high-scorer was T/Sergeant Tom Dye, with eight victories credited. Dye, originally trained as a radio operator, volunteered to become a ball turret gunner. Without benefit of any gunnery training, he flew five missions, claiming two victims, before

100 Tail turret in a Martin Marauder of the 12th Air Force USAAF serving in Tunisia.

higher authority decreed he should attend gunnery school. Having *failed* his training course, Dye rejoined his old crew and completed his operational tour, claiming six more Luftwaffe fighters. One gunner, M/Sergeant Hewitt 'Buck' Dunn of the 390th Group, though credited with only one Fw190 destroyed, set a record for the number of combat missions flown in the European Theatre of Operations (ETO), racking up a final tally of 104 sorties. His first 28 missions had been as either tail or top turret gunner, the remainder as bombardier/nose gunner. In contrast, Sergeant De Sales Glover set a different kind of record. Enlisting in the USAAF in October 1942 by lying about his true age of 14 years, by early 1944 he had completed six missions over Germany as a gunner before the authorities discovered his true age – by then 16 – and reluctantly but firmly grounded him.

In terms of bomber operations throughout the 1939-45 war, in any theatre of operations around the globe, the American daylight offensive against Germany must rank as the most intensive, in the context of pure aerial combat gunnery. Whether in self-defence or simply adding his weight of lead to the rest of his box formation's

102 *Nose turret of Liberator (B-24) of the 458th BG which was based from January 1944 to June 1945 at Horsham St Faiths airfield (now Norwich City airport).*

103 *Another 458th BG Liberator at Horsham St Faiths, undergoing maintenance between missions, January 1944.*

defensive barrage, the Fortress, Liberator or Marauder gunner faced a constant slugging match each time he crossed over into German-defended skies. In sheer numbers alone, the USAAF offensive saw more gunners in combat than any other Allied bomber force, including the RAF, during the years 1942-45. Though the un-wittingly over-exaggerated combat claims by American gunners in the ETO can never be rationalized to a completely accurate figure, they at least give some guidance to the number of occasions that each man was in action against Luftwaffe fighters. To these must be added the unknown actions of the many hundreds of gunners who

104 *Tail damage to a B-17 Fortress, piloted by 2/Lt Frank E. Valesh, which force-landed at an RAF airfield after a mission to Germany.*

105 *B-17 Fortress, 43-38172 of the 398th BG, on return to Nuthampstead after the Cologne raid of 15 October 1944. A flak shell went straight through the chin turret and exploded in the upper bombardier's compartment. Yet the pilot (Lt Lawrence de Lancey) brought it home. Note bombardier's .50 Browning still hanging on wreckage.*

failed to return – men like T/Sergeant Harris, the top turret gunner in a 306th BG B-17 mortally crippled by flak during a raid on St Nazaire. A shell sliced away the entire nose, taking the bombardier and navigator with it. Then, just north of Brest, the Fw190s closed in, leaving the cripple only when it began its final plunge downwards towards the sea. Four parachutes only were seen to leave the B-17, but it was obvious to other members of the group that the pilot, Lieutenant Charles Cranmer, was still at his controls. Levelling out, Cranmer ditched his aircraft smoothly but the gaping nose section let the sea in immediately and the huge bomber started sinking within seconds. Yet, until the waves closed over him, Harris in the top turret kept aiming his guns upwards, still firing at his tormentors until the ocean claimed him. His fighting spirit was recognized by the award of a posthumous Distinguished Service Cross (DSC).

13. Mission to Regensburg

Lieutenant-Colonel Beirne Lay, Jr was one of the original seven USAAF officers (then a Captain) who landed in England on 20 February 1942 to become the initial HQ staff of the Eighth Army Air Force, USAAF, under the direction of Brigadier General Ira C. Eaker. A pilot in his own right, Lay remained a staff officer for well over 18 months, but occasionally flew as 'observer' in various operational bombers. It was as co-pilot of B-17F, *Piccadilly Lily* of the 351st BS, 100th BG, that he flew on the notorious Regensburg mission of 17 August 1943. His classic description of that mission illustrates vividly the form of massive gun battles fought by the aerial gunners of the 8th AAF against the Luftwaffe while doggedly pursuing the USAAF's rugged policy of daylight bombing offensive. On 11 May 1944, when commanding a B-24 Group, the 487th BG, Lay was forced to bale out of his crippled Liberator, but evaded capture subsequently.

17 August 1943

When our group crossed the coast by Holland at our base altitude of 17,000 feet, I was well situated to watch the proceedings, being co-pilot in the lead ship of the last element of the high squadron. With all of its 21 B-17Fs tucked in tightly, our group was in handy supporting distance of another group, ahead of us at 18,000 feet. We were the last and lowest of the seven groups that were visible ahead on a south-east course, forming a long chain in the bright sunlight – too long it seemed. Wide gaps separated the three combat wings. As I sat there in the tail-end element of that many-miles-long procession, gauging the distance to the lead group, I had the lonesome foreboding that might come to the last man to run a gauntlet lined with spiked clubs. The premonition was well founded.

Near Woensdrecht I saw the first flak blossom out in our vicinity, light and inaccurate. A few minutes later two Fw190s appeared at one-o'clock level and whizzed through the formation ahead of us in a frontal attack, nicking two B-17s in the wings and breaking away beneath us in half-rolls. Smoke immediately trailed from both B-17s but they held their stations. As the fighters passed us at a high rate of closure the guns of our group went into action. The pungent smell of burnt powder filled our cockpit and the B-17 trembled to the recoil of nose and ball-turret guns. I saw pieces fly off the wing of one of the fighters before they passed from view.

The members of the crew sensed trouble. There was something desperate about the way those two fighters came in fast, right out of their climb without any preliminaries. For a few seconds the interphone

147

106 *Boeing B-17G-I-BO of the 535th BS, 381st BG, based at Ridgewell, early 1944;*
displaying nose, upper, waist, ball and tail turrets. Later, cheek guns were added on
the side of the nose, and glazed flexible windows in the open waist locations. The chin
turret was operated by 'remote' controls; just visible in the upper nose perspex
compartment.

was busy with admonitions: 'Lead 'em more . . . short bursts . . . don't
throw rounds away . . . there'll be more along in a minute.'

Three minutes later the gunners reported fighters climbing up from all
around the clock, singly and in pairs, both Fw190s and Me109Gs. This
was only my fourth raid, but from what I could see on my side it looked
like too many fighters for sound health. A co-ordinated attack followed,
with the head-on fighters coming in from slightly above, the nine- and
three-o'clock attackers coming from about level, and the rear attackers
from slightly below. Every gun from every B-17 in our group and the
one ahead was firing, criss-crossing our patch of sky with tracers to
match the time-fuse cannon shell puffs that squirted from the wings of
the Jerry single-seaters. I would estimate that 75 per cent of our fire was
inaccurate, falling astern of the target – particularly the fire from hand-
held guns. Nevertheless, both sides got hurt in this clash, with two
B-17s from our low squadron and one other falling out and several

fighters heading for the deck in flames, or with their pilots lingering behind under dirty yellow parachutes. Our group leader pulled us up nearer to the group ahead for mutual support.

I knew that we were already in a lively fight. What I didn't know was that the real fight, the onslaught of the Luftwaffe 20 mm cannon shells, hadn't really begun. A few minutes later we absorbed the first wave of a hailstorm of individual fighter attacks that was to engulf us clear to the target. The ensuing action was so rapid and varied that I cannot give any chronological account of it. Instead I'll attempt a fragmentary report, salient details that even now give me a dry mouth and an unpleasant sensation in the stomach when I recall them. The sight was fantastic and surpassed fiction.

It was over Eupen that I looked out of my co-pilot's window after a short lull and saw two whole squadrons, 12 Me109s and 11 Fw190s, climbing parallel to us. The first squadron had reached our level and was pulling ahead to turn into us, and the second was not far behind. Several thousand feet below us were many more fighters, with their noses cocked at maximum climb. Over the interphone came reports of an equal number of enemy aircraft deploying on the other side. For the first time I noticed an Me110 sitting out of range on our right. He was to stay with us all the way to the target, apparently reporting our position to fresh squadrons waiting for us down the road. At the sight of all those fighters I had the distinct feeling of being trapped – that the Hun was tipped off, or at least had guessed our destination and was waiting for us. No P-47s were visible. [Luftwaffe fighters by then deliberately waited until Allied bombers were beyond fighter escort range before attacking.] The life expectancy of our group suddenly seemed very short, since it had already appeared that the fighters were passing up preceding groups, with the exception of one, in order to take a cut at us. [German tactics almost invariably concentrated on the lowest bomber groups first.]

Swinging their yellow noses around in a wide U-turn, the 12-ship squadron of Me109s came in from 12 to 2 o'clock in pairs and fours, and the main event was on. A shining silver object sailed past over our right wing. I recognized it as a main exit door. Seconds later a dark object came hurtling through the formation, barely missing several props. It was a man, clasping his knees to his head, revolving like a diver in a triple somersault. I didn't see his 'chute open. A B-17 turned gradually out of the formation to the right, maintaining altitude. In a split second the B-17 completely disappeared in a brilliant explosion, from which the only remains were four small balls of fire, the fuel tanks, which were quickly consumed as they fell earthward. Our aeroplane was endangered by hunks of debris. Emergency hatches, exit doors, prematurely opened parachutes, bodies, and assorted fragments of B-17s and Hun fighters breezed past us in the slipstream.

I watched two fighters explode not far below, disappearing in sheets of orange flame, B-17s dropping out in every stage of distress, from engines on fire to control surfaces shot away, friendly and enemy parachutes floating down, and, on the green carpet far behind us, numerous funeral pyres of smoke from fallen fighters marking our trail. On we flew through the strewn wake of a desperate air battle, where disintegrating aircraft were commonplace and 60 'chutes in the air at one

time were hardly worth a second look. I watched a B-17 turn slowly out to the right with its cockpit a mass of flames. The co-pilot crawled out of his window, held on with one hand, reached back for his 'chute, buckled it on, let go, and was whisked back into the horizontal stabilizer. I believe the impact killed him. His 'chute didn't open.

Ten minutes, 20 minutes, 30 minutes, and still no let-up in the attacks. The fighters queued up like a breadline and let us have it. Each second of time had a cannon shell in it. The strain of being a clay duck in the wrong end of that aerial shooting gallery became almost intolerable as the minutes accumulated towards the first hour. Our B-17 shook steadily with the fire of its .50s and the air inside was heavy with smoke. It was cold in the cockpit, but when I looked across at our pilot – and a good one – sweat was pouring off his forehead and over his oxygen mask. He turned the controls over to me for a while. It was a blessed relief to concentrate on holding station in formation instead of watching those everlasting fighters boring in. It was possible to forget the fighters. Then the top-turret gunner's twin muzzles would pound away a foot above my head, giving an imitation of cannon shells exploding in the cockpit – while I gave an even better imitation of a man jumping six inches out of his seat.

A B-17 ahead of us, with its right Tokyo tanks on fire, dropped back to about 200 feet above our right wing and stayed there while

107 *Tail and side-hatch guns of a B-24 J-10-FO Liberator.*

seven of the crew baled out successively. Four went out of the bomb bay and executed delayed jumps; one baled from the nose, opened his 'chute prematurely and nearly fouled the tail. Another went out of the left waist-gun opening, delaying his 'chute opening for a safe interval. The tail gunner dropped out of his hatch, apparently pulling the ripcord before he was clear of the ship. His 'chute opened instantaneously, barely missing the tail, and jerked him so hard that both his shoes came off. He hung limply in the harness, whereas the others had shown immediately some signs of life after their 'chutes opened, shifting around in the harness. The B-17 then dropped back in a medium spiral and I did not see the pilots leave. I saw it just before it passed from view, several thousand feet below us, with its right wing a solid sheet of yellow flame.

After we had been under constant attack for a solid hour it appeared certain that our group was faced with annihilation. Seven had been shot down, the sky was still mottled with rising fighters, and target time was still 35 minutes away. I doubt if a man in the group visualized the possibility of our getting much farther without 100 per cent loss. I know that I had long since mentally accepted the fact of death, and that it was simply a question of the next second or next minute. I learned first-hand that a man can resign himself to the certainty of death without becoming panicky. Our group fire-power was reduced to 35 per cent, and ammunition was running low. Our tail guns had to be replenished from another gun station. Gunners were becoming exhausted and nerve-tortured from the prolonged strain, and there was an awareness on everybody's part that something must have gone wrong. We had been the aiming point for what seemed like most of the Luftwaffe and we finally expected to find the rest of it primed for us at the target.

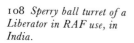

108 *Sperry ball turret of a Liberator in RAF use, in India.*

109 *The XB-40, a much modified B-17F, intended as a long range escort 'fighter'. Fore-runner of 20 YB-40 versions, it carried no bombs, but doubled armament and ammunition as a form of flying arsenal to escort bombing formations. YB-40s saw only brief operational service in mid-1943.*

Fighter tactics were running fairly true to form. Frontal attacks hit the low squadron and lead squadron, while rear attackers went for the high. The manner of their attacks showed that some pilots were old-timers, some amateurs, and that all knew pretty definitely where we were going and were inspired with a fanatical determination to stop us before we got there. The old-timers came in on frontal attacks with a noticeably slower rate of closure, apparently throttled back, obtaining greater accuracy than those that bolted through us wide open. They did some nice shooting at ranges of 500 or more yards, and in many cases seemed able to time their thrusts to catch the top and ball turret gunners engaged with rear and side attacks. Less experienced pilots were pressing attacks home to 250 yards and less to get hits, offering point-blank targets on the breakaway, firing long bursts of 20 seconds, and in some cases actually pulling up instead of going down and out. Several Fw pilots pulled off some first-rate deflection shooting on side attacks against the high group, then raked the low group on the breakaway out of a sideslip, keeping the nose cocked up in the turn to prolong the period the formation was in their sights. I observed what I believe was an attempt at air-to-air bombing, although I didn't see the bombs dropped. A patch of 75 to 100 grey-white bursts, smaller than flak bursts appeared simultaneously at our level, off to one side.

One B-17 dropped out on fire and put its wheels down while the crew baled. Three Me109s circled it closely, but held their fire, apparently ensuring that no one stayed in the ship to try for home. I saw the

Hun fighters hold their fire even when being shot at by a B-17 crew from which the crew were baling out. Near the IP one hour and a half after the first of at least 200 fighter attacks, the pressure eased off, although hostiles were near by. We turned at the IP with 14 B-17s left, two of which were badly crippled. They dropped out after bombing and headed for Switzerland. The No. 4 engine on one of them was afire, but the plane was not out of control. The leader of the high squadron received a cannon shell in his No. 3 engine just before the start of the bombing run, but went into the target with the prop feathered.

Eventually, at dusk, with red lights showing on all of the fuel tanks in my ship, the seven B-17s of the group still in formation circled over Bertoux [the B-17s on this mission had been pre-briefed to carry on southwards after bombing, to head for North African coast airfields; rather than return to England and run the gauntlet of Luftwaffe opposition twice] and landed in the dust. Our crew was unscratched. Sole damage to the aeroplane: a bit of ventilation round the tail from flak and 20 mm shells. We slept on the hard ground under the wings of our B-17, but the good earth felt softer than a silk pillow. . .

14. The Sun Goes Down

It was in the final stages of the sprawling Pacific war that integrated aerial gunnery reached its peak during the 1939-45 war. While the RAF and its many allied air services were primarily engaged in the re-conquest of Burma, the USAF was directly engaged in the rolling tide of victory northwards across a seemingly endless chain of islands towards its ultimate goal, the Japanese homeland. A mounting aerial assault, stemming from Doolittle's initial carrier-borne bomber raid on Tokyo, had reached massive proportions by early 1945. Chief weapon in the USAF's aerial armoury was the Boeing B-29 bomber, known as the 'Superfortress'. First flown in prototype form in September 1942, from a three-years' development programme, the B-29 was originally mooted for operations against Germany. In 1943, as the first Service units to be equipped with B-29s were formed, however, it was decided to employ the new long-range 'hemisphere' bomber solely in the struggle against Japan. Accordingly, the subsequent island-hopping campaign by American ground forces was undertaken, mainly to establish suitable landing fields for operational B-29 units, with the objective of creating a bomber assault on Japan itself.

From the outset of B-29 development it was intended to incorporate a defensive system of power-operated gun turrets, remotely controlled by a central fire controller; thereby integrating all fire-power to a peak of efficiency. Initially used for daylight bombing operations in a manner similar to those flown by the B-17 Fortresses in Europe, from March 1945 the B-29 became used by night for devastating incendiary fire-raising attacks on principal Japanese cities – probably the most destructive bombing attacks of the whole war. Though continuing mainly as a night bomber, occasional high

110 *Boeing Superfortress – ultimate in World War Two remotely-controlled gun systems for defence.*

altitude daylight sorties were undertaken, and opposition from Japanese fighters continued almost until the final days of the war.

With its nominal armament of twelve .50 machine guns spaced, among four remote-controlled gun turrets, plus a single, rearward-firing 20 mm M2 Type B cannon, the B-29 was a veritable death-trap for any enemy fighter. Its mode of defence is best described by ex-T/Sgt Raymond Pritchard, Jr, the CFC (Central Fire Control) on a B-29 of the 6th Bomb Group (VH) during the final weeks of the Pacific war:

The advent of the Boeing B-29 ushered in the first major change in aerial gunnery with its remote-controlled, computer-aligned, GE (General Electrics) system. For the first time[1] aerial gunners on a production-built operational bomber could aim and fire turrets of up to four calibre .50 machine guns that were as much as 60 feet from them, and furthermore could fire as many as three of those turrets, two at a time. No longer did he have to figure windage, and lead or lag his target, not worry about any other ballistics, as this was all done for him by a 'black box' computer. Besides the back of the pilot's seat, it was the only other thing in a B-29 protected by built-in armour plate. The gunner using his remote control electric sight was free to concentrate on aiming directly at his target by keeping it framed in his reticle of lighted dots, and trying not to burn up his guns by firing short bursts. A formation of B-29s could throw out a deadly field of fire such as no attacking fighter pilot had ever had to face before.

Before one accepts this over-simplification as meaning that nearly any idiot could close his eyes and become an ace-gunner in a B-29, I'd better review some of the requirements and training required of a remote-control turret gunner, as his MOS (Military Occupation Speciality) called him. Most B-29s had a gunnery crew consisting of a 'gunnery commander' (CFC) who occupied the top rear-sighting blister just ahead of the upper rear turret. The upper forward plexiglass dome near the upper forward four-gun turret was actually an astrodome sighting station for the navigator, not a gunsight position. There were two side gunners, known as left and right blister gunners, and a tail gunner who was isolated in his 'office' except when the aircraft was not pressurized. The other sighting station was in the nose over the bomb sight, and primarily operated by the bombardier.

All of these gunners went through the regular Air Force aerial gunner schools, plus the additional familiarisation and light maintenance on the General Electrics gunnery system. The CFC gunner who, according to the TO, was responsible for maintenance of the whole system in his B-29, also had to take a six weeks' cram course on the electronic and mechanical design, maintenance, and operation of the system. This school operated on 24-hour basis at Lowery Field, Denver. After this he went through the regular aerial gunnery school skeet range course, firing from a pickup truck, standing at a swivel-mounted

[1] The claim for the B-29's system as the 'first' such is questionable historically. Remote-controlled turret guns had been used operationally in RAF and Luftwaffe bombers in Europe by 1944.

shot gun. In the air the prospective gunner flew in B-24s, in our case at Buckingham Field, Florida, firing both hand-held waist guns as well as all the turrets, at both water targets and towed sleeves. We even had a bit of firing at armoured P-39s and P-63s painted up like zebras, but we used a special frangible ammunition which shattered on impact, though with enough force to record a hit on the target aircraft. In addition to this we went on to fire the GE system mounted in rebuilt B-24s.

Although very little else about the gunnery set-up on B-29s resembled a mission in Europe-based B-17s, the pre-flight arming procedure was pretty similar. Ground crew armourers actually did most of the maintenance of the guns themselves, and remote-control turret maintenance specialists kept the GE system tuned in top condition. In our 6th Bomb Group the aircrew gunners usually went down to the flight line several hours before a mission and loaded the ammunition cans, checked and armed the guns in the turrets, and generally pre-flighted the system. Although we had been taught that the guns and turrets could be freed of malfunctions in flight, it proved to be almost impossible, and jammed guns and inoperative turrets stayed that way until return to base.

On 8 August, 1945, the 6th Bomb Group participated in the mission to Yawata, with the Sasebo Naval Base and shipyards and the steel mills as the targets. This turned out to be the last large B-29 mission of the war where any great fighter opposition from the Japanese was mounted against the 20th Air Force bombers. Once airborne, the

111 *The initial three-gun tail turret in a Superfortress – twin .50 Brownings and single 20 mm cannon – which was little used operationally.*

gunners on board the B29s didn't have much to do on the long flight up to the mainland of Japan, normally about a seven-hour flight across about 1,700 miles of Pacific Ocean from our bases in the Marianna Islands, since no enemy opposition was normally expected until some 100 miles off the coast.

The B-29 was such a tremendous improvement over anything previous, especially in creature comforts with its pressurized, air-conditioned and heated crew compartments, that it was really more like a flight in an airliner of today, as compared to the box car-like accommodations on B-17s and B-24s where at altitude over Europe, even in summer, it was pure freezing misery to the gunners. At altitudes of up to 35,000 feet and higher, we wore ordinary summer flight suits over T-shirts, unencumbered by gloves or jackets, or even headgear except for baseball caps. Needless to say, this made for much greater combat readiness.

The B29s flew in formation over Japan by day, and singly at night like the RAF bomber trains. As we were timed to pass over the target at high noon, we began endless circling in sight of Japan as the forming up by squadrons and groups began. Although this was the most vulnerable and dangerous time when fighter attacks could have played havoc, the desperate fuel situation of the Japanese Air Forces was evident, since we did not receive even one pass by an enemy fighter while we were forming up off the coast. They preferred to save fuel and wait for their fighter controller to try and determine our targets before vectoring them in to intercept.

It was not until just before we reached the forming-up area that gunners manned their gunsight positions. On signal from the pilot, we slipped into flak vests and steel infantry helmets, and alerted ourselves and our gun positions. I was CFC, or top gunner, on our aircraft and climbed up into my plywood seat which was mounted on a round, elevated platform, also plywood, and thrust my head up into the little plastic bubble where my sight was located. Each gunner was given his primary turret as I activated his sight by throwing the switches in the master gunnery control panel which in turn activated the whole system. The tail gunner was back all alone in his separated pressurized position under the great rudder, sealed in by the airlock door. He still had two .50s, although his 20 mm cannon had been permanently removed since the low-level Tokyo raids in March. They were never too effective in combination due to their different trajectories.

Since the bombardier was primarily busy getting set up for his main job, the CFC gunners rigged the switches so that both upper turrets were tied into the CFC gunner's sight. However, the bombardier could claim his upper forward turret on demand by pressing his primary control on the sight, as well as having secondary control of the lower forward turret in case of frontal attacks. Both the bombardier and CFC had command of six .50s on demand. The side blister gunners had primary control of the lower forward and aft turrets and could swap them about so that either could use both, depending on which side was under attack. They could also take over the tail turret in the event of the tail gunner being knocked out. However, their sights were useless for dead aft aiming, except for blind spraying.

With all the preliminaries out of the way, and now completely

112 *The more normal operational tail turret of a 'Superfort' – two .50 Brownings.*

formed up by squadrons and groups, the armada began its track towards Yawata, and thereby committed itself to fighter attack which was not long coming. We in *Myas' Dragon*, No. 40 of the 39th Squadron, were on the left outside position of the Vee of Vees of 18 aircraft. The 12 o'clock to 6 o'clock area was of main concern to us in regards to possible fighter attack. We could hear the other aircraft begin to call in fighter sightings. A couple of twin-engined Nicks or Irvings had been flying alongside us, about two miles out, for several minutes, radioing our course, altitude and speed. Every few miles a ground flak unit fired up white trailing phosphorous shells, visually marking our position as well. The whole Japanese Fighter Command appeared to be setting us up for the kill.

We bore on towards our IP on Shimonosenki Straits under a cloudless summer sky, eyes and heads swivelling like mad. Our formations contained about 200 B-29s stacked up between 15,000 and 18,000 feet. The gunners in our particular group of 18 had command of 216 .50 calibre machine guns, mounted in the finest turret system available. The possible hail of gun-fire from such a formation was enough to make any fighter pilot in his right mind a bit gun-shy. One twin-engined Nick started the ball rolling by diving straight down from the sun, right through the middle of our formation so fast that no one even fired at him and he made no hits either. Another came barrelling through head-on with a combined closing speed of about 700 mph, as we were cruising at about 325 mph indicated. Once again no hits, but everyone had their adrenalin up by now, and we know we were going to get a workout – as predicted.

We had been briefed that we would have an escort of P-51s and P-47Ns from Iwo Jima, but so far no show. Suddenly the navigator called out at P-47 at 10 o'clock high. I couldn't spot him at first and felt a little panicky because he kept calling him out and I still didn't see him – I was looking too far – finally saw him, and the great red 'meatballs' on his side hit me right in the eye. 'That's a Frank,' I shouted, 'Not a P-47!' To give it its more formal name it was a Nakajima Ki.84 Hayate, unpainted except for the honamaru insignia ('meatballs'), and was out only about 1,000 yards pulling up ahead for a pursuit curve attack. I barely had time to get him in my sight – we left them set for 37 feet wingspan – when he pulled up and over, coming in inverted with all his cannons winking red. I clamped down on the trigger, firing all six guns in the upper turrets. Right away he was hit and off flew his cowling with a black plume of smoke shooting back underneath. Everybody was banging away at him as he flashed below to complete his breakaway, still inverted. 'He's starting to spin,' yelled the tail gunner.

Our brief moment of elation was ruined by the B-29 right off our right wing calling out that he was hit and feathering No. 3 engine, which caused him to drop behind right away. We were swearing because we thought the Frank had hit him after all. Tail gunner called out that the Frank was still spinning and trailing black smoke, we went off and left him long before he reached the ground – no parachute though. The hit B-29 was dropping back fast and was down about 1,000 feet. Another pilot was almost demanding that he be released to drop back and cover him. He was refused by the Group commander and told to tighten up and the whole formation ordered to increase speed to 330. We found out later that the cripple made it back to Okinawa,

113 *B-29 Superfortress* American Maid *of the 21st Bomber Command, at 29,000 ft during a raid on Nagoya, Japan, on 3 January 1945. The 'object' hanging from the waist hatch was the gunner, Sgt James R. Krantz, who was literally blown out of his hatch by Japanese fighter fire, but was saved from certain death by his personally-devised safety harness. Hanging in mid-air by just one leg, five miles high above Japan, he was eventually pulled back into safety some 15 minutes later, and survived his ordeal, despite severe frostbite injuries.*

fighting all the way, and getting credit for shooting down five Navy Georges. He took many hits but luckily no one was wounded on board – the aircraft never flew again.

Our burning Frank didn't get him after all; it was a Nick that dove straight down from the sun getting through the middle of the formation so fast no one hit him, most didn't even see him. One hundred and seventy-five individual fighter attacks were reported on our formation, with no other B-29 losses that day.

We were coming up on the IP fast now, and the flak began at this point and the fighters pulled off. A couple of cruisers in the harbour were really laying up the flak along with the area defence batteries. A formation off to our left at 7 o'clock had a carpet of black so thick under them you could walk on it – luckily it was 100 feet too low. By now some 250 B-29s were unloading ten tons of 500-pounders apiece on Yawata at high noon – some lunch hour! Radar Spook reported bomb bay doors closed and bomb bay clear. Where were those escorts? We had never had any before anyhow! Now five Tonys in echelon pulled up about 1,500 yards off at 9 o'clock. They had a lot of black paint on them, red meatballs on white. They just flew along looking us over for a few moments. We were really tensed up for this one. I thought they would turn in on the formation, instead only the leader tipped up – and all hell broke loose. Every plane on our side of the formation cut loose on him, and pieces were flying off him as he flashed, under us diving away. Now came No. 2, same thing, but he broke away further out. The other three decided to linger out there while getting up nerve.

What happened next shows just how effective the GE system was over the old power turrets and hand-held guns, few of which had a range effective over 800 yards away. The three Tonys still sat out there in formation, with us about 1,200 yards away. As the next one looked like he might come in, I fired at him away out there. My tracers, which we used every 12 or so rounds for scare, flashed right by his nose. He straightened up for a moment and then dove away to the left, quickly followed by No. 4. I'm sure I got hits on him away out there.

Now No. 5 was out there all by himself. I don't blame him for thinking it over, but he concentrated too long. A P-47 dove on him from behind, firing as he came. The Tony pilot yanked the stick back into his stomach, going into a tight loop with the '47 looping right outside him firing bursts all the way. They want around three times like this before the Tony stalled and fell off into a tight spiral, turning into a spin. That was the only fighter I ever saw shot down by another fighter, and I saw no other Thunderbolts. As we bored down Shimonosenki Straits heading back towards the east coast of Honshu, and the long haul home, a large formation of P-51s flashed by towards Yawata, 5,000 feet below us – a little late, fellows!

In a few more minutes we cruised on by a sight I will never forget – the incredible desolation of Hiroshima. No one said a word on the air, or the intercomm for five minutes at least. Our 250 B-29s had not begun to do to Yawata what that one bomb dropped by the lone *Enola Gay* had done.

15. An Infinite Variety

To attempt to relate even a worthy proportion of the tales of air gunners in every type of operational role, in every corner of the 1939-45 global conflict, is patently beyond the scope of any single volume. Perhaps inevitably many such experiences would be similar in basic character, differing only in the contexts of geographical location, aircraft and opponent. Nevertheless the rich aggregation of selected experiences which follows may exemplify to some degree the wide variety of the air gunner's lot. Hopefully these glimpses into the 'routine' tasks of the gunner will also demonstrate in no small way a few of the unique problems – and hazards – which were a permanent corollary to those tasks. If these brief stories have anything in common it is primarily unadulterated courage, allied with a stubborn determination always to fight to the very last no matter what the odds or circumstances. Such courage is usually translated by all Services' bureaucracy in the cliché-phrase 'Devotion to Duty'; but such a non-explicit description fails to explain the instinctive fighting spirit of the men behind the guns.

The only operational RAF fighter in World War Two to employ a gun turret was the Boulton Paul Defiant. First designed and built in 1936, the Defiant was originally intended for the role of interception of bomber formations, whereby the 'normal' single-seat fighters employed their usual tactics, and the Defiant was to fly alongside the bombers using its four-gun BP turret on beam fire. The concept was ill-starred, based essentially on 1918 concepts of two-seater fighter tactics. When, in 1940, Defiants commenced operations against the Luftwaffe, however, they were used as fighters in their own right – a role never intended for the design – and suffered accordingly. First to equip with Defiants was 264 Squadron, based at Martlesham, in December 1939, and on 10 May 1940 the squadron was based at Duxford, ready for operations. Two days later A Flight was detached to Horsham St Faith (now Norwich City Airport), and within hours of arrival flew the unit's first operational sorties, along the Dutch coast, where one Junkers Ju88 was claimed as destroyed – the Defiant's 'first blooding' – while seconds later a Heinkel HeIII was shared between another Defiant and three escort Spitfires from 66 Squadron.

On 13 May B Flight made its first sorties and six Defiants set out to attack enemy troop movements in Holland. In the process they

attacked a gaggle of Junkers Ju87s and claimed four of these, but were then 'bounced' by a batch of Messerschmitt Bf 109s who swiftly shot down five of the six Defiants, leaving the sixth (Pilot Officer Kay/LAC Jones) to land at Knocke and later return to England. Of the five Defiant crews shot down, only two crew members survived by parachute. It was a foretaste of the destruction to come for 264's doughty crews. On 23 May the squadron moved to the forward airfield at Manston for cross-Channel operations, and during the following five days claimed six enemy aircraft without loss to the squadron. On 28 May, however, three Defiants were lost during a battle with nearly 30 Bf 109s, of which 264 crews claimed six shot down.

Undoubtedly the Defiant's rough resemblance to the Hawker Hurricane was responsible to a large extent for its relatively light losses – and high successes – during these early clashes, but the Luftwaffe's fighter pilots learned quickly from their errors. On 29 May the Defiant crews claimed a total of 37 German aircraft in the course of two fighting patrols that day; all for just one Defiant damaged. Postwar examination of Luftwaffe records shows that in fact only 14 aircraft were actually lost – yet even this figure was a contemporary record for a single fighter unit. By the end of May 264 had claimed a total of 65 enemy aircraft to date for the loss of 14 Defiants. Squadron Leader Philip Hunter, commander of 264 Squadron, was awarded a DSO shortly after, and the unit was with-

drawn to Kirton-in-Lindsey for re-equipment to full strength again, having lost seven Defiants on 31 May.

The second unit to receive Defiants was 141 Squadron, which was declared fully operational on 3 June. On 19 July, based at Hawkinge, 141 went into action when nine of its Defiants set out to patrol south of Folkestone just after mid-day. Out of the blue they were jumped by ten Bf109s of the crack II/JG2 'Richthofen' Geschwader – and decimated. Recognizing the Defiants for what they were, the Bf109 pilots attacked from below, dead astern – a Defiant's blind spot – and in less than 60 seconds had sent five down in flames. The four survivors limped back to base where one crashed, and a second was found to be so severely damaged that it was written off charge on the spot. Such a crippling loss forced Fighter Command to withdraw 141 Squadron from first-line operations and send it north to Prestwick on 21 July. Meanwhile 264 Squadron, engaged in spasmodic patrols in the northern zone, was preparing to join the Battle of Britain further south, and on 22 August flew to Hornchurch, with Manston as its forward landing ground. When one considers the stark slaughter perpetrated on 141 Squadron only weeks before, it is difficult – to say the least – to understand why 264 should have been thus committed to frontline battle again.

Two days later the squadron had nine Defiants on Manston airfield when a German raid developed. Taking off hurriedly the

Defiants engaged individually and lost three crews, including their commander, Philip Hunter. Later that day three more Defiants were lost; two of these in an air collision. Seven German aircraft were claimed as destroyed. On 26 August, led by Flight Lieutenant A. J. Banham, 264 was sent off from Hornchurch to intercept a formation of Dorniers near Herne Bay. As they were about to close with the bombers two *Gruppen* of Bf109s, some 50 in total, fell on the Defiants and shot three down. The after-combat report reflects the course of this brief engagement:

Flt Lt Banham, after destroying a Dornier 17, received an explosive shell in his cockpit which set fire to the aircraft. He rolled on his back calling to his gunner to bale out, and then baled out himself. He was picked up after 1½ hours in the sea; his gunner, Sgt B. Baker, is missing. Plt Off Goodall was attacked by a Bf109 and after beating off the attack made an overtaking attack on a Do17 which he saw catch fire, and also saw two of the crew bale out. Plt Off Hughes, in his first engagement with the enemy, successfully destroyed two Do17s by converging attacks. Sgt E. R. Thorne and Sgt F. J. Barker put up a magnificent show by destroying two of the Do17s, and while attacking a third were in turn attacked by a Bf109 and their machine developed oil and glycol leaks. Taking evasive action they spun away and were preparing to make a crash landing near Herne Bay when the Bf109 again attacked them at 500 feet. The aircraft caught fire but before crashing Sgt Barker fired his remaining rounds into the enemy which crashed a few fields away. Both Sergeants Thorne and Barker escaped with minor injuries. Campbell-Colquhoun, after attacking a Do17 which dived smoking from both engines, was attacked by a Bf109 and was unable to confirm the destruction of the Dornier. Fg Off Stephenson's Defiant was set on fire by a Bf109; the pilot baled out and was picked up from the sea and taken to Canterbury hospital with minor injuries. His gunner, Sgt W. Maxwell is missing.

Sergeants Thorne and Barker proved to be 264 Squadron's most successful fighting partnership, being eventually credited with 13 victories, and each receiving a DFM award. But as a day fighter the Defiant was clearly a failure. On 29 August, having lost two more aircraft, with four others damaged on the previous day, 264 Squadron was withdrawn to Duxford. Along with the re-formed 141 Squadron, the unit was allocated to night-fighting duties thereafter. In all 13 squadrons were eventually equipped with Defiants for night interception during 1941-2; while several training units continued to employ the type until the end of the war. Basically the Defiant was an anachronism – a throwback to the magnificent Bristol F2b Fighter of 1917-18, when a pilot and gunner, back to back, became a superb fighting team. In 1940, however, the Defiant lacked the speed and manoeuvrability of its opponents, and was therefore doomed from the outset. Like so many other aircraft designs in history, any successes achieved by Defiants were directly attributable to the tenacity and uncommon courage of their two-man crews.

Warrant Officer S. Magee was not really an air gunner – his trade was Armament, and had been for many years, and he was well over the age for aircrew duties anyway. Thus when he was posted to 107 Squadron at Wattisham in late 1940 it was as Squadron Armament Officer; responsible to the squadron commander directly for all facets of armament within the unit. A regular of the old school, Magee soon made his presence felt and, though his standards of discipline might have been considered by some of the younger airmen as quasi-Draconian, he applied such standards equally to all technical facets of the Armoury, resulting in the unit's Blenheim IVs being possibly the best-serviced aircraft in 2 Group, RAF Bomber Command. It was not very long before every armourer, down to the meanest AC2 mechanic, felt himself to be a segment of an élite body. And at a period when even the squadron commander's mode of personal transport comprised a humble Service-issue bicycle, Warrant Officer Magee mysteriously contrived to run an 18 hp Wolseley car around the Suffolk countryside (at alarming speeds) with seemingly inexhaustible supplies of petrol, despite severe fuel rationing.

At this period RAF Wattisham appeared to be a constantly attractive target for Luftwaffe bomber crews – indeed, like the aircraft carrier *Ark Royal*, the station had the dubious distinction of being 'destroyed', according to the enemy propagandist 'Lord Haw-Haw' (William Joyce) in one of his regular radio broadcasts. Magee, whenever an air raid warning was sounded, and when other more

116 *Bristol Blenheim gunner of 211 Squadron in 1941, taking on board a camera. His Bristol turret was armed with a solitary VGO 'K' gun.*

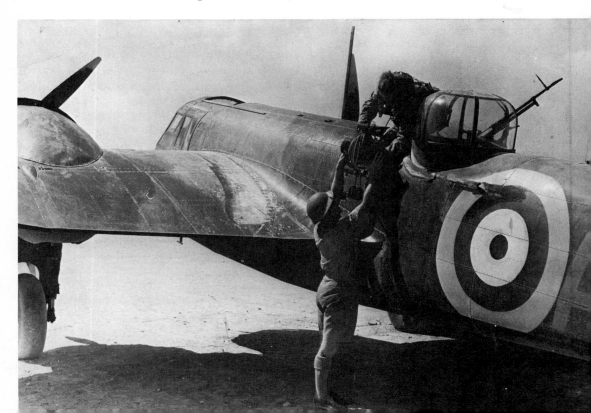

prudent souls sought immediate shelter, had an uncompromising routine. Marching (not, be it noted, walking or running) from his office to a clear spot in front of one of the hangars where he had an unrestricted view of the airfield, Magee would set up his very private counter-measure – a .303 VGO 'K' machine gun, with a wooden butt specially shaped for his shoulder, and a modified trigger mechanism. By his side would be that day's unfortunate duty armourer, whose sole task was to replenish ammunition pans to pass to his Warrant Officer. As most German raids were made at low level, Magee would next proceed liberally to spray the surrounding air with bullets as soon as enemy aircraft hove into view. True, he never succeeded in shooting down any enemy aircraft, but wherever Magee went, his VGO went too.

In May 1941 the squadron, which had been at Leuchars since March, moved south again to Great Massingham, a satellite airfield to West Raynham, and commenced a series of low-level daylight sorties over enemy-occupied Europe. Magee, with his armoury now working with silk-like precision and thus needing little personal guidance, turned his attentions to the possibilities of more active service. By persistence and subtle persuasion Magee eventually obtained permission from his squadron commander to be allowed to fly as a 'passenger' on operations. In a Blenheim IV there was little space to spare for an extra body, and certainly no spare seat. It meant Magee having to sit crouched for hours on a small ledge just aft of the bomb bay, almost in darkness. His only vision access to the outside was a small perspex panel in the centre of the wireless operator/air gunner's escape hatch, where normally a vertical camera could be fitted. Invariably when 'Mr' Magee went on operations he took with him his beloved VGO with several magazines loaded with 100 per cent tracer bullets, and, parked carefully on a nearby ledge, a 40 lb GP bomb. Once above the target, Magee would remove the escape hatch, hand-launch his 40 lb bomb, and then blast away as much tracer ammunition as time permitted. It was never discovered exactly why he decided on this course of action, or what satisfaction he derived from it.

Though designated as low-level, 107's Blenheim sorties only flew at zero heights over enemy-occupied territory, and thus all crews carried parachutes. One morning, Magee, who was short-sighted, was struggling into the B Flight commander's Blenheim with his equipment, when he made the most common error of picking up his parachute pack by its D-release ring instead of the carrying loop handle. The parachute spilled out, and Magee impatiently cast it aside and climbed into the aircraft. The sortie was an attack on Hanover and the Flight commander's Blenheim did not return to base. Only months later was it learned via the Red Cross that the Flight commander was a prisoner of war, but Warrant Officer S. Magee – part-time air gunner and squadron legend – had been killed in the bomber's crash, being buried in Hanover.

No. 458 Squadron RAAF, in 1943, was one of many units of the
Middle East Air Force engaged in anti-shipping patrols, reconnaissance and strikes around Sardinia and in the Tyrrhenian Sea.
Equipped with Wellington bombers converted to carry and launch
air torpedoes, the Aussie crews had made a particularly prodigious
effort during July that year; totting up a total of over 1,000 hours
of operational flying in the course of 134 sorties, and sinking or
damaging a dozen enemy vessels. Nearly all had been flown into the
teeth of intense flak opposition and prey to any marauding enemy
fighters, and these operations cost the squadron four aircraft shot
down. During the first two weeks of August two more Wellingtons
and their crews were lost, from which there was only one survivor,

*117 Rear turret in a
Wellington XIV of 36
Squadron, RAF Coastal
Command, at Chivenor,
1944.*

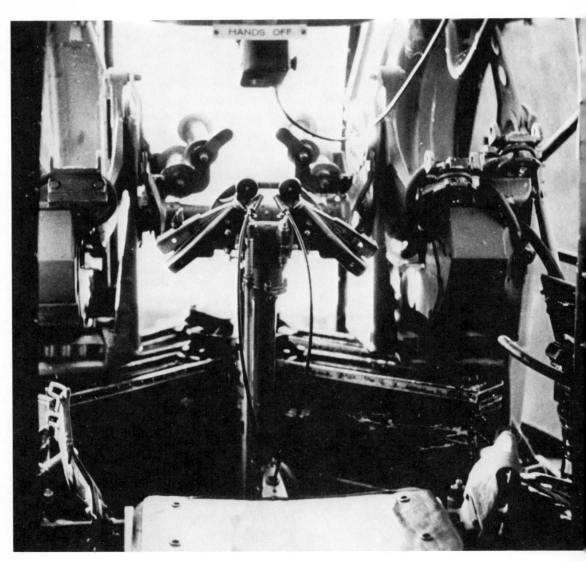

a Wireless Operator/AG, Sergeant (later Warrant Officer) B. A. Watson, RAAF.

An ex-grocer's assistant from Norseman, Western Australia, Watson was one of a mixed nationality crew on the night of 4 August. Skipper of the crew was a fellow Australian, Flight Sergeant R. G. Spencer, whose co-pilot was Flight Sergeant B. E. Adams, RAF. The navigator Flight Sergeant L. McKay, Wop/AG Flight Sergeant J. M. Fischer were also Australian; while the third Wop/AG was another RAF man, Sergeant C. Ebbage. One of six squadron 'Wimpys' detailed for a shipping recce over the Tyrrhenian Sea, Watson's aircraft left base at Protville, Tunisia, at about 10 pm and nothing was heard from them until minutes after midnight, when a signal came through, 'Returning to base, engine trouble.' Only eight minutes after sending the signal the Wellington's port engine coughed and then cut completely. With the port propeller feathered, Spencer set course for base, and jettisoned his torpedo to lighten the aircraft.

Unable to maintain height on one engine the bomber became unmanageable and Spencer told his crew to stand by for ditching – only to hit the sea almost immediately afterwards. Watson meantime had just had time to open the astro-hatch dome – and the next thing he knew he was under water, struggling to reach the surface for air. He had no recollection of how he got out of the Wellington – probably through the astro-hatch. On finally surfacing and gratefully gulping in fresh air to his bursting lungs, he looked around him for signs of his friends. Oil was burning on top of the sea, while some 20 yards away floated an uninflated dinghy. With bruised body and battered arms, Watson dog-paddled and forced himself towards the dinghy, and after half an hour's exhausting labour he finally reached the dinghy, inflated it and managed to get into it. A second crew member, Ebbage, came into view, spotted Watson, called to him, and eventually scrambled into the dinghy.

Ebbage was severely injured in the crash, so Watson, despite his own injuries, found the dinghy's ration box and tried to open it for morphia for Ebbage. The physical effort was too much for him and Watson fainted. Two hours later he recovered consciousness – but his companion was dead by then. For two days Watson kept Ebbage's body with his in the dinghy, but then, reluctantly, gently, slid the body over the side. For the next six days Watson continued to drift in the dinghy, a human micro-dot on a seemingly endless vista of water. By day he kept himself cool by dipping his clothing in the sea; and kept up his spirits by singing to himself. Food and fresh drinking water was provided in the dinghy by tins of water and yet more tins of Horlick's tablets; and Watson strictly rationed himself on these from the start.

Throughout his eight days' ordeal Watson saw several aircraft, including German, pass over, but none appeared to notice the tiny dinghy below. Then, on 12 August, just after mid-day, a Catalina,

118 *A 1941 Wellington rear gunner, with his personal insigne.*

escorted by an American Lightning, appeared over the horizon. Standing unsteadily in his dinghy, Watson waved a red flag furiously. The Catalina banked, circled, and landed nearby. A rope was thrown to Watson and he was hauled aboard, where he was plied with hot coffee and cold tomato juice as the flying boat flew back to Bizerta. Watson was then transferred to the 96th General Hospital where his injuries were treated, and after a short convalescence, he returned to operations. The cool-headed appraisal of his desperate position shortly after ditching, which led to his self-imposed strict rationing of his meagre food and water supplies undoubtedly contributed largely to his survival – indeed, when finally rescued, he still had five tins of water and four tins of Horlick's tablets left. Even more certain is that without his stubborn refusal to surrender to his circumstances, even after the chilling experience of having the body of a close friend at his feet for two days and two nights, Watson might still have not lived to tell the tale.

It was 29 May 1945. The European war was over, with VE Day celebrations still lingering on in most parts of the free world; while in a ruined Europe millions of men and women were dazedly trying to reconstruct shattered lives. To 'Curly' Copley – his Christian name was Cyril, but who ever called him that? – seated in the rear turret of his 358 Squadron Liberator in the early hours of that May morning, the war was still very real. Japan had yet to be conquered or beaten into unconditional surrender, and either prospect seemed very unlikely in the immediate foreseeable future. Fanatics do not reason; logic means nothing to the obsessed. To Yorkshire-born Curly Copley, carefully scanning the sky as he rotated the twin .50 guns' turret of 'P-Peter', the war was still 'on'. High over enemy-occupied Thailand (Siam), Copley's aircraft had left its base at Jessore, Calcutta hours earlier on a top-secret mission – to drop three American officers in enemy territory, where they could join up with the Thai underground forces well behind Japanese front-lines.

Copley glanced at his watch. It was 6.30 am; nearly at rendezvous point for the drop. Then his whole body jumped as the bomb-aimer's voice crackled in his ear-phones, 'Two fighters starboard, skipper!' Quickly peering around his field of vision Copley saw two other fighters above, then another pair, then three more – at least nine fighters, which began forming up in three Vics of three ahead of the Liberator. Harry Smith, his Canadian skipper, sized up the situation, yelled, 'Watch 'em, gunners, they're coming in', then began weaving the bomber to spoil the fighters' aim. Within seconds Copley heard – and felt – the first hail of cannon shells slashing along the flanks of the bomber's fuselage; then, as it broke away downwards to port, he got his first glimpse of an Oscar. Before he could bring his gyro gunsight to bear, a second Oscar was flashing past, its fire having hit the co-pilot up front and wounded the navigator. By now Copley's guns were in action, squirting brief bursts at each fleeting fighter as it veered by him. A shell blew away the elevator trimming tab past his turret, and Copley became aware of a plume of white smoke going by at one side – a ruptured engine.

The Japanese fighters had been thorough, queueing up in line astern and successively attacking from head-on. Their fire shattered each engine in turn, tore jagged holes in the wings and fuselage, smashed the pilot's windscreen, wounded most of the crew and killed the co-pilot. The skipper, frantically struggling to maintain his 6,000 feet altitude in an aircraft rapidly becoming uncontrollable, was given no alternative but to lose height. As the matted green jungle carpet came closer, he yelled over the intercomm, 'Prepare for crash-landing!' Copley heard this, evacuated his turret, and moved up the fuselage to his crash position. It was too late to bale out, and less than a minute later came impact as the mauled Liberator ploughed through tree-tops and hit the jungle floor, smashing its way through the undergrowth. Hurled backwards by the jolt, Copley blacked out.

As he regained consciousness Copley realized dazedly that he was still in the fuselage – or at least part of it. He could smell burning petrol and knew that the broken section he was lying in must be on fire. One foot was wedged tight amongst the mangled metal, but fear

gave him strength and he dragged the trapped foot out of its shoe, then got out through a gap in the side. Once clear, he looked around and saw the scattered debris in every direction, while from the main pile of burning wreckage came a sickening odour of burning flesh. He could see no other survivors. Then the full irony of the situation hit him – after four years away from England, in the Middle East and now Far East theatres of war, this was to have been his ultimate operational sortie. He had already been planning ahead for that beautiful boat that was going to take him back home – now he was alone, hundreds of miles deep in enemy-occupied territory, without a hope of ever seeing his native Yorkshire moors again.

At that moment he was astonished to see his pilot, Harry Smith, totter from the other side of the wreckage, his head pouring blood from a scalp injury; followed seconds later by one of the wireless operators, 'Timber' Woods, also injured by the crash. Despite the flames and detonating ammunition, all three set about retrieving the other members of the 14-man crew and passengers. Though in various degrees injured and/or burned, ten of the 14 men had survived

119 *Liberator tail 'tin' turret of a Middle East RAF unit. with its twin .303 Brownings.*

120 *The Emerson electrically-controlled nose turret in an RAF Liberator in India, 1944. Twin .50 Brownings had replaced the earlier smaller calibre guns by then.*

both fighter attacks and the subsequent crash-landing. A hasty conference resulted in general agreement that they must put as much distance as possible between themselves and the shot-down Liberator; its location would almost certainly have been reported by the Jap fighters. Setting off for the nearest hill range, they hoped eventually to contact the Thai underground forces in some way. Five days later, after a variety of adventures, they reached Bangkok, where – to their astonishment – the Thai police helped screen them from the Japanese occupying the city.

Spending his first night in a police cell-dormitory, Copley was sharply awakened in the early hours of the morning by his skipper, and introduced to – of all people – two American OSS officers! Until that moment Copley had resigned himself to, at best, internment by the Thai authorities. Now – to his utter astonishment – he was told of the secret Free Thai underground movement, with its headquarters actually here in the heart of Bangkok. Though legally at war with the Allies, the Thai Regent was in fact head of this underground force, supplying military intelligence to the Allies, and preparing a nationwide revolt against the Japanese occupiers. Naturally the presence of the American passengers in Copley's Liberator was an embarrassment – if the Japanese discovered them, the repercussions might wreck the whole underground objective. The OSS men had already spirited their fellow Americans away, and six days later arranged for Copley and his pilot to be taken out of the city. Reaching Ban-Pe airfield, Copley was taken by light aircraft to another air-strip, where, next day, a 357 Squadron Dakota dropped in and Copley and Harry Smith were taken aboard and flown to India; less than three weeks since their crash.

Epilogue

With the close of hostilities in August 1945 the days of the true air gunner became numbered. In every leading air service in the world the jet engine was about to supersede the piston power plant in aircraft designs, with a startling increase in performance as the prime and immediate result. Only in the dwindling quantity of war-surplus piston-engined aircraft was there any provision for gun turrets and air gunners. Even here the operational efficacy of the gunner, attempting to track and intercept an opposing jet fighter, was drastically impaired. Radar sighting and interlocked turret controls may well pick up a fighter, estimate its correct range and bearing, calculate true deflection angles, even fire the cannons or machine guns. The inefficiency lay mainly in the types of gun or cannon available to the gunner – obsolete conceptions of weaponry lacking sufficient rates of fire or muzzle velocity to inflict any significant damage on a fleeting target which closed at a speed perilously close to that of sound. With the advent of fighter-borne missiles and long-range rockets for air-to-air combat, the conventional turret-gun was hopelessly out-ranged; leaving the air gunner as a last-ditch, slightly desperate measure of bomber defence.

Within the RAF in the immediate post-1945 years, Bomber Command was forced to rely on wartime Lancasters and the larger Lincoln derivant as its mainstay equipment, supplemented by a few retreaded Boeing B-29s from the USA and retitled Washingtons. This dying era of the piston-engined bomber was to last until the late 1950s, until jet-powered Canberras and the later V-bomber designs appeared in first-line squadrons. Nevertheless, the demise of the RAF air gunner came officially on 1 January 1955. From that date the RAF aircrew category Air Gunner was declared defunct, and all existing, serving air gunners were offered a choice of various ground trades, while a relative few – mainly those of younger years – were permitted to undertake further training as a Signaller (aircrew). Once qualified in the latter flying category, Signallers were required to man the existing gun turrets should the occasion arise. The remainder became physical training instructors, administrators and/or disciplinary trades.

In other world air services the air gunner also drifted into other full-time employment duties. While it is true that a slight resurgence in air gunnery emerged in the many post-1945 conflicts and open wars, e.g. Korea and Vietnam, aerial gunnery never resumed its former status. All aircrew personnel are instructed in basic weaponry and general armament as part of their normal training, hence it needs little more than an intensive 'refresher' period of practice to produce a reasonably competent gunner. This is borne out by the myriad of other-trade personnel who wielded multi-barrel machine guns and other hand-operated 'free' guns from helicopters and so-termed 'gun-ships' during the protracted American war in Vietnam. It is no slur on such men to say that they were not air gunners in the context of the traditional definition of that aircrew category – it was not their sole, trained role in their respective air services.

Thus, the true air gunner is now part of aviation history – in function, as dead as the dodo, due to the ever-escalating graph of aeronautical research, design, and progress. It is a measure of the sheer magnitude of that astonishingly rapid development that at the time of writing there are many thousands of men still living who flew as air gunners in a hundred different conflicts stretching back to the very birth of man-powered aeroplanes. The oldest of these, who as vibrant young men fought an enemy from the fabric-skinned, wooden-framed gunner's cockpit of a World War One biplane, are now witnessing man's first ventures into the cosmos of space and the infinite outer reaches. With the seemingly unlimited capacity of man for aggression against his fellow man, is it perhaps too fanciful to imagine a war in space, far into the distant future, with space 'fighter' tackling space 'bomber'? And is it too fictional to consider the possibility that – in a future era beyond man's present projection of imagination – there may yet be another breed of 'aerial gunners', doing battle with weapons yet to be conceived, attempting to destroy an opponent yet to be discovered?

Glossary

RANKS:

AC2 *Aircraftman 2nd Class (RAF)*
AC1 *Aircraftman 1st Class (RAF)*
LAC *Leading Aircraftman (RAF)*
Cpl *Corporal*
Sgt *Sergeant*
F/Sgt *Flight Sergeant (RAF/RAAF/RCAF/RNZAF)*
WO *Warrant Officer (RAF/RAAF/RCAF/RNZAF)*
Plt Off *Pilot Officer (RAF/RAAF/RCAF/RNZAF)*
Fg Off *Flying Officer (RAF/RAAF/RCAF/RNZAF)*
Flt Lt *Flight Lieutenant (RAF/RAAF/RCAF/RNZAF)*
Sqn Ldr *Squadron Leader (RAF/RAAF/RCAF/RNZAF)*
Wg Cdr ('Wingco') *Wing Commander (RAF/RAAF/RCAF/RNZAF)*
Grp Capt *Group Captain (RAF/RAAF/RCAF/RNZAF)*
A/Cdre *Air Commodore (RAF/RAAF/RCAF/RNZAF)*
MRAF *Marshal of the Royal Air Force*
AOC *Air Officer Commanding*
AOC-in-C *Air Officer Commanding-in-Chief*
M/Sgt *Master Sergeant (USAAF)*
S/Sgt *Staff Sergeant (USAAF)*
T/Sgt *Top Sergeant (USAAF)*

DECORATIONS/AWARDS:

CBE *Companion of Order of the British Empire*
CGM *Conspicuous Gallantry Medal (UK forces)*
DCM *Distinguished Conduct Medal*
DFC *Distinguished Flying Cross*
DFM *Distinguished Flying Medal*
DSC *Distinguished Service Cross*
DSO *Companion of the Distinguished Service Order*
MC *Military Cross*
MM *Military Medal*
VC *Victoria Cross*

GENERAL:

AGI *Air Gunnery Instructor*
AMO *Air Ministry Order*
AWL *Absent without leave*

BS *Bombardment Squadron (USAAF)*
BG *Bombardment Group (USAAF)*
CO *Commanding Officer*
E/a *Enemy Aircraft*
ETO *European Theater of Operations (USAAF)*
GOC *General Officer Commanding*
ITW *Initial Training Wing (RAF)*
MU/AG *Mid-Upper Air Gunner*
OC *Officer Commanding*
OSS *Office of Strategic Services (USA)*
OTU *Operational Training Unit (RAF)*
PBO *'Poor Bloody Observer' (RFC/RAF)*
RAAF *Royal Australian Air Force*
RAF *Royal Air Force*
RCAF *Royal Canadian Air Force*
RFC *Royal Flying Corps*
RNAS *Royal Naval Air Service*
RNZAF *Royal New Zealand Air Force*
USAAF *United States Army Air Force*
U/t *Under training*
WAAF *Women's Auxiliary Air Force*
WAG *Wireless Air Gunner (RCAF)*
W/T *Wireless Telegraphy*
WOP *Wireless Operator (RAF)*

Bibliography

The following works were those chiefly consulted during the preparation of this book. For space reasons they do not include literally hundreds of features and articles published in the past 60 years directly, or in part, relevant to the general subject of aerial gunners.

Aircraft Armament, M. Olmsted: Sports Car Press, 1970
Air Gunner, M. Henry: Foulis, 1964
Air Gunners at War, J. Bushby: Unpublished MS
Armament of British Aircraft, H. F. King: Putnam, 1971
Bomber's Eye, D. Saward: Cassell, 1959
Battle over the Reich, A. W. Price: Ian Allan, 1973
For Valour – The Air VCs, C. Bowyer: William Kimber, 1978
Gunner's Moon, J. Bushby: Ian Allan, 1972
Guns of the RAF, G. F. Wallace: William Kimber, 1972
Hell in the Heavens, A. G. J. Whitehouse: W. & R. Chambers, 1938
I Hold my Aim, C. H. Keith: Allen & Unwin, 1946
Observer, A. J. Insall: William Kimber, 1970
New Zealanders with the RAF (3 Vols), H. L. Thompson: WHB, New Zealand, 1959
RAAF over Europe, Ed. F. Johnson: Eyre & Spottiswoode 1945
RAAF Official History (4 Vols), Australian War Memorial, 1963
RCAF Overseas (3 Vols), OUP 1949
So Few, D. Masters: Eyre & Spottiswoode, 1945
Strike and Return, P. Firkins: PB Pty Ltd, 1965
The Crowded Hours, A. Richardson: Parrish, 1952
The Dangerous Sky, D. H. Robinson: Foulis, 1973
The Mighty Eighth, R. A. Freeman: Macdonald, 1970
Nous Y Serons (107 Sqn History), Ed. B. S. Northway: 1963
We Find and Destroy, P. Alexander: 485 Sqn Council, 1959

OFFICIAL PUBLICATIONS (All HMSO unless otherwise indicated)

Air Publication (AP) 1641C, .303 Browning Machine Gun
AP 1641F, 20 mm Hispano Gun
AP 1641L, .50 Browning Machine Gun
AP 1659, Aeroplane Gun Turrets
AP 1661D, Ammunition
AP 2580A, 'Bag the Hun'
AP 2768E, Type 17 Gun Turrets

AP 2799F, R & T Nose & Tail Turrets for Sunderland & Lancaster aircraft

AM Pamphlet 132 Gunnery Sense

Air Forces Manual No. 20, May 1944, USAAF Publication

Armament Notes for Aircrews, 1944

Standard Notes for Air Gunners, 1940-44, Various editions

Standard Notes for Armourers, 1942-44, Various

The Complete Lewis Gunner, Gale & Polden, 1918

Strategic Air Offensive against Germany (4 Vols), Webster/Frankland, 1961

Index